Tweed rins tae the Ocean

A Walk along Scotland's Border

Alasdair Allan (signature)

Alasdair Allan

With a foreword by Cameron McNeish

TP

ThunderPoint Publishing

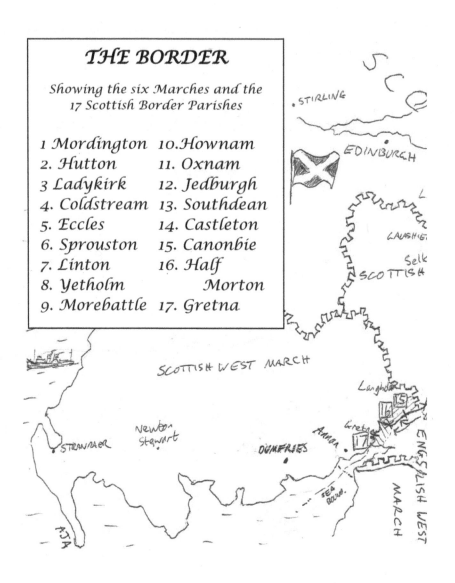

THE BORDER

Showing the six Marches and the
17 Scottish Border Parishes

1 Mordington
2. Hutton
3 Ladykirk
4. Coldstream
5. Eccles
6. Sprouston
7. Linton
8. Yetholm
9. Morebattle

10. Hownam
11. Oxnam
12. Jedburgh
13. Southdean
14. Castleton
15. Canonbie
16. Half Morton
17. Gretna

Map 1: Southern Scotland and northern England, showing some traditionally boundaries. These include the Border itself, with the small historically-disputed sections at each of its ends, and also the six 'marches' which were administered by the two countries from the thirteenth century until 1603. Also marked is the line of Hadrian's Wall.

The Scottish East March very broadly corresponds to the old county of Berwickshire. The Scottish Middle March takes in most of Roxburghshire, Peeblesshire and Selkirkshire. The Scottish West March includes most of Dumfriesshire and Galloway. The English East and Middle Marches corre-

spond very roughly with Northumberland, while the English West March lies in Cumbria.

A general indication is also given of the seventeen traditional Scottish parishes which border England, as these are largely the communities through which our walk takes us. A case could also be made for mentioning the parishes of Dornock, Annan and Cummertrees (as we walk through those areas in Chapter 8).

Remembering my grandparents:

James Allan (1897-1964)
Grace Simpson (1902-2003)
Jock Tait (1913-2006)
Margaret Brown (1910-2003)

who lived their lives along the Border, and worked where I only walked.

Tho' the Borders may be an imaginary line,
Yet it's a' the mair real for that, of course,
And deeper than Ordnance Surveys divine.

(From Hugh MacDiarmid: 'The Borders')

First Published in Great Britain in 2021 by
ThunderPoint Publishing Limited
Summit House
4-5 Mitchell Street
Edinburgh
Scotland EH6 7BD

Front Cover Image © Lisa Jarvis / Welcome to Scotland / CC BY-SA 2.0
Back Cover Image © Taras / British Railways sign at the Anglo-Scottish Border
Licensed under the Creative Commons Attribution-Share Alike 4.0 International
license.

Cover Design © Huw Francis

ISBN: 978-1-910946-75-6 (Hardback)
ISBN: 978-1-910946-76-3 (eBook)

Printed and bound in Great Britain by Clays Ltd, Elcograf S.p.A

www.thunderpoint.scot

Permissions

Fergus of Galloway by Guillaume Le Clerc, translated by DRR Owen, © Birlinn Limited reproduced with permission of the Licensor through PLSClear.

The excerpts from *The Borders, A Drunk Man Looks at a Thistle* and *Little White Rose of Scotland* by Hugh MacDiarmid reproduced with permission of © Carcanet Press.

My Ancestress and the Secret Ballot by Les Murray, reproduced with permission of © Carcanet Press.

Addresses Against Incorporating Union 1706-1707 by Karin Bowie, reproduced with permission of © The Scottish Historical Society.

Feachd a'Phrionnsa by George Campbell Hay from *Collected Poems and Songs of George Campbell Hay* edited by Michel Byrne, © Edinburgh University Press, reproduced with permission of the Licensor through PLSClear.

The Border Feud diagram on p90 reprinted by permission of HarperCollins Publishers Ltd © George MacDonald Fraser 1971.

Oran na Cloiche by Donald MacIntyre reproduced with permission of the Gaelic Texts Society.

Scotland by Alexander Gray from *Selected Poems* reproduced with permission from the Gray family.

The Declaration of Arbroath Crown copyright. National Records of Scotland, SP13/7.

All extracts from *The New Minstrelsy of the Scottish Border* reproduced with permission of Walter Elliot.

With thanks to Niall Taylor of the HV Morton Society, Alastair Moffat of Deerpark Press, Pippa Little and Walter Elliot for their kind permission to quote their works.

Contents

Acknowledgements

My sincere thanks are due above all to Malcolm Fleming, who agreed to walk much of the Border with me (days 1 to 3 and 8 to 11, plus the additional two-day walk along the Solway), and who put up with me cheerfully along the way.

I would also like to thank my other friends who walked with me, namely Grant McLennan (days 4 and 5), Stuart Rivans (day 5), Grant Moncur (day 6) and Alan Masterton (day 7). I should apologise to Alan in particular for the injuries which he sustained while walking with me. Equally due appreciation are all those – not least my mother – who dropped us off or picked us up by car at some of the unlikely and rain-swept places where we started and stopped.

I should thank Michael Russell MSP for telling me (after much procrastination on my part) just to get on with writing, and for then looking over this text, offering very helpful comments. I am also indebted to a number of others who similarly provided views, material, ideas and corrections. Of these, I would particularly mention Malcolm Fleming, Dr Duncan Sneddon, Prof Murray Pittock, Mr Walter Elliot and Dr Frances Murray, as well as the very patient Seònaid and Huw Francis of ThunderPoint Publishing.

I am also grateful for information provided by Ian Hamilton QC, Dr Guy Puzey, Shamus McPhee, David Shanks and Aileen Bathgate, and appreciate the help given by staff at the National Library of Scotland. A number of authors or editors, including Walter Elliot and Pippa Little, as well as Annabel Gray (granddaughter of the late Sir Alexander Gray) have been very helpful in offering the free use of quotes.

Factual errors, like any opinionated conclusions which I may have drawn in the passing, are my own responsibility.

I am grateful to Bordersprint, Selkirk, for engaging Louise Scott of Louise Scott Textile Design, Ettrick, to render my illegible sketches into proper maps. In doing so, I am very pleased to acknowledge that Louise has made a major contribution to the book in her own right.

Finally, it is a real honour to have a foreword provided by Cameron McNeish, and I would like to thank him for being kind enough to contribute this.

Any moneys due to me from this publication are being divided equally between two small Scottish charities. The first of these is the Western Isles Cancer Care Initiative, which works in partnership with Macmillan to provide support around the specific issues (and costs) faced by cancer patients and their families throughout the Outer Hebrides:

https://www.facebook.com/wiccioffice/

The other is the Mamie Martin Fund, which raises money to allow girls in northern Malawi to access secondary school:

https://mamiemartin.org/about-us/

Finally, by way of defensive explanation, I should add that writing this book did *not* interfere with my day-job as Member of the Scottish Parliament for Na h-Eileanan an Iar (The Western Isles). The book was researched on occasional stray weekends over a period of two and a half years, and then mainly stitched together on my laptop while I was offline and in the air, somewhere high over the Great Glen or Loch Tay, on my twice-weekly journeys between home in the Isle of Lewis and Parliament in Edinburgh.

A.J.A.

Isle of Lewis, July 2021.

Foreword by Cameron McNeish

Many years ago, I seriously considered walking the full length of the Border between Scotland and England.

A light-hearted book called *Walking the Scottish Border* by a BBC television presenter called Bob Langley made me think this would be quite a good ploy, a helpful addition to Scotland's at that time mediocre list of long-distance trails. Bob Langley was fond of pubs and wearing denim jeans and his journey was plagued by bad weather, but his seemed to be an intriguing journey. Sometime later, a good pal of mine, the broadcaster Eric Robson, made a similar journey from the Solway Firth to Berwick-upon-Tweed. He too endured a fair share of rain and boggy ground, but Eric was well-seasoned in stoicism and patience. He had to be – he had been the ever-patient television companion of the legendary curmudgeon Alfred Wainwright.

For various reasons, I never did get round to tracing the Border in the way the two broadcasters did. I think perhaps their constant references to bad weather and boggy ground put me off, as did my own long-term preoccupation with mountains, but Alasdair Allan has walked every inch of the way, exhibiting a similar fortitude and tenacity in dealing with changing conditions and navigation as Robson and Langley, although it would appear Alasdair's companions were infinitely more pleasant and tolerable than the dour, iconoclastic Wainwright.

Unlike the broadcasters, Alasdair chose to walk from east to west, betraying perhaps the effect of his years living in the land of the Gael. A native Borderer, Alasdair is an MSP representing the good people of the Na h-Eileanan an Iar constituency (the Western Isles), who all know that heaven itself lies in the West. Celtic traditions have it that in the far West, off the edges of all maps, lies the Otherworld, or Afterlife. The great religions of the world all point in that direction too – the West represents movement towards the Buddha or enlightenment. Ancient Egyptians believed that the Goddess Amunet, protector of the Pharaoh, was a personification of the West. It surely makes sense to walk from east to west. It's going home.

There is of course an excellent, and official, trail, the Southern Upland Way, which runs between Cockburnspath, a few miles north of Berwick-upon-Tweed, and lovely Portpatrick near Stranraer, and ranges across some magnificent landscapes. This route, however, Scotland's longest official long-distance trail, is a bureaucratic creation designed for popularity and comparative ease of travel and doesn't actually follow the line of the Border. The Border route, unpathed, unofficial and unspoiled by the erosion of countless pairs of hiking boots, contains sections that even the most experienced long-distance hiker would find daunting.

Scotland's Border with England runs for just under a hundred miles between the River Tweed and the Solway Firth. It represents Scotland's only land border and it has rarely been a peaceful line. There has been a long history of raiding and plundering, battling and frays between those with mixed allegiances. Border families frequently changed sides, swearing allegiance to whoever was in their best interests at the time. Indeed, the Borderers tended to show more loyalty to their family than their nation, but they were aye Borderers!

It has even been said that, at battles like Ancrum Moor in 1545, Borderers changed sides mid-battle to curry favour with the likely victors, and at the Battle of Pinkie Cleugh in 1547 it is said that the Scottish and English Borderers blethered to each other in the midst of engagement, and, on being spotted, put on a show of fighting.

I never did manage to walk the Border line, but I do have a passion for the borderlands. One of the most delightful things about this little country of ours is its huge diversity of landscape. Running parallel to that diversity comes a multiplicity of culture. You only have to compare the windswept, rolling landscapes of Banff and Buchan with the jagged upthrusts of Wester Ross, or contrast the mastiff-like Cairngorms with the serrated skyline of the Skye Cuillin to appreciate that diversity. I suspect that's why I love to frequently visit the polar opposite of my own home area of the Scottish Highlands.

The Borders are familiar, yet as different as rugby is from shinty. I feel comfortable there, with abiding interests in the traditional Border ballads and the history of the reivers. I've always felt at ease amongst the rolling Border hills with their cleuchs, haughs and heathery braes and, at the end of each winter when the highland hills are still streaked with snow, it's always a joy to travel south to where springtime is more advanced, where daffodils sway in yellow dance and the new-born lambs gambol on a green sheen of new growth.

On one occasion we visited the Stob Stones near Kirk Yetholm. These are known locally as the 'Gypsy Stobs' and the name relates to the tradition that the stones mark the spot where the Gypsy kings and queens were crowned. This point on the Border was regarded as fixed as far back as 1222. Today, an old wall and fence nearby mark the present national border, the man-made line that separates two distinct nations, two distinct cultures and two very distinct parliaments. Beyond the Stob Stones, we followed the fence line over White Law to the summit of Black Hag where another grassy track runs downhill to Old Halterburnhead and Kirk Yetholm.

Next day, being so close to the Cheviot, we decided it would be a tad churlish not to climb it. From the Scottish side, you get a largely peat-bog-free ascent, and a much prettier one than from the Northumberland side. Indeed, the walk-in from Sourhope Farm in the Bowmont Valley is a sheer delight, wandering through narrow valleys that are rich in ancient remains and traversing sheep-grazed slopes by good paths.

We left our vehicle near Sourhope Farm, so we could follow farm tracks all the way up to the Border ridge just south of Black Hag. From there, the ridge carried us over the Schil, past the mountain refuge at Auchope, and onto Auchope Cairn from where it was just over a mile of peat-plodding to the summit of the Cheviot itself. From there, we resumed our ridge-wandering south, over Score Head and King's Seat and onto Windy Gyle, almost ten miles from the Schil. From Windy Gyle a track runs north down Windy Rig to Kelsocleuch Farm and the farm road past Cocklawfoot and back to the start. It had been a phenomenal day of hillwalking, far removed from Munro or Corbett-bagging, but so typical of what the Borders have to offer the enthusiastic hill-goer as opposed to the dedicated peak-bagger.

Kirk Yetholm's chief claim to fame is an unusual one. It's the northern terminus of the Pennine Way, England's long-distance trail that runs up the spine of the country from Edale in the Peak District all the way to the Cheviots. A few years ago, I chose Kirk Yetholm as the starting point for a route I walked for television, the Scottish National Trail, a 470-mile journey that linked up a host of existing trails and footpaths to make one continuous route between the Scottish Borders and Cape Wrath.

Kirk Yetholm has a second claim to fame. Being situated so close to the national border line, the village was often used as a refuge for groups and individuals fleeing from one country to the other, particularly Gypsies. In the late nineteenth century, Scotland's last Gypsy king, Charles Faa Blythe, was crowned here. It's said the coronation carriage was drawn by six donkeys!

It was on the slopes close to Carter Bar that I fully realised the difference between walking in Scotland and in England. My companion walked on one side of the border line and was legally trespassing, while I, only a few feet away, thanks to the Land Reform (Scotland) Act 2003, was lawful. To the south of us, the sinuous twists of Redesdale dropped down to the Catcleugh Reservoir, deep in its conifer-covered cradle. Eastwards, straddling the Border, lay the broad slopes of Redeswire, famous for its sixteenth-century skirmish, and way beyond it, across the crumpled borderlands, lay the massive bulk of the Cheviot.

Grand as these views were, it was the view north that was most heart-warming. Yellowed moors led the eye to the fabled Eildon hills. From the Lammermuirs to the Moorfoots to the Tweeddale, Teviotdale and the Ettrick hills, everything was gleaming brightly fresh in the springtime sun. It didn't take much imagination to see that rumpled land rolling onwards, beyond the Central Belt and into the glorious Highlands. And it was here on Carter Bar that the words of the author H.V. Morton came to mind:

> How can I describe the strange knowingness of the Border? Its uncanny watchfulness. Its queer trick of seeming still to listen and wait. I feel that invisible things are watching me. …Out of the fern silently might ride the Queen of Elfland, just as she came to Thomas of Ercildoune in this very country with 'fifty silver bells and nine' hanging from her horse's mane.[1]

There is nowhere else in Scotland I sense this 'uncanny watchfulness' as intensely as I do in the Borders. It lurks on every hill-top, in every cleuch, and in every castle ruin, and Alasdair Allan has, almost magically, captured this essence of the Border. It's a landscape that requires us to use our imagination, helping us to reconcile those things that lurk in our mind's eye and events that may, or may not have shaped history. This is the land of Thomas the Rhymer, Merlin the Wizard and that other acclaimed wizard Michael Scott (also known as Michael Mathematicus, the court astrologer and physician to the Holy Roman Emperor Frederick the Great). Sir Walter Scott mentioned Michael in his *Lay of the Last Minstrel* and James Hogg, the Ettrick Shepherd, wrote about him in *The Three Perils of Man*.

Wizards, elves and rhymers may have shaped the culture of the Borders but this, above all, is a region of battles, fights, skirmishes, wars and general fisticuffs, and it seems you can't go round a corner without encountering some visible relic of times gone by. Perhaps that's why so many good rugby players come from the Borders – fighting and struggling is in their blood.

It's also the region of the Border Ballads, tales of yore told in bothy and fairmhoose since time immemorial. My own introduction to the Borderlands was through the singing of the Border Shepherd, one Willie Scott, as great a collector of native ballads as Hamish Henderson or Ewan MacColl. I'm delighted many of these ballads are still in circulation and some of them are quoted by Alasdair to give character to some of the places he passes. Many of these were once important locations, now lost to the re-alignment of paths and tracks or to the deadening monotony of commercial timber plantations.

[1] H.V. Morton: *In Search of Scotland*.

I wish I'd read this book forty years ago. Chances are I would have taken up the challenge and attempted it for myself, rather than be put off by the experiences of others. At one point Alasdair even admits to liking rainy weather, which might suggest a certain masochism in his character, but he is a politician after all! I suspect most of us who go to the hills and wild places have an inkling of such masochism in our system, but the good news is that Alasdair Allan has walked the Border and recorded it in such detail that you don't have to get your feet wet – unless you really want to! And if you do, I'm sure there is an experience of a lifetime awaiting you on this historic line that separates the nations of England and Scotland.

Cameron McNeish
Newtonmore, June 2020.

Cameron McNeish is deservedly Scotland's best-known hillwalker and mountaineer, having presented many award-winning series of hillwalking and outdoors programmes on television. He has also written over twenty of the most authoritative and widely-read books on Scotland's hills and landscapes and is an honorary fellow of the Royal Scottish Geographical Society. Cameron McNeish has climbed many of the world's highest mountains and is presently on his way round Scotland's 282 Munros for an impressive third time.

Key to Maps

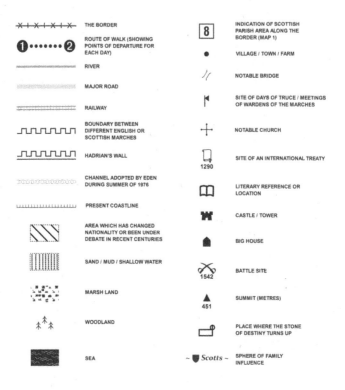

×—+—×—+—×—+—×	THE BORDER
❶ ••••••• ❷	ROUTE OF WALK (SHOWING POINTS OF DEPARTURE FOR EACH DAY)
	RIVER
	MAJOR ROAD
	RAILWAY
⊓⊔⊓⊔⊓⊔	BOUNDARY BETWEEN DIFFERENT ENGLISH OR SCOTTISH MARCHES
⊓⊔⊓⊔⊓⊔	HADRIAN'S WALL
	CHANNEL ADOPTED BY EDEN DURING SUMMER OF 1976
	PRESENT COASTLINE
▨	AREA WHICH HAS CHANGED NATIONALITY OR BEEN UNDER DEBATE IN RECENT CENTURIES
	SAND / MUD / SHALLOW WATER
	MARSH LAND
⋏⋏⋏	WOODLAND
	SEA
8	INDICATION OF SCOTTISH PARISH AREA ALONG THE BORDER (MAP 1)
●	VILLAGE / TOWN / FARM
//	NOTABLE BRIDGE
⚑	SITE OF DAYS OF TRUCE / MEETINGS OF WARDENS OF THE MARCHES
+	NOTABLE CHURCH
⊔ 1290	SITE OF AN INTERNATIONAL TREATY
📖	LITERARY REFERENCE OR LOCATION
♜	CASTLE / TOWER
⬛	BIG HOUSE
⚔ 1542	BATTLE SITE
▲ 451	SUMMIT (METRES)
⬓	PLACE WHERE THE STONE OF DESTINY TURNS UP
~ 🛡 Scotts ~	SPHERE OF FAMILY INFLUENCE

Map 1 is by Alasdair Allan. Maps 2 -7 (as well as this key) are by Louise Scott, based on rough sketches by Alasdair Allan. The maps in Chapter 4 are by Alasdair Allan, making use of an outline map purchased from istock.

Introduction: Against the Prevailing Wind

This is a book about a line on a hillside.

A real line along a wind-torn ridge, and up the stony beds of a narrow burn and a broad salmon river, and over a fertile haugh. At times, the line is lost in yellow whins or dank bog. At others, it is the perforated white paint of a B-road. It follows a broken fence and a dry-stane dyke, into the dark interior of a massive commercial forest, and out eventually onto the shifting sands of a glistening firth. This, then, is the Border between Scotland and England.

I was once smugly told by a British Empire Loyalist – posing at that point in his political career as an internationalist – that the Scottish Border cannot be seen from space. As if that proved something. As a Scottish Borderer, I can only retaliate that I would certainly see the Border very clearly from space. Indeed, given the opportunity, I would happily delineate it in some detail to my fellow astronauts, if the weather were good that day.

Despite prevailing winds and opinions, I decided to walk this line from east to west, choosing that direction for my own reasons. I now forget what those reasons are.[1]

The line in question is, of course, not just one on a map. Contrary to what anyone might try to tell the reader, this is a far from imaginary border, not least because Scotland is a far from imaginary country. That said, Scotland is certainly an *imagined* country too, as this book seeks to explore. So this is an attempt both to *walk* and to *read* my way along the Border. As I go, I will try to indicate where many (sometimes very obscure) points on this line intersect with Scotland's history and literature.

In doing this, I have cast my literary net fairly wide – an exercise which will no doubt irritate many of the unrelated species which find themselves caught together in it. Working relentlessly from east to west means, for instance, that Hugh MacDiarmid will probably find his cosmic lyrics mentioned in the same sentence as a jokey village bard or the mutterings of a Dumfriesshire minister. The reader may perhaps feel that this seemingly arbitrary way of categorising literature earns for me the same ridicule as was once directed at a dictionary of Shakespeare which infamously contained the entry: 'Gulls: not mentioned by Shakespeare'.[2]

---

[1] The truth is that I had written out most of my own detailed route-plan for the walk before I remembered the issue of the prevailing wind, and by then I could not face the task of re-writing everything in reverse.

[2] The nearest I can source to this legendary quote is one by Emma Phipson, in *The Animal Lore of Shakespeare's Time* (1883). She says of the gull that, 'This beautiful frequenter of our coasts is not once mentioned by name by Shakespeare', an observation of questionable relevance, by anybody's standards.

However, had the Border only ever produced three writers – James Hogg, Sir Walter Scott and Hugh MacDiarmid – then its contribution to Scottish (and wider) literature would have been immense. Add to that the philosophers, John Duns Scotus and David Hume, plus the Border ballads themselves, and the literary story of an extremely thin sliver of Scotland[1] becomes truly remarkable.

I will attempt, therefore, to take the reader on something like two parallel journeys – the one walked and the one read. Throughout this book, my definition of 'literature' will be broad, and takes in ballads, historical writing, poetry, and a stray opera, as well as popular literature, folklore, philosophy, travel writing and novels.

My definition of the Border, by contrast, will be more dogmatic. So, although I will sometimes refer to places that lie a few miles to one side of my path or other, I will usually do so only because they are relevant to something I actually see – or perhaps read – on my way. The places I will talk about in any detail are, at the very most, ten miles from the Border line, and generally less than that. It should be stressed that this is not primarily another book about *the Borders*; others have written about that region extensively. It is a book about the *Border* and what the places along it bring to mind – to my mind at least. The majority of places mentioned are in Scotland, partly for the simple reason that more of the southern edge of Scotland is populated than can be said of the northern edge of England. However, this emphasis is also because this book is really about what the Border means to Scotland.

The Border, if we learn to celebrate it, is – I contend – not only real, but a valuable (and often overlooked) part of Scotland's cultural inheritance. Indeed, it is highly unusual among the world's international land-frontiers. Chiefly this is because of its quite exceptional age,[2] but also because of its endless literary and historical associations, and its impressive (and, in a few parts, relatively undiscovered) landscapes. It is, I suggest, a Border worth exploring, not least at a time when Scotland is slowly but surely remembering who she is.

What began as an annotated route-map very quickly turned into a private and highly-opinionated guide for those who had agreed to come walking with me. By the time I started walking, it had formed the beginnings of this book.

What type of a book this adds up to is for others to judge. However, it is probably best, in the interests of transparency and good manners, for me to identify now some groups of readers who are likely to be disappointed or even offended, in order to save them the trouble of reading further.

---

[1] While Hogg and Scott both lived their lives a whole 25 miles north of the Border line, they each have so much to say about it that they more than qualify for inclusion here.
[2] I will explore in Chapter 4 and elsewhere how the Border came to be where it is now.

This is a book about a much-interrupted, and very largely un-signposted walking trip, but it is not a hillwalker's guide. There are far safer and more authoritative sources of information for walking in Scotland than this one,[1] filled with far wiser practical advice. I positively seek to indemnify myself against ill consequences befalling anyone who tries to use this book as such a guide. Less flippantly, I urge anyone walking the Border hills and forests to respect what some parts of that landscape can be like, especially in winter.

Nor is this book *too* much of a personal reflection, although, as will become clear, I cannot reasonably disentangle long sections of the Border from my own family origins. The book reflects in places the fact that three sides of my family have always – I use the last word advisedly – lived in the Scottish Borders. Many of them have worked the land within daily sight of the Border itself for the greater part of their lives. The fourth side of my family, my maternal grannie's, was English, and her family hailed from the northern part of Northumberland.

I grew up in the village of Ashkirk,[2] near Selkirk, which – from the viewpoint of any anxious cattle – is in fact a relatively safe few hours away from the Border on horseback. Most weekends of my youth, however, involved visiting relatives who lived, in several senses, a great deal closer to the edge than I did. All of that personal explanation given, I hope nonetheless to have steered clear of the very worst self-absorption seen in certain travel writers.[3]

In places, I will make a fair bit of use of the Scots language.[4] If the reader asks why, then I can only respond *whit for no?* Given the subject matter, it seems no less arbitrary than using English. If the reader doesn't like that kind of thing, please don't purchase.

Despite my every effort, the book inevitably becomes political in places. It is very difficult to think about the Border long enough to follow it through a forest without doing some reflecting. This is a book about a political boundary by a political activist in political times. In places, it is impossible (for me at least) not to draw certain conclusions about the present and the future from the past.

All of that said, this account makes much more modest claims for itself

---

[1] The books of Cameron McNeish represent such an authority, and one to be recommended.
[2] Ashkirk is around eighteen miles from the Border at the Carter Bar.
[3] The most brilliantly extreme example of this is found in the nearly-real person that is Alan Partridge, in *Nomad* (Orion Publishing, London, 2016). This is Partridge's description of a walk from Norwich to Dungeness Power Station (where his late father once applied for a job).
[4] A glossary is provided at the end of the book.

than any of that. This is ultimately just the story of a small adventure with some friends.

There is, it would seem, a venerable tradition of opinionated accounts of journeys through the Borders. Generally these come from the opposite point of view to my own. I will mention a few of of these in Chapter 3, but one of the earlier of these is Daniel Defoe's 1727 account, which opens by complaining that:

> Hitherto all the descriptions of Scotland, which have been published in our day, have been written by *natives* of that country, and that with such an air of the most scandalous partiality, that it has been far from pleasing to the gentry or nobility of Scotland themselves.

Defoe would, I trust, have been suitably disappointed by the present account on very much those same grounds, and no doubt on others too.

Opinionated as it is, however, *Tweed rins tae the Ocean* is not a political treatise. My account of this walking expedition professes to offer no solution to any political, social or economic problem. I was on my holidays.

CHAPTER 1
From the North Sea to the Solway: One Route to Take

Some brief, vague, but helpfully-intended information for other Border-walkers.

The least contentious plea I will make over the next hundred miles – at least as much to myself as to others – is to come offline for a wee while, go outside, and walk. That plea is all the more sincere for being made at a time when the world is still feeling the impact of a global pandemic.

As the famous scene in *Trainspotting*[1] at lonely Corrour station illustrates, a great many Scots do not explore their own countryside – at all. Many do not have the opportunity. Just as troublingly, however, many other Scots who *do* have that opportunity are simply not convinced that there is anything whatsoever in Scotland to see.

In 2018, my old friend Malcolm Fleming and I wanted to explore, though. We debated at length over a pizza whether either of us still had the youth, strength or available annual leave for a ten-day walk. We both failed by a number of these measures, and it was decided instead to attempt the journey in several parts. In the end, Malc joined me for seven of the eleven days[2] which the journey eventually took.

The walk described here could in fact probably be done in eight days, if the reader were really keen, though that would not leave a lot of time or energy for them to form any opinions about what they were actually seeing. The route is broken down fairly arbitrarily here into eleven walks of wildly-varying length and difficulty. These range from a scarcely-worth-mentioning four-mile section of the Border to a respectable seventeen-mile treck over pathless hills.

I have tried to give the reader enough cursory sat-nav-like information between my anecdotes to allow them, should they wish, to plot a similar route.

---

[1] The scene in question, famous from the 1996 film adaptation of Irvine Welsh's novel of the same name, shows the story's heroes stepping off the train onto the magnificent Rannoch Moor. They are torn between feelings of overwhelming national pride and a somewhat bleaker, if considered, assessment that: 'It's shite being Scottish! We're the lowest of the low…It's a shite state of affairs to be in, Tommy.' Concluding that fresh air will not solve that problem, they are not sure what they are supposed to do on a mountainside: 'What now?… This is not natural,' one of the characters wonders. They get back on the train.

[2] I am not, for the moment, including in this the afterthought I subsequently had of following the Border line still further beyond Gretna to the point at which it actually stops on the Solway Firth (see Chapter 8).

The maps I used were OS Explorer 346, OS Landranger 74, and OS Explorer maps OL16, OL42, 324, 323 and 322. I have throughout (following the example of medieval charters) described my route by the things I passed, rather than by grid references, though the latter are easy enough to trace. I have *not* made use of the *What3words* app, which with all the self-assuredness of a nineteenth-century colonial power, has renamed every spot on earth with three random (and, needless to say, English) words.[1]

If the reader does plan to take the same road as I did, then they should be aware that, while there is plenty of accommodation to choose from at each end of the Border (i.e. in Berwick and Gretna/Annan), this is not true of anywhere in between. The places to stay mentioned in the account are not quite the only options, but they are not far off it. There are, for instance, a Bed-and-Breakfast and campsite in Kielder, and a couple of B-and-Bs to choose from in both Coldstream and Yetholm, the last of which villages also has a bunkhouse and campsite. There is a B-and-B at Cocklawfoot Farm in the Cheviots, and one or two places to stay in Canonbie and Newcastleton, as well as the bothy at Kershopehead. There is also a bunkhouse at Mounthooly, a mile or two from the Pennine Way. Beyond those places, however, most other alternatives would involve wandering a long way from the Border by carefully-positioned car each evening. If the reader is planning to sleep in a bed rather than a ditch, book early.

Mentions of where I stayed should not be viewed as product-placement, but the Mason's Arms in Norham and the Border Hotel in Kirk Yetholm can both be particularly recommended, based on my own experience.[2]

If the reader is prepared to carry a tent, then wild-camping is an option, subject to all the usual injunctions about good practice that go with that. The law on roaming the countryside is considerably more liberal in Scotland than in England (England has a law of trespass) but, in both countries, all the obvious rules about shutting gates and not damaging crops apply.

In general, the East and West Marches are comparatively leisurely walking, stotting from pub to pub, if the reader chooses to. Large sections at each end of the Border could probably be cycled, with a little modification to the route described here, and with some of the advice about pubs cautiously revoked.

---

[1] This app redesignates my walk's starting point near Marshall Meadows Bay as tornado.beak.crucially. The Kirk of the Steill at Ladykirk becomes troll.launched. workloads. If this device is not intended to be a way of wiping clean the cultural hard drive of the word's place names, it would be a pretty handy tool for anyone so minded. It reminds me of the person who once asked me for 'a poetic Gaelic name' for their new holiday house in the Hebrides. He was mystified when I told him that, if he asked any of his elderly neighbours, he would find that the spot already had a much more interesting *genuine* Gaelic name than any fake one we could come up with between us.
[2] The Powfoot Hotel also makes a fine roast lunch.

Cyclists would, however, have to be prepared patiently to pick up and discard bikes several times if, like me, they enjoy traveling one-way along political boundaries.

The fifty miles or so of the Middle March are a much more challenging prospect, however, for modern walkers and medieval armies alike. So food and warm clothes need to be carried, and journeys have to be planned properly. Decent boots, maps, compasses, and back-up batteries for mobiles should *not* be regarded as optional, and the mishaps described in Day 7 of my walk should, in seriousness, be avoided.[1]

Distances referred to are approximations, and come with that health warning, but the Border itself, from Marshall Meadows Bay to Gretna, is around 96 miles long.[2] My own walk was probably about 104 miles in total (if I do not include either of the times I was lost, or the additional walk along the Solway described in Chapter 8).

The rest of the information after this point in the book becomes notably less practically useful in character. Some of the commentary is, in its very border-conscious tone, probably subliminally influenced by the annual tradition of the ridings of the marches in the Border towns.[3] As border-inspections go, however, this one was friendly in its diplomatic intentions.

---

[1] Additionally, a glance at tide tables, if walking along the Solway coast, would be very sound safety advice. Although the Solway can, with some difficulty, be forded at points, nobody should attempt this without great forethought. The tidal rise is over 20 feet, and the tidal bore can travel at seven knots.

[2] Like most people, I will generally (and inconsistently) measure heights in metres, but distances in miles.

[3] Common ridings are of course a practice intended originally to check that local boundaries had not been encroached upon.

CHAPTER 2
Day 1: *Lowpin-on Stanes*[1]

Breathes there the man?; The train there; Anomalous Berwick; The Border begins.

Many things in Scotland were either created by Sir Walter Scott or named after one of his creations. Edinburgh's Waverley Station is one of the latter. Today, as reminder of that fact, the heaving crowds hurry past billboards that have been put up in the station to carry quotations from Scott himself:

> Breathes there the man, with soul so dead,
> Who never to himself hath said,
> This is my own, my native land!
> Whose heart hath ne'er within him burn'd,
> As home his footsteps he hath turn'd,
> From wandering on a foreign strand!
> If such there breathe, go, mark him well;
> For him no Minstrel raptures swell;
> High though his titles, proud his name,
> Boundless his wealth as wish can claim;
> Despite those titles, power, and pelf,
> The wretch, concentred all in self,
> Living, shall forfeit fair renown,
> And, doubly dying, shall go down
> To the vile dust, from whence he sprung,
> Unwept, unhonour'd, and unsung.[2]

The rest of the travelling public today may not have much time to consider these stirring injunctions. I do though, because I am on a rare weekend off. I have been looking forward to it. My journey began two days earlier at my home in an opposite corner of the country – the Isle of Lewis.

As I wait for the train to Berwick, an earnest and angry-looking young man suddenly charges along the platform opposite me, a determined little ice-

---

[1] A *lowpin-on stane* (a 'jumping-on stone'), according to my late father, was any large boulder designated in the past by people with horses as a place from which they might leap up into the saddle.
[2] Sir Walter Scott: *Lay of the Last Minstrel*, from its sometimes unduly-derided Canto VI.

breaker against arctic flows of commuters. Politically-badged, red-bearded and kilted, he marches, apparently straight from the pages of Scott's *Waverley*[1] and onto the Plymouth train. I am not sure what it is he has planned for Plymouth. Fair play to him, anyway. He provides a strangely appropriate, if slightly uncanny, image with which to begin my own expedition.

I turn around. Malc has arrived, as planned. We heave our modest rucksacks onto the train. In Malc's case, he says it is the same rucksack he used when we once walked (in one youthful go) the two hundred miles of Scotland's Southern Upland Way.[2] Malc and I have variously been student flatmates, hillwalking partners, political brothers-in-arms, and expert first-foots.

I have been nursing the idea of this new walk for some time. Malc is seemingly undeterred by grim memories of the first (and I think last) real test of our long friendship, which was in 1995. This was when, several days and numerous flasks of tea into the Southern Upland Way, Malc discovered that I had absent-mindedly been storing our supply of new tea bags in a small plastic bag. Unfortunately it was the same plastic bag which he had, at the outset, clearly explained to me was designated for the environmentally-responsible storage of the discarded sticking-plasters from our feet. Malc, happily, has been able to put that experience somewhere nearer the back of his mind, and agree to this new trip.

Soon, we are on the train. Glancing down, we each separately follow the dot, as it moves by jumps and starts in time with the flickering broadband. It speeds out over the fast-shifting landscape of *Google Map* and on towards the broken red line. Outside and offline, it is not raining. The spring morning makes no bolder claim for itself than that. It is not mild or bright, not promising or 'trying'. It is just not raining.

The train hurtles around deep gashes in Berwickshire's black clifftops. The day is fair enough to see an Eyemouth fishing boat out against the pale horizon. It is probably going to be a good day.

The expedition we have planned is definitely not to be reckoned in the same sentence as Mungo Park's malaria-ridden expedition to the source of the River Niger, but it has probably been equally long in the planning. I have deaved Malc by email for weeks about it. Fortunately, given the amount of time we are going to spend in each other's company this week, the pair of us are happy proving Charles Lamb's dictum that 'tis the privilege of friendship to talk nonsense, and to have that nonsense respected.[3]

Equally, it is of course another such privilege to feel no need to make

---

[1] (Or, indeed, directly out of my own unduly-intense youth).

[2] Given his tendency towards frugalness, I readily believe this.

[3] E.V. Lucas: *The Life of Charles Lamb*. London, G. Putman & Sons, London, 1905.

conversation at all.

We have, in any case, silently decided against opening up the old debate about the burgh (or perhaps borough[1]) of Berwick. So, when we get to Berwick Station, we will dutifully make our way back north to this breezy place we are passing right ... *now* ... on the cliffs. For this is the easternmost point of the Scottish-English Border.

***

Over half a century ago, the general firebrand and noted eccentric Wendy Wood[2] physically moved the border sign on the A1 three miles south from here to the middle of the bridge over the Tweed, beyond Berwick. This, she said, was an act of protest at England's annexation of the town in 1482. I do not intend to try to follow her example this week.

Berwick is, nonetheless, a famously anomalous place. As one old rhyme puts it:

> They talk about England and Scotland, indeed.
> But it's England and Scotland and Berwick-upon-Tweed.

In 1551, Berwick was recognised as an 'independent borough', apparently part of neither Scotland nor England, but definitely administered by the latter. Continuing uncertainties about what exactly that might mean led to clarifications in the *Wales and Berwick Act* of 1746. There remained for some time, however, a degree of lingering mystery which was sometimes expressed in almost spiritual terms by saying that Berwick was *of* the Kingdom of England but not *in* it.

Similar existential questions led to the famous story that the town is today still at war with Russia. The claim runs that Queen Victoria declared war on Russia in 1854 as 'Queen of Great Britain, Ireland, Berwick-upon-Tweed and the British Dominions beyond the sea'. In declaring peace however, the Government forgot to mention Berwick, an error that was not discovered until the rather crucial moment of October 1914.

---

[1] Even the spelling here is not without significance; Scotland has burghs, but England has boroughs.

[2] While canvassing in an election campaign, I once met an elderly voter who told me that he had made a mental note, sometime in the 1950s, never to vote for my party, the SNP. His resolution was based on his experience of having been lectured in the street about his patriotic duties by a solitary tartan-clad lady. From his description, this was certainly Wendy Wood. She had insisted that he buy, for a shilling, a pamphlet about the Darien Disaster of 1700.

Proclamations of this kind did at one time often make specific belt-and-braces mention of Berwick, although this particular story has perhaps become a little enhanced in the re-telling. I do not, however, grudge Berwickers or anyone else a good anecdote. In any case, the Mayor of Berwick and a Soviet representative signed a 'treaty' of goodwill a century afterwards, to seek to put the matter to rest.

We discard a second-hand newspaper – which gives prominence to Russia's present and less conciliatory international intentions – pick up our bags, and set foot on Berwick Station.

***

Scots traditionally have an unusual interest in the actual moment of 'The Bells'[1] at Hogmanay. We prepare carefully each year to cross a very undisputed boundary between the past and the future. With a similar exactness, we wait for a first-foot to cross the clear boundary of our threshold.[2] Crossing the Scottish Border is, likewise, a definite, sudden and significant matter. Berwick, however, (I have never heard any Borderer call it 'Berwick-upon-Tweed'[3]) is a place of genuine ambiguities.

Among these is the fact that Berwick Rangers play in the Scottish football league. The club still celebrates beating the 'Big Gers' – Glasgow Rangers – in 1967, in much the same way as Scotland fans still recall beating the reigning World Cup champions (England) in a game that same year.

Still more confusingly, Berwick's barracks are home to the museum of the King's Own Scottish Borderers Battalion of the Royal Regiment of Scotland.

With a similar illogicality, the Royal Border Bridge (as the railway bridge over the Tweed here is called) is clearly not on the modern Border at all. It stands beside James VI's bridge, which that wily (but far from lion-hearted) monarch ordered to be built, immediately upon arriving in his new English kingdom in 1603. He had been badly scared crossing the rickety wooden bridge which then stood there. On James's new bridge, the battlement above the sixth arch is raised above the others because it marks the boundary between the old county of North Durham and the town of Berwick. It might be said, only a little more provocatively, that it also marks where England stops and

---

[1] i.e. midnight at New Year.

[2] My grandmother took this latter tradition so seriously that, on New Year's Day, she would keep me standing outside her door in Duns until someone who did *not* have red hair could cross the doorstep before me. Red-haired first foots are less propitious than most other types, with the exception of ministers and undertakers.

[3] At one time, many people in Scotland apparently referred to Berwick as 'South Berwick', to distinguish it from North Berwick in East Lothian.

the Danzig-like statelet of Berwick begins.

I have heard it suggested that there might be different national identities associated with different sub-groups within the town, though I cannot verify that. Certainly, the multiple different versions of the Church of Scotland operating here in the nineteenth century suggest a very Scottish interest in religious schism. There is still one 'Scottish' congregation here, whose church is at Wallace Green.[1]

To Scottish ears, the Berwick accent is definitely English. Yet many Berwickers do – unusually for most English people outside the West Country – traditionally put an 'r' sound after the vowel in words like 'car' or 'hair'. The 'Berwick burr', as this is called, while it occurs in this same context as a rolled Scottish 'r', sounds (if I may crudely approximate here) more like the letter 'w'.

Most anomalously of all, however, the Scottish county of Berwickshire has not contained Berwick for over five centuries. Berwickshire has in fact struggled ever since to decide which of its comparatively small remaining settlements should replace Berwick as county town.[2]

I do not claim to know how exactly this situation is seen in Berwick itself, but, in Berwickshire and the easternmost part of Roxburghshire, the town is viewed in a very specific way. On a long eastern stretch of the Border, where national identities change very clearly within a matter of a few yards, Berwick is nonetheless still viewed as the 'local' market town. No other town in England is viewed in this light. People living near borders will of course always shop and work in other countries as, to a more limited extent, happens further west in Carlisle. Berwick, however, is not Carlisle. It is not going too far to say that there is still some dim recollection – at least in the Merse – that Berwick was once one of the four great cities of Scotland.

But this is a historical connection, not a political one. For me, none of this friendly (if complicated) relationship between Berwick and Berwickshire creates any kind of basis for the lengthy constitutional arguments, occasionally still rehearsed, which seek to prove that Berwick is in Scotland. It isn't.[3]

---

[1] This street where the Church of Scotland stands is beside the city walls, suggesting the name was once simply 'Walls Green'. A much better story, however, is that it gets its name because it was here that one of the severed limbs of William Wallace was displayed by Edward Longshanks. This is a scene to which the film *Outlaw King* (2018, Netflix) does some justice.

[2] The County of Berwickshire (or its successor, Berwickshire District Council) was formally abolished in 1996, though its existence is still widely acknowledged as a local identity.

[3] In the early 2000s there were in fact opinion polls conducted in Berwick which suggested that a majority of Berwickers were in favour of rejoining Scotland. This question was largely framed at that time in terms of the different public services available in Scotland and England. This was, however, before there was any immediate prospect of Scottish independence. Any similar future debate in Berwick, if there is

As we will see, one of the great advantages for Scotland is that, unlike many other re-emerging countries, its borders are not disputed. For the moment, we should probably accept that fact, or as the Scots proverb puts it more vividly, *dinna claw whaur it's no youkie.*[1] Berwick is the exception on the Border, not the rule.

***

The construction of Berwick railway station in 1847, while it spared the town's Elizabethan walls, involved largely flattening its medieval castle. Here was where Edward I of England imprisoned the Countess of Buchan in a publicly-displayed iron cage for four years, for having dared set the crown on the head of Robert Bruce. Here too was where Edward required all the nobles and officials of Scotland to kneel before him in his newly-invented role as Lord Paramount of Scotland, and to sign the 'Ragman Rolls'[2] as homage.

When the station was built, some tourist guide books[3] warned that the spirit of King Edward I is condemned, for his innumerable crimes, to wander irritatedly up and down a railway platform here, looking forever both psychopathic and late for work.

We come out of the station and catch the Duns bus. We head back north for a few minutes, crossing the intriguingly-named Conundrum Roundabout as we do. I think – not for the final time in my expedition – of a family story.

A brother of my Northumbrian great-grandmother married a native of one of England's very few inhabited islands, Lindisfarne or Holy Island, not far down the coast from here. She drove a milk float round the island for many years into her old age, and it was eventually put to her that she should get a driving licence. In due course, during her test in Berwick, she was told by the driving examiner to 'go straight across the roundabout'. She revved up and did literally as she was told, ploughing over the top of the large green hill in the middle and onto the busy junction beyond. I hope it was this roundabout, with its strangely appropriate name. I hope she passed.

I mention all this to Malc, who remarks darkly that I have form, on this type of trip, when it comes to roundabouts. The reader, at this early stage, cannot possibly know what relevance roundabouts have to matters. Roundabouts, however, will be raised several times in the course of my

---

one, will no doubt be held in a completely new political context.

[1] 'Don't scratch where it's not itchy'.

[2] From the name of which document, incidentally, we (may well) get the word 'rigmarole.'

[3] Maurice Lindsay quotes this story in *The Lowlands of Scotland.*

expedition – both mysteriously and annoyingly. I will not try the reader with an explanation, just at the moment.

To our left now lies Halidon Hill. Here in 1333, during the Second Scottish Wars of Independence, the Scottish commander Sir Archibald Douglas was defeated by Edward III of England, who was was supporting the claim of Edward Balliol (the son of King John Balliol)[1] to Scotland's crown. Balliol, some months earlier, had declared himself King of Scots, only to flee almost immediately to England, half-naked and promising half of Scotland to Edward III[2]. Halidon Hill was England's attempt to overthrow Scotland's nine-year-old King David II with this evidently more pliable alternative. England won the battle, but not the war; Edward Balliol is not a name you will see on many lists of Scottish kings and, after several attempted coups, his claim was abandoned. He is believed to be buried under a post office in Doncaster.

I said I would be *reading* my way westwards, not just walking. So, before I go much further, I will pause to take a sceptical look at some of the travel writers who have come this way before us.

For the moment, though, Malc and I are happy enough to get off the bus at New East Farm. We are still in England. We run across the busy A1 road (walking across it here would be fatal), and into Marshall Meadows Farm. Here, a caravan site stretches down to the sea's edge from near England's most northerly hotel. Walking north-eastwards for a couple of hundred yards through the farm, we head onto the little bridge over the railway. Crossing it, we turn left, and emerge onto a coastal path which follows the eastern side of the railway line. Just beyond Marshall Meadows Bay, a sign on the path welcomes us to Scotland and tells us that we are now out of Berwick and into Berwickshire.

We are standing on the Border. Our walk has begun.

---

[1] John Balliol is generally accredited as having been Scotland's least-rated king.
[2] See the 'Roxburgh Promise' mentioned in Chapter 4.

CHAPTER 3
Mostly Lost: Travel Writers and the Border

James Logan Mack; Pope Pius II; Boswell and Johnson; H.V. Morton; Rory Stewart; Nigel Tranter.

The long tradition of travel-writing about the Borders should now be acknowledged, though I admit that I do so here only very selectively.

Much of what has been written about the region (mainly by visitors) has assumed that the Scottish Borders are somehow 'neither in Scotland nor England', or that they are a 'middle country'. A great deal of this writing takes it as read therefore that the Border line somehow doesn't *really* exist. Some writers wonder aloud in a state of perceptible bafflement about the Border, and all those who live by it.[1] I am unable to oblige the reader by falling into this tradition, as I very markedly do not subscribe to its key premise.

In plotting a path for my walk, I looked at the accounts of some people who said they had walked the Border. In a number of cases, I found they had gone nowhere near the Border at all. One honourable exception is James Logan Mack who, over the course of no fewer than seventy expeditions to different sections of the Border between 1916 and 1922, probably gathered more meticulous information on it than has any other individual. Mack took his commission so literally that at times he leaves the impression that he chose to walk through bogs and burns, rather than deviate an inch from the Border. In the process, he produced a very fine book, *The Border Line*, to which I am greatly indebted.[2] My own route will not take quite such a diligent route as J.L. Mack's and will use paths and roads wherever these are available. For the most part though, I will stick as inflexibly and unreasonably close to the Border as seems physically practicable.

Much travel writing about the Border takes a less rigorous approach than J.L. Mack's. There is probably no better way to demonstrate that point than by reading the account of one of the most eminent, if unlikely, people to walk (some of) this way before us: Pope Pius II.

***

---

[1] In some cases, this confusion is almost certainly partly the product of the surprisingly widespread belief that England is an island, sceptred or otherwise. Many English people (and the rest of the world too, to be fair) have little idea of the distinctions between the U.K., Great Britain and England.

[2] I will refer to J.L. Mack so often that I will allow myself the familiarity of doing so without giving full citations.

Aeneas Silvio Bartolomeo Piccolomini, to use his own name, visited Scotland in 1435, some years before his election as Pope Pius II. He probably enjoys the accolade of having been the only Pope ever to have crossed our Border, other than in an aeroplane. He deserves a mention here for that strange fact alone. By a happy coincidence, he is also one of only a couple of Popes ever to have written an autobiography. It makes curious reading.

Aeneas arrived in Scotland by ship from Bruges, during which journey he had been blown off-course towards Norway. A north wind eventually blew him back to the coast of East Lothian, from where he walked barefoot to the shrine at Whitekirk to give thanks.

Aeneas believes that Scotland is an island, though he also says it is 'connected with Britain'.[1] He observes that the men are 'short and brave'. The women, meanwhile, are 'fair and easily won, thinking less of a kiss than Italian women think of a touch of the hand'. People in the north-west speak a different language. In the winter, he claims, the day is barely four hours long. The chief delight of Scots, he concludes, is to hear verbal abuse directed against England. He dispels a story (which had seemingly reached Italian ears) that there are trees in Scotland whose fruit, if it falls into a river, is transformed into birds. He concedes that this type of thing might possibly still be going on in Orkney.[2]

Aeneas eventually made his way over the Border, somewhere in the Merse, and headed for Newcastle. Immediately after crossing into Northumberland, one incident which he records illustrates (among other things) the terror which people there had for the Border reivers:

> Two young women showed Aeneas into a chamber strewn
> with straw, planning to sleep with him, as was the custom of
> the country, if they were asked. But Aeneas, thinking less
> about women than about robbers, who he feared might
> appear at any minute, repulsed the protesting girls, fearing
> that if he committed a sin, he might have to pay the penalty
> as soon as the robbers arrived. So he remained alone, among

[1] The *Mappa Mundi*, the map in Hereford Cathedral produced around 1300, also delineates Scotland as an island. Both Berwick and Edinburgh lie to the north of what is marked ambiguously either as a narrow stretch of sea or perhaps a river which (somehow) runs between the North Sea and the Atlantic. Earlier mapmakers like Matthew Paris, however, still imagine a *'regio invia et aquosa'* ('damp and impassable region') further north, and still think of the land north of the Forth and Clyde as an island, or as good as one. Paris's map of c1250 marks this as *'Scocia Ultra Marina'* ('Scotland beyond the sea'), noting that *'Albania dicta est'* ('This is called Alba').
[2] This story has echoes of the (then widely-accepted) belief that barnacle geese were born of barnacles.

the heifers and the nannygoats, which prevented him from sleeping a wink by their stealthily pulling the straw from out of his pallet.[1]

Aeneas goes on to describe the panic in the household, when the door is hammered in the middle of the night, though these particular 'reivers' (it turns out) are just rowdy visitors. He attributes his escape to his moral 'continence'.

Pope Pius II is in fact widely rumoured to have fathered a child just on the Scottish side of the Border and, on that basis, presumably has descendents somewhere near Duns or Jedburgh to this day.

***

The eighteenth century's Great Englishman, Samuel Johnson, and his Scottish chronicler James Boswell, famously toured together as far north as the Hebrides. Boswell was in fact a man not without feelings for his native country, but his first and famous words to Johnson ring down the ages as the definitive statement of cringing cultural inferiorism from the mouth of a specific type of Scot:

> Mr. Johnson, I do indeed come from Scotland, but I cannot help it.

Johnson's response is more perceptive:

> That, Sir, I find, is what a very great many of your country-men cannot help.[2]

A century after Boswell, the English travel writer H.V. Morton wrote two hugely popular books: *In Search of Scotland* and *In Scotland Again*. These detail long car expeditions around Scotland (including the Borders) in 1928 and 1932. Elegantly-written, these books are even authentically – Scottishly – couthie in places. Like Boswell's accounts, they had a significant impact on how Scotland was seen by tourists.

Very sadly, however, Morton's biographer feeds the nagging fear that many parts of Morton's most attractive travel accounts are inventions from beginning to end. I fear that Morton's story about the curator of the Burns

[1] Pope Pius II: *Commentaries*, from *Memoirs of a Renaissance Pope*, translated by Florence Gragg and Leona Gabel.
[2] James Boswell: *Life of Samuel Johnson.*

Museum in Alloway bursting into tears and reciting 'To Mary in Heaven' (because his own wife had died the day before Morton's visit) may well fall into this category. Cautioned by such disappointments, I will try my best to be broadly truthful in my own anecdotes.[1]

***

A more recent travel writer I want to mention is Rory Stewart. His book *The Marches,* like this one, recounts a walk along the Border, but with the opposite starting and end points to mine (both in terms of the route walked and the conclusions reached).

Mr Stewart and I have perhaps rather different backgrounds and world-views (he is a former Conservative MP[2]). His book opens by talking about his childhood routine of fencing practice in Hyde Park. Searching politely for some common ground here, I could relevantly mention some of the fencers in my own family too. In fact, many of the Border fences I will follow along the Cheviots were probably put up by my Great Uncle Geordie, who worked as a fencer in Yetholm into his eighties.

Mr Stewart's book is, above all else, a very dignified and touching tribute to his late father. He has a very learned understanding of an earlier period of history, before Scotland and England were states or concepts. Yet they have been both concepts and states for a very long time now, as Mr Stewart seems unwilling to acknowledge. Moreover, neither the Border nor Scottishness were invented by the SNP, as Mr Stewart often seems to imply. So our paths must diverge, in terms of our respective views about what the Border means (or, in his view, does not mean) today.

Entitled as Mr Stewart is to his thoughts on all this, the BBC's decision to broadcast them on prime-time television[3] as a three-part series in the weeks running up to the Scottish Independence Referendum of 2014 was fairly remarkable.

---

[1] The H.V. Morton Society admits coyly on its website that: '[Morton was] 'a creature of his time, a product of the Edwardian certainties of class, sex and race... [he had] a darker side [with] right wing sympathies.' His biographer Michael Bartholomew is less circumspect, and mentions Morton's statement – as late on in the day as 1941 – that 'Nazi-ism has some fine qualities.' From *In Search of H.V. Morton* by Michael Bartholomew (Methuen, London, 2004), as reviewed by Max Hastings in the *Daily Telegraph,* 9 May 2004.

[2] A strange coincidence is the fact that Mr Stewart (former MP for Penrith and the Border) was writing his book at the same time as I was first giving thought to this one, unbeknown to each other. An even stranger coincidence is the fact that we have both subsequently done exactly the same job in our two respective governments (indeed, the same job as the hapless politician in the film *In the Loop*), namely Minister for International Development.

[3] *Borderland: The story of Britain's lost Middleland,* BBC, 2014.

***

Graham Robb, Alistair Moffat and Ian Crofton are three other modern writers who, whenever they talk about the meaning of the Border, all seem to nail their colours to fairly similar masts to Mr Stewart's. In his own book on the Border, Eric Robson regularly offers assessments which are depressing, not so much for their take on Scottish independence as for their casual dismissal of Scotland in general:

> ...of course anyone of Scottish Nationalist persuasion would take a rather different view. Proud, independent Scottish nation and all that. But talk of full-blown independence for a tiny underpopulated bit of offshore Europe seems to be straying dangerously close to Prisoner of Zenda territory. With Jimmy Logan rather than Ronald Coleman playing the lead. But I wouldn't like you to get the impression I've any strong view about these things.[1]

I respectfully suggest it is time to even up the score a little when it comes to writing about the Border. The balance is presently weighted very much against writers who view the Border as the now-peaceable meeting place between two venerable countries, and in favour of those who see the Border (and by implication Scotland) as not really being there at all.

One travel writer, however, who I am going to claim is on my side on this issue, is Nigel Tranter. His *Illustrated Portrait of the Border Country* was described by its publisher as:

> ...biased, dogmatic, opinionated, but then so is the Borderland. It is one man's picture of the most essentially controversial area of these islands – and he takes sides. Any portrait of the Borders which sought to stay calm, sober, reasonable, impartial would be a travesty.[2]

I take these remarks as licence for what follows.

---

[1] Eric Robson: *The Border Line: The Story of the Anglo Scottish Border.*
[2] This is how Tranter's publishers described his book in a notice on the back cover of Godfrey Watson's *The Border Reivers.*

CHAPTER 4
Aye Bin?[1] Origins of the Border Line

(This chapter is best read in conjunction with the Timeline at the end of the book)

Hadrian's Wall and All That; Romans, Picts, Britons, Angles, Scots; Origins of the line; From the Battle of Carham to the Treaty of York – the Border settles on its modern line; Wars, promises and treaties; Berwick, the Debatable Lands and the Union of Crowns; The Border since 1603 – a Parliament adjourned and reconvened; The world's oldest national land border?

Hadrian's Wall and All That

I recall once visiting Hadrian's Wall as a child. A good-natured tourist, from not much further south in England, made the mistake of joking to my father that the wall had been 'built by us guys, to keep you guys out'.[2] It is, needless to say, not quite as simple as that.

Nonetheless, when the Border is spoken of (very often by people who don't quite believe that Scotland *really* exists in the modern world) it is often referred to jokingly as 'Hadrian's Wall', as if the wall might be where the two countries meet.

Strangely enough, many Scots and most English people have only a very general idea of where the Border actually is. Few have even a slight idea of how long it has been there. As long ago as the eighteenth century, the author Tobias Smollet observed this confusion in one of his characters:

> She was so little acquainted with the geography of the island, that she imagined we could not go to Scotland but by sea; and, after we had passed through the town of Berwick, when he told her we were upon Scottish ground, she could hardly believe the assertion – If the truth must be told, the South Britons in general are woefully ignorant in this particular. What, between want of curiosity, and traditional sarcasms, the effect of ancient animosity, the people at the other end of the island know as little of Scotland as of Japan.[3]

---

[1] *'It's aye bin'* (It's always been) is traditionally offered in the Borders as an answer to almost any question beginning with the word 'why'.
[2] I recall my father responding dryly to this that the wall had actually been built by the Romans, 'after they conquered you guys'.
[3] Tobias Smollet: *The Expedition of Humphry Clinker.*

In this chapter, I will attempt to untangle as much of this confusion as I can, before our walk begins in earnest.

Figure A) 700 AD

AD 130 – 843: Romans, Picts, Britons, Angles, Scots

Before I leave the reader with any impression that the Scots are all that much better informed about the Border than the English are, I should say that quite a number of Scots who followed my walk on Facebook asked me – apparently seriously – why I had not just walked along the top of Hadrian's Wall.

In fact, the wall, completed around AD 130, predates both Scotland and England. Although at its western end it begins more or less exactly on the modern Border, by the east coast it is some 68 miles too far south[1] (and several hundred years too early) to have any real bearing on this walk or this book. In any case, the Antonine Wall, running between the Forth and Clyde, was probably the one more effectively defended by the Romans while they were here.

Of the various ethnic and linguistic groups competing for territory after Hadrian's Wall was abandoned, in the course of the fourth century, there are many local tribal names that could be listed. However, the three significant broad categories of people are (as history generally names them) the Britons, the Scots and the Angles. These names are not completely transparent without a word of explanation.

By the Britons are meant the Brythonic[2] people in the west, who spoke a Cumbric language closely akin to modern Welsh. They had a kingdom, initially known as Alt Clut and latterly called Strathclyde, which came eventually to include much of south-west Scotland from Dumbarton southwards into modern Cumbria.[3]

The Angles[4] arrived at the end of the fifth century, and their language ultimately provided us with both Scots and English. The Anglo-Saxon kingdom of Northumbria latterly stretched, on the east coast, from the Humber to the Forth.[5] To the west, Northumbria also initially included the Dumfries and Galloway areas,[6] until some point in the ninth or early tenth

---

[1] See Map 1.

[2] Or Brittonic. To confuse matters further, they are often referred to (even in what is now Scotland), as 'Cumbrians'. This name is itself one and the same as 'Cymru' (the modern Welsh name for Wales).

[3] When I refer to 'modern Cumbria' I do not mean the swathe of once-Brythonic speaking peoples in southern Scotland and northern England, but specifically the local authority area formed in 1974 out of the former counties of Cumberland, Westmoreland and some other adjacent areas of England.

[4] Or Anglo-Saxons.

[5] It is important to say that the Kingdom of Northumbria was neither part of the Kingdom of England nor of Scotland. Nor was it coterminous with the modern English county of Northumberland.

[6] This explains why at Ruthwell, just beyond the very end of our walk, an eighth century cross is scratched with runic lines from the Old English poem 'The Dream of the Rood'.

century, when these areas (along with modern Cumbria) came back under Brythonic influence, and probably even under the direct rule of the Kingdom of Strathclyde.[1]

By the Scots are meant – for the moment only – the people the Romans called the *Scotii*, the Gaelic-speaking people who were found both in Ireland and in the west of Scotland. Their kingdom, Dalriada, centred on Argyll, at its height stretched from the Isle of Skye to the Antrim coast. A traditional (though now much-questioned) take on their story would be to say that, having broken their political ties with Ireland, the Scottish Gaels united in 843 with the Picts in the north-east. However exactly it happened, a kingdom called *Alba* or *Scotland* was formed, encompassing a very large chunk of the country we now know by those names.[2]

---

[1] Historical sources for the Kingdom of Strathclyde are scant, so any description of its borders must be couched in these vague terms. It must also be said that, whether run by Angles or Britons, or by the Kingdom of Scotland, Galloway was in fact a multicultural place, and had a significant number of Gaelic speakers until the sixteenth century.

[2] Gilbert Márkus provides a cautionary note about all this. In *Conceiving a Nation* he rightly warns that 'The idea that in the early medieval insular world there were strong and long-lasting kingdoms united by language, shared ancestry, [and] territorial integrity ... is a seductive view of the world for historians both medieval and modern.' Bede and others have popularised down the centuries the idea of Gaelic having come to Scotland from Ireland, when it probably evolved on both sides of the water simultaneously. Likewise, the union of Pictland and Dalriada is not quite so straightforward as my traditionalist maps would have the reader believe. There were in fact significant incursions by the Picts into Dalriada, while Dalriadan influence on Pictland was as much about cultural assimilation as it was military or dynastic conquest. But over-simplifications have a venerable tradition in Scottish history, and so I repeat them here, albeit with all the above caveats.

Figure B) 954 AD

843 – 1018: Origins of the Line

In setting out on our expedition in 2018, Malc and I felt that some official pretext was required. Thousandth anniversaries do not often present themselves but, for us, one very happily and relevantly did.

In 1018, Malcolm II of Scotland (aided by King Owain the Bald of Strathclyde) prevailed at Carham against the Earl of Northumbria.[1] The battle essentially bisected Northumbria between Scotland and England – very broadly

[1] The Kingdom of Northumbria, weakened by Viking incursions to its south, came to an end in 954, after which it was only a semi-independent Earldom under increasingly effective English suzerainty.

along present lines.

Although modern Scotland can credibly claim some ancient national origins before this time, it only makes sense to start talking about the *Border* when we reach the point in history where there are two clearly-defined countries called Scotland and England, along something like their present boundaries. Carham begins to give us that, with a Border whose eastern half at least is now very familiar to us. Even when footnoted with all the qualifications the historians can muster, we now have a very old border indeed to talk about and walk along.

Figure C) 1030 AD

1018 – 1237: From the Battle of Carham to the Treaty of York – The Border settles on its modern line

It is likely that, for thirty years after Carham, earls of Northumbria made (probably successful) attempts to withhold from Scotland at least some of what we now think of as the Scottish Borders region. Ultimately, however, the battle came to secure for Scotland something resembling our familiar Border, or at least its eastern half.

At some time not long after Carham, Malcolm also gained control over the Kingdom of Strathclyde (including modern Cumbria), all of which was then absorbed into Scotland.[1]

After 1066, a large number of refugees from northern England settled in Scotland, following the Norman conquest.[2] Then, in 1092, Scotland lost her hold over what is now Cumbria.[3] From 1097 to 1107, Edgar, King of Scots also briefly acknowledged the king of England as overlord of Lothian (by which was then meant that part of the former kingdom of Northumbria which lay to the north of the Tweed).

There then followed a short period of Scottish expansion, between 1139 and 1157, when David I and Malcolm IV effectively held sway on the east coast as far south as the Tees. The 1136 and 1139 treaties of Durham also granted either David I or his son Henry large swathes of modern Cumbria, as far south as Lancashire. In reality, the Scottish king had to acknowledge the English king as feudal superior in these southern possessions, but I have included them as part of the Scottish realm in Figure D.

---

[1] That said, Fergus, Lord of Galloway (who, as we will find later, lent his name to a character in medieval literature) does also appear to have claimed some kind of semi-independence for Galloway from the Scottish Crown in the twelfth century.

[2] The Normans came to Scotland too, though here they did so perhaps more clearly on the terms of their hosts than was the case for them in England (a country which they simply conquered).

[3] This is why there is no mention of Carlisle in the 1086 *Doomsday Book*; the town was at that time not in England.

Figure D) 1139 AD

None of this lasted long. In 1157, Henry II of England made Malcolm IV of Scotland give up what are now Cumbria and Northumberland, creating a boundary that looks – again – very like the one today. There then endured for a century a period of (relative) peace and stability along the Border line. So, the decades following the Battle of Carham gradually created a border that we can begin to recognise, and a Scotland which increasingly had a functioning central authority.[1]

---

[1] All of that said, of course, for centuries afterwards much of the Highlands was in reality well beyond the day-to-day control of any Scottish government. That certainly did not stop people there from thinking of themselves as Scots. Indeed, the eighteenth-century Gaelic poet Alasdair Mac Mhaighstir Alasdair talks of Lowlanders as an (implicitly deviant) subculture within Scotland, in much the same way as many Lowlanders then viewed Highlanders. Samuel Johnson remarked on his Highland

Figure E) 1157 AD

The Border was, of course, still contested in matters of detail. As an effort at resolving such questions, a series of border surveys was authorised by the English authorities between 1222 and 1249. Our walk will follow at least some of the paths taken by those surveyors. These surveys describe the eastern half of the Border pretty much exactly as it now stands (save that they mark Berwick as Scottish). Similar surveys of the East March were authorised in 1245 and 1246.[1]

tour of 1773 that Lowlanders were as ignorant of the Highlands as they were 'of Borneo or Sumatra'. Further back, in the medieval era, many local leaders in parts of the Highlands – for example those in Moray – would have thought of themselves as kings in all but (or sometimes including) name.

[1] For a fictionalised account of these surveys and of the negotiations that preceded them near Newcastle in 1244, see Nigel Tranter's *Sword of State*.

The year 1237 is probably at least as good as any other to identify as the date when our modern Border (or something extremely like it) was defined in law. This is the date of the Treaty of York. Taken together with the 1266 Treaty of Perth (which ended Norwegian overlordship of what had until that point been the Kingdom of Mann and the Isles), the treaty recognises a Scotland that looks on the map essentially as it does today.[1] The Treaty of York is the Border's birth certificate, even if it in fact mainly confirms in law a border that had already been a political reality (off and on) for perhaps eighty years.

A rather gossipy account by the English chronicler Matthew Paris survives of the meeting in York, at which Alexander II of Scotland and Henry III of England sat down with the papal legate to negotiate the Border line. The Treaty deals not only with the Border but also with questions of suzerainty. The 1174 Treaty of Falaise[2] had introduced such claims by England over Scotland to some extent. These had to be untangled, and in return Scotland gave up any lingering claims to northern England.

1237 – 1482: Wars, Promises and Treaties

At this point, conscious of the reader's anxiousness to start walking again soon (and of the danger of their attention fading meantime) I recall the collective boast which Malc and I make that, in our youths, we managed to gatecrash Robert the Bruce's funeral. It is as well for any writer, from time to time, to check that his readers are looking at his footnotes. The above wild claim, surely requiring some explanation, provides just such a convenient prompt.[3]

---

[1] Though Scotland at this time includes Berwick and the Isle of Man, and is as yet without Orkney and Shetland. After the Treaty of Perth, the Hebrides were under the Scottish Crown, a fact which did not stop the MacDonalds there from acting quasi-independently at times, to the extent that in 1462, John, Lord of the Isles attempted to contract a treaty *against* Scotland *with* Edward IV of England.

[2] Falaise in Normandy was where William the Lion, King of Scots was held captive by the English king. Suzerainty (i.e. overlordship) over Scotland, and various parts of Scotland in particular, was the price which William paid in this treaty for his liberty. In practice, Scotland bought out the treaty in 1189, and the claims to overlordship were effectively ended then. They seem, however, to have been brought up again at York by the English.

[3] Robert the Bruce's embalmed heart, at his request, was taken on crusade to the Holy Land after his death in 1329, but only made it as far as Teba in Spain. From there, it returned to Scotland to be buried at Melrose Abbey. In the months leading up to the reconvening of the Scottish Parliament in 1999, a lead casket was found buried beside the high altar there which was widely believed to contain Bruce's heart. This was then reburied at a small official ceremony to which – by means that are not altogether clear to posterity – Malc and I both managed to appropriate tickets.

Figure F) 1266

I mention all this also because it is worth emphasising now that Bruce's victory over Edward II[1] at Bannockburn in 1314, did not mean that the shape of Scotland *de jure* was never afterward challenged *de facto* by English kings. The first three Edwards made sustained military incursions into southern Scotland in the sixty years of warfare after 1296.

In 1332, for instance, the 'Roxburgh Promise' was made. The promise was

---

[1] The nature of Edward's eventual assassination, at least as it was luridly reported by chroniclers of the time, can possibly be inferred from the name of the 1980s English melodeon band *Edward the Second and the Red Hot Polkas*.

offered by Edward Balliol (son of King John Balliol), making use of the highly-debatable status which he had in his own mind as King of Scots. Edward Balliol thus 'gifted' the English king territory including the three Lothians, plus the counties of Roxburgh, Selkirk, Peebles, Berwickshire and Dumfries. This was, in other words, an attempt to give away everything that had been won at Carham, and more. Edward Balliol was willing to cede sovereignty over this huge and fertile chunk of Scotland (plus overlordship over the rest) in exchange for the return of much of his own personal property.

Shortly afterwards, at the Battle of Halidon Hill (1333), Edward III of England sought to make good this promise. In the words of one metrically-questionable English ballad:

> Scottes, out of Berwick and Aberdeen
> At the burn of bannock, ye were far too keen.
> King Edward has avenged it now
> And fully too, I wean.[1]

Balliol's promise was codified in the Treaty of Newcastle of 1334, the most substantial legal threat to the 'traditional' Border in recent centuries. This allowed Edward III, for a time, to regard the Border as effectively running from Cockburnspath in Berwickshire, through the Pentlands and Lammermuirs, to Carlops and Crosscryne in Peeblesshire, before that line usurped its way towards the Ayrshire coast:

> At Karlinlippis and at Corscryne,
> Thare thai made the marches syne.[2]

Another treaty, at Berwick in 1357, bought back David II from English captivity. Edward III became distracted elsewhere and so, in the end, Scotland regained virtually all this land from England by 1370, although the castles of Roxburgh and Berwick continued to be in English hands for a while after that.

Rather astonishingly for a Scottish Borderer, the writer Alistair Moffat makes the following claim about this period, which I had better just leave without my trying to offer further comment:

> Looked at from a Border perspective, Bannockburn was a
> disaster. If Edward I had defeated Robert de Brus, then

---

[1] Traditional.
[2] Wyntoun's *Cronikkil.*

Scotland might have moved closer politically to England, or more likely the frontier would have shifted safely north to the Lammermuirs.[1]

As it turned out, despite all these invasions, the Border did *not* move to the Lammermuirs. It returned, again and again, to its familiar, legally-understood (if, in places, fairly hazy) line.

1482 – 1603: Berwick, the Debatable Lands and the Union of Crowns

As our walk will show us, in recent centuries, there have been two significant exceptions to the picture I have been drawing of a relatively stable modern Border line.

The first of these is the three miles of Border that lie furthest east, on the northern bank of the Tweed, and which comprise the town of Berwick. Berwick changed hands thirteen times and has been under English control since 1482. In that year, Edward IV of England sent his brother Richard into Scotland in an effort to depose James III (and replace him with James's biddable brother, Alexander). This caused the burning of numerous places along the border line,[2] and raised the real possibility of large areas of southern Scotland being ceded to England all over again. The price of getting the English forces to leave Scotland was essentially to give them Berwick.

The other exception to my rule is the 'Debatable Lands'. These are a ten by three-and-a-half-mile tract of untamed land (and people) around the little village of Canonbie, near the very western end of the Border. The very uncertain border line here was finally fixed legally only as recently as 1552.

From some point in the thirteenth century, up to the Union of the Crowns in 1603, the regions on each side of the Border were by international agreement policed by their respective countries' wardens of the West, Middle and East Marches. This was an attempt, by means of these six uncommonly warlike civil servants, to create some kind of official buffer-zone in both countries, and to contain the many lawless activities of the inhabitants on both sides of the Border. Wardens, it should be said, did not always stand very far outside the fray of Scottish Border family politics. The Humes generally held the office in Scotland's East March, and the Kerrs that in the Middle March, while either the Johnstones or the Maxwells often held sway in the west.

---

[1] Alistair Moffat: *The Borders.*
[2] Yetholm was one such place.

Amid all this lawlessness, some further official surveys took place in the 1550s. These settled the line along the watershed in the Cheviots, instead of along some of the other (very nearby) places mentioned in earlier surveys. The changes we are talking about here, however, are generally better reckoned in yards than in miles.

The Border since 1603: A Parliament adjourned and reconvened

Although the Union of the Crowns brought to an end the period of Border history known to us for its reivers, battles and ballads, the Border remained, in a less bloody sense, an international frontier until 1707. That said, from 1603 to 1707, the King of Scots and the King of England did not always manage to maintain the most straightforward of relations with each other, in spite of their now being one and the same person.

The Union of Parliaments in 1707 was what eventually ended Scotland's independence. It was marked in London by a service of thanksgiving, in Dumfries by a crowd publicly burning the relevant legislation, and in Edinburgh, by the bells of St Giles ringing out the popular tune 'Oh why am I so sad, upon my wedding day?'

This was a union subject to a series of guarantees, each of which continued to give the Border some political meaning. Scotland and England each maintained their own education systems, their own very different established churches, and their own legal and judicial systems.[1] Somehow, despite the growing trend over the next hundred years to refer to Scotland as 'North Britain', both the Border and Scotland survived. Indeed they remained alive as ideas throughout the 'Long Adjournment'[2] of the Scottish Parliament between 1707 and 1999.

The Scottish Parliament was reconvened (albeit this time in devolved rather than independent form) in 1999. After this, an increasing number of areas of public policy diverged significantly at the Border line, on issues as varied as access to old folk's care and the cost of going to university. For a short while, train conductors asked passengers to put out their cigarettes as they left Berwick station going north, when the laws in each country differed regarding smoking in public places. Nowadays, there are differing laws about what times

---

[1] These are the three guarantees of 1707 that are generally quoted, as they are the three that were (more or less) adhered to. In the absence of a written constitution, it is in fact ultimately as easy for the UK Parliament to change things in the Act of Union as it is for them to change speed limits.
[2] The quotation marks here are slightly deceptive. I have not heard this phrase used before. I coin it shamelessly now.

you can buy a beer on the train.

Rather more substantially, from this point onwards, the question of Scottish independence became the ideological dividing line within the Scottish body politic. Questions about how the Scottish Border might operate practically in the future were raised both in the run-up to the 2014 Independence Referendum and in the chaotic aftermath of the 2016 referendum on UK membership of the European Union.

Today, paradoxically, many of the unionist politicians who most vehemently deny the Scottish Border's reality are the very people who have helped build far less porous borders between the UK and Europe.

The world's oldest national land border?

In the last four and a half centuries, any uncertainties about parts of the Border have been extremely minor in nature. They are so minor, in fact, that listing these places (as I will, as I walk through them) serves only to emphasise how little this border really has changed, when compared to most others across the world.[1]

Such modern changes and uncertainties have often related to questions in the minds of map-makers about where exactly the Border crosses uninhabited stretches of land. There were a few small areas of this kind marked on some maps as 'disputed' as late as the 1840s. Other fluctuations involved a field or a hill changing hands between two landowners, sometimes in disputed circumstances.[2]

However, it does not seem that even these few small patches of hillside have been in any debate now for a century and a half, since the Ordnance Survey became the conclusive arbiter on all such matters.

This stability does not prevent some commentators from arguing that the Scottish Border is neither an old nor indeed a stable line. By pointing to the lack of a recognisable Scotland along familiar borders *before* the middle ages, Rory Stewart, for example, sets an impossibly high bar for Scotland to meet in order to qualify for nationhood. Eric Robson, likewise, manages to pray modern border disputes (some of them barely football-pitch-sized) in aid of his claim that:

[1] That, paradoxically, of course comes down in large part to Scotland's very lack of independence during much of this period. This has meant the 'fossilising' of an ancient line, for want of political reasons to dispute it. In the modern era, Scotland has had no Schleswig-Holstein question of its own to contend with as a consequence.

[2] It was often assumed after 1603 (now that the detail of the Border was not to be settled by armies) that the line would, for practical purposes, be marked out by the march dykes of individual landowners' estates.

...it took 1720 years to fix the border line, a frontier dispute of Balkan proportions.[1]

Graham Robb sets similarly far-fetched standards, by complaining that the Scottish Border cuts across an area inhabited by the Selgovian tribes of the fourth century:

> As the day of the [2014] referendum drew near, I often looked at the map of Selgovia. The Solway Firth, where one nation seems to draw away from another, was not an ancient border after all.[2]

I can only add that, if we all have to have borders which have remained unchanged since the fall of the Roman Empire, then not many countries are going to qualify as countries. Indeed, if we are playing the antiquity game, and Scotland's Border (recognised on virtually its present lines since at least 1237) is not good enough for us, then it is difficult to think how many nations in the world would make the grade. Certainly the UK would not, given that its current borders date only from 1922, and considering how Scotland has only been involved in the business since 1707.

I offer this brief race through the history of the Border in order to provide some context, but also to make a point. Despite all the wars, treaties, invasions and unions, the Scottish Border has generally always settled back more or less where it was confirmed legally to be in 1237. Scotland does indeed have one of the oldest and most enduring national land-borders anywhere in the world.[3] Indeed, the part of the Border that has been most stable of all[4] seems to have lain exactly where it does now – the middle of the River Tweed – for something like eight and a half centuries.

And all of these interesting facts are what bring me to Marshall Meadows Bay, this damp spring morning.

---

[1] Eric Robson: *The Border Line.* I struggle to work out, using such criteria, how long it therefore took England to be formed. I suspect that if an Englishman were told that his present borders were historically suspect because of the loss of Calais in 1558 or the gain of Kirkandrews in 1552, he would rightly see this as rather a shaky line of argument.

[2] Graham Robb: *The Debatable Land.*

[3] Of the currently *independent* countries in the world, tiny Andorra lays claim to the oldest land border. Its 75-mile circumference was agreed in 1278.

[4] The section that lies between Paxton Toll and the Redden Burn at Carham.

CHAPTER 5
The East March

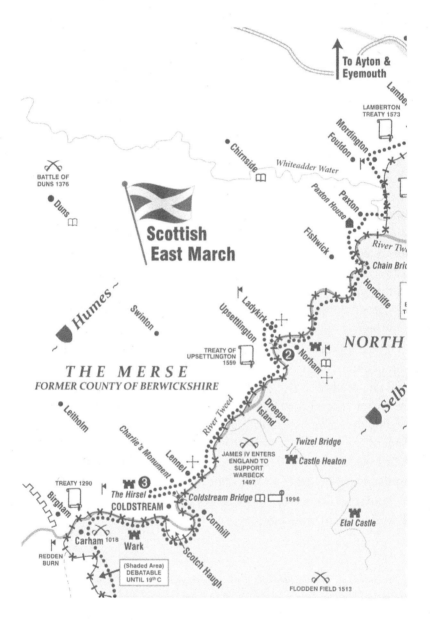

Map 2: Scotland and England's East Marches, from Berwick to Coldstream.

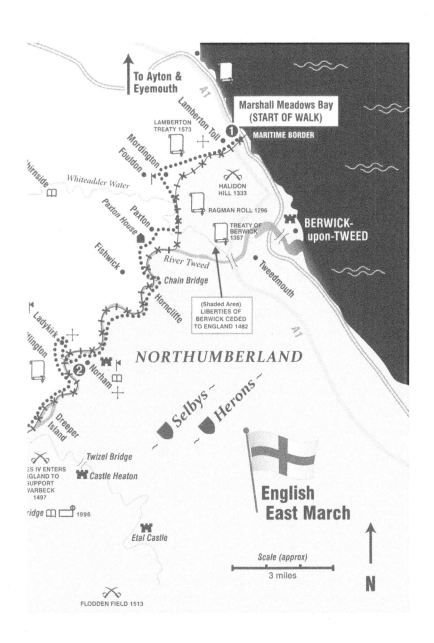

To Ayton & Eyemouth

A1

Lamberton Toll

LAMBERTON TREATY 1573

Marshall Meadows Bay
(START OF WALK)

MARITIME BORDER

Mordington

Fouldon

Chirnside

Whiteadder Water

Paxton

Paxton House

HALIDON HILL 1333

RAGMAN ROLL 1296

TREATY OF BERWICK 1357

BERWICK-upon-TWEED

Fishwick

River Tweed

Chain Bridge

Horncliffe

Tweedmouth

A1

(Shaded Area)
LIBERTIES OF
BERWICK CEDED
TO ENGLAND 1482

Ladykirk

tlington

② Norham

NORTHUMBERLAND

~ *Selbys* ~

~ *Herons* ~

Dreeper Island

ES IV ENTERS
IGLAND TO
SUPPORT
WARBECK
1497

ridge 1996

Twizel Bridge

Castle Heaton

**English
East March**

Etal Castle

Scale (approx)

3 miles

N

FLODDEN FIELD 1513

45

Day 1 (Continued): From the North Sea to Norham
(Circa 11 miles)

Marshall Meadows Bay; The Lamberton betrothal; Ayton and Linton; Black Agnes; Witches; Paxton and a Polish bear; David Hume; The Merse and the Tweed; Norham Castle.

Our Border expedition begins at Marshall Meadows Bay. Unfortunately, we can't wet our feet in the North Sea here to mark the occasion, as at this point there are sixty feet of sheer cliffs down to our right. J.L. Mack does suggest that it is possible to get down to the sea from near here 'with the risk of a broken limb', but that does not sound like a very sensible way to begin our walk. I actively counsel the reader against it.

There is however one other way to get to the sea, and that is to tunnel. Somewhat incredibly, there is a 240-foot tunnel from Marshall Meadows Farm. It was constructed, as far as anyone can establish, in the 1840s to bring kelp from the beach up, underneath the original[1] course of the railway line, to be used on the land as fertiliser. Sometimes referred to as the 'seaweed railway', because of a belief that the kelp was hauled up on rails, the tunnel descends from a suspicious-looking hole beside the caravan park, out through the cliffs to an opening some 40 feet above sea level, a few yards inside England. This is a bizarre route by which to get to the very easternmost point of the Border, and not one I have yet tried. Anyone who does so is advised to exercise extreme caution.

On the rocky foreshore down on our right, two edges of Scotland meet: one wet, one dry. To our left we see the well-known border sign on the East Coast railway line. The word *England* still stands, but a vengeful hand, elemental or otherwise, has ripped away the one saying *Scotland*. The sign's golden English lion and silver Scottish unicorn shake hands, but avoid eye contact, and are visible for a flashing heraldic millisecond to all railway passengers who make the effort to look up from their phones.

Beyond the railway, on the main road, is Lamberton Toll where a line of saltires announces Scotland to motorists. In 1769, the Welsh travel writer Thomas Pennant commented on this view into Scotland, from somewhere along this road, as he looked over towards the village of Ayton. He evidently had mixed feelings about the state of the Borders' economy at that time:

> The entrance into Scotland has a very unpromising look; for

---

[1] The tunnel has been curiously redundant for a century and a half. Shortly after it was dug, the railway line was moved a little inland, following an accident right on the Border, where a train went over the cliff. A local story suggests that parts of the locomotive can still be seen in the rocks at very low tides.

it wanted, for some miles, the cultivation of the parts more distant from England: but the borders were necessarily neglected; for, till the accession of James VI and even long after, the national enmity was kept up, and the borderers of both countries [were] discouraged from improvements by the barbarous inroads of each nation ... but on reaching the small village of Eytown, the scene was greatly altered; the wretched cottages, or rather hovels of the country, were vanishing; good comfortable houses arise in their stead; the lands are inclosing, and yield very good barley, oats, and clover ... [though] there is still a mixture of the old negligence left amidst the recent improvements, which look like the works of a new colony, in a wretched impoverished country.[1]

Near the very end of the Border, there was once a toll house. Somewhere around here, a century ago, J.L. Mack advises there was a pig sty which sat exactly on the Border, and which became the subject of a celebrated dispute with Berwickshire County Council. At risk of over-simplifying the matter, the question of which country the pig's owner was liable to pay his rates in apparently hung on whether that liability was based on where the pig slept or where it ate.

Immediately to our left, beyond the railway, the boundary dyke stretches west, making a strange double-right-angled turn for a few yards. At some point in the nineteenth century, it was proposed to simplify cultivation here by straightening out the dyke. One of the proprietors (it is not clear in which country) was not keen to pay his half of the cost, and allegedly made this excuse:

> God forbid that I should alter the boundary of my native land.[2]

And so this odd, tiny little zig-zag in the Border remains here to this day.

***

Looking in the other direction, across the black waves that break below us, is the maritime border. Maritime borders are a different beast, and not part of this book's scope. However, it would be remiss not to point out here that, until 1999, Scotland's sea border with England headed due east from here,

---

[1] Thomas Pennant: *A Tour in Scotland, 1769.*
[2] Quoted by J.L.Mack.

far into the North Sea. The line was moved then by the UK Government, in contentious circumstances, on the eve of Scottish devolution.[1] Since then, the line has bent north-eastwards from here. It now – curiously – excludes some of Scotland's oil and gas fields from Scottish territorial waters.

Following the coastal path into Scotland takes us to another bridge, brings us back inland over the railway line, and lets us cross the A1 again. We are still some two-and-a-half miles south of 'Scotland's first village' at Burnmouth, with its little fishing harbour and its appropriately-named pub, 'The First and Last.'

Just beyond Burnmouth lies Ayton, where a number of international treaties were signed. Among these were a formal truce agreed at Ayton's St Dionysius' Kirk in 1380, and another in 1497.[2] The diarist James Boswell records spending an unhappy evening in Ayton in 1762 when the wheel came off his coach. He remarks on staying in:

> ...a cold ale-house in a dirty little village. We had a beefsteak ill-dressed and had nothing to drink but thick muddy beer.[3]

We keep to the Border. This decision means, sadly, that we do not visit the nearby fishing village of Eyemouth. Eyemouth could (and indeed has) justified books all of its own, not least on the fishing disaster of 1881. In a single storm that year, 189 fishermen from villages between Newhaven (near Edinburgh) and Burnmouth, here on the Border, lost their lives. 129 of these were from Eyemouth. A few days after the disaster, Rev Walter C. Smith published this telling verse in *The Scotsman*:

> There's Elsie sits dazed-like and dumb
> And Janet moans aa the day through.
> I try tae keep haud o Thee Lord;

---

[1] *The Scottish Adjacent Waters Boundaries Order 1999*, moved a huge chunk of the North Sea from Scottish to English jurisdiction, for reasons that were never made clear. The boundaries of UK waters (the UK's Exclusive Economic Zone) are now delineated out to roughly 200 nautical miles by the 1982 UN Convention on the Law of the Seas. This superseded much more limited concepts of territorial waters, going back to the 17th century, which defined anything beyond a three-mile cannon-shot of land as essentially international waters. The 1982 Convention does continue to recognise three and twelve-mile limits for certain purposes. However, the division of Scottish waters from English, Northern Irish and Manx waters remains up to the UK Government to determine.

[2] The 1497 treaty brought to an end James IV's Perkin Warbeck adventure (which we will encounter tomorrow) and eventually led to the airily-misnamed 'Treaty of Perpetual Peace' of 1502, which married James IV to Margaret Tudor.

[3] James Boswell: *London Journal*.

But aa that I get for my pains
Is to drift farther into the mist
Midst the wail o the women and weans.[1]

***

We turn into the road-end for Lamberton, passing under a set of whale's jaw bones, relics of Berwick's days as a great whaling port. Actually, 'under' is not quite the word, as all that now remains of the jawbones is a pair of decayed stumps. They stand, seemingly admonishing young whales to brush their teeth.[2]

One of the many remarkable things about the line we are now walking is the number of tiny places on it which, like Ayton, give their names to treaties. Lamberton is another example. In 1573, the Treaty of Lamberton allowed English mercenaries to take Edinburgh Castle on behalf of the Scots (a proposal that is not altogether easy to picture or untangle in the mind).

Mr Christison, the minister of this parish (Foulden), writing in 1845,[3] reports yet another treaty being concluded in nearby Foulden Kirk[4] in 1587. This, he says, sought to justify the execution of Mary Queen of Scots. In the same article, incidentally, Mr Christison also regrets the recent arrival of tea in his parish:

> ...a change which, from the cost and for other obvious reasons, is much to be regretted.[5]

More vehement even than his view on tea is Christison's disdain for the number of people coming over the Border to get married at irregular Gretna-like ceremonies at Lamberton Toll.

A very particular form of land-tenure was set up in Foulden and Lamberton after the First World War for some of the soldiers who had been promised that

---

[1] Collected in Walter Elliot: *The New Minstrelsy of the Scottish Border.*
[2] Lamberton, as a geekish aside, is (along with the nearby villages of Paxton, Ladykirk, Foulden, Mordington and Fishwick), a postcode anomaly within an anomaly. Berwick has a 'Scottish' postcode beginning TD15. However, TD15 also identifies the above (Scottish) villages as part of (English) Berwick. It is probably wise not to think about it overly long.
[3] *New Statistical Account of Scotland.*
[4] Foulden is also noted for having one of only two surviving 'tithe barns' in Scotland, into which a tenth of the local harvest was paid for the use of the Kirk.
[5] There were instances some years before this around Scotland of illicit tea-drinking parties being broken up by elders who presumably initially assumed tea to have been a narcotic of some kind.

they would come home to land of their own. The 'Lamberton Colonies' were formed under the Land Settlement (Scotland) Act 1919, and involved smallholdings of land being parcelled out from the remnants of the estate of the ancient Renton family. Certain tasks were undertaken in common among smallholders for many years, though few of the holdings are still used in this way today.

The ruins here of Lamberton Kirk, once dedicated to St Lambert, an eighth-century Bishop of Maastricht,[1] have been abandoned for over three centuries, other than for their use as a burial lair.

This is a good place to stop for a minute, though I reflect it may be a little early in our campaign to stop anywhere very long. The line stretches out ahead of us westwards, across prosperous fields, for another hundred miles. Yet we stop here at the lichened remnants of Lamberton Kirk, and look out from this hillock of graves across the wide Merse. This place was once the scene of an event that fundamentally changed the fates of both Scotland and England.

In more recent times, English brides crossing the Border have been running from their parents. Lamberton, however, is most associated with a betrothal that was very much arranged.

***

In 1503 King James IV of Scotland sought a wife and a peaceful accommodation with England. His answer to both questions was Margaret Tudor, the fourteen-year-old daughter of King Henry VII of England.

Margaret met James's representatives here, just inside Scotland. From Lamberton Kirk, Margaret (who had already been married in London by proxy), was ushered onwards to Holyrood, to be married there in person to Scotland's king.

William Dunbar, Scotland's pre-eminent makar,[2] penned 'The thrissil and the rois' and 'To the Princess Margaret', to describe the event in allegorical terms. James appears in the poems variously as a thistle, a lion rampant and an eagle, while Margaret is depicted as a red-and-white Tudor rose:[3]

---

[1] A less exotic explanation is that the village was simply called after someone local named Lambert.

[2] *Makar:* a Scots word for 'poet'. Most associated with the courtly Scots writers of the fifteenth and sixteenth centuries, and more recently with the title of Scotland's official 'poet laureate'.

[3] The mercat cross at the village of Cockburnspath, fifteen miles up the coast, is held by local tradition to have been built to commemorate this marriage. It is certainly decorated with thistles and roses, though some writers have concluded that it was built later to mark the 1603 Union of Crowns.

Welcum the Rose bothe rede and whyte,
Welcum the floure of oure delyte!
Oure secrete rejoysyng frome the sone bein,
Welcum of Scotland to be Quene;
Welcum of Scotland to be Quene![1]

Both royal families were aware of what this marriage might mean. It was always recognised as a possibility that Margaret's Scottish descendants might eventually inherit the English throne. Indeed, Henry VII had to reassure his ministers that, if such a thing ever happened, 'the greater would always draw the less'.[2] In other words, if a Scot ever became King of England, he need not be considered Scottish for very long.

In any case, as things stood in 1503, Margaret had two brothers, either of whom could have been expected to found a line of English kings. As it turned out, Margaret's eldest brother Arthur died aged sixteen. Her other brother, later Henry VIII, had a noted career as a serial husband which gave him children, but no grandchildren. By this chance series of events, when Henry VIII's daughter Queen Elizabeth I died (exactly a hundred years after Margaret Tudor came to Lamberton) the nearest heir to the English crown was indeed Margaret's great-grandson, King James VI of Scotland.

James then made his triumphant way south, passing not far from Lamberton and into his new English kingdom. This was the dynastic union of 1603, the so-called 'Union of the Crowns'. Despite what unionists sometimes now jokingly say, 1603 was anything but a takeover by Scotland of England. On that point, if on that point alone, Henry VII was right about Scotland. The greater was to draw the less.

It is strange to stop in these ruins though and consider for a moment just what a random series of political miscalculations and royal illnesses Scotland's fate hinged on in the end.

If Edward VI had (hypothetically) had his measles jag, his immune system would quite probably have been in a condition to fight off tuberculosis, and he would most likely have survived to have heirs. If Queen Mary I of England's much-publicised phantom pregnancy had not, in all likelihood, really been a cancerous tumour, or if Elizabeth I had decided against a diplomatic policy

---

[1] William Dunbar: 'To the Princess Margaret on her arrival at Holyrood', from *The Poems of William Dunbar* (Edinburgh, William Paterson). Dunbar himself had a hand in the negotiations which led to the marriage.
[2] Hume Brown: *The Legislative Union of England and Scotland* (Ford Lectures, Oxford, 1914).

of non-marriage, their descendants might still be on their throne. If Prince Arthur had consummated his marriage before he died, he might have given the House of Tudor a successor. If any single one of these factors had been slightly different, the Union of the Crowns could have been avoided.[1]

I digress. There is quite a distance still to walk. Malc reminds me, directly, about the circumstances in which his auntie might have been his uncle. We set off again through the fields.

***

We follow the fence and a row of hawthorns up the hill from Lamberton Kirk towards Woodhills Farm.[2] Today – as it generally will be for the rest of our journey – England is on our left. On our right stretches the wide expanse of Berwickshire.

Daniel Defoe, who had not long previously served as an English spy in Scotland, gives an account of crossing the Border somewhere near here (probably at Lamberton Toll) in 1726. He expresses bafflement, verging on outrage, that the place is so *Scottish*:

> Mordintown lying to the west, the great road does not lie thro' it, but carries us to the brow of a very high hill, where we had a large view into Scotland: But we were welcomed into it with such a Scots gale of wind, that, besides the steepness of the hill, it obliged us to quit our horses, for real apprehensions of being blown off ...it blew directly in our faces ...I never was sensible of so fierce a wind, so exceeding keen and cold, for it pierced our very eyes, that we could scarcely bear to hold them open. ...The first town we come to is as perfectly Scots, as if you were 100 miles north of Edinburgh; nor is there the least appearance of anything

[1] Admittedly, all this probably belongs in the same category of historical conspiracy theory as a question I once heard expounded – apparently seriously – in a pub in Glasgow as to whether, if the Union of Parliaments had not occurred in 1707, Scotland might have been neutral in the First World War. A much more credible 'what if' is to speculate that the Jacobite uprisings might well not have taken place had Queen Anne had aspirin available to her. This would have stood a good chance of addressing some of Anne's ongoing medical complaints long enough to have ensured a different outcome to some of her tragic eighteen pregnancies. At least one child would surely have survived her. Being brought up as a Protestant, that child would then probably have been acceptable to both her Scottish and English parliaments, and quite likely also to a great number of the devotees of the House of Stuart.
[2] Just beyond us now is what is claimed to have been the site of Scotland's first race course, on Lamberton Moor.

English, either in customs, habits, usages of the people, or in their way of living, eating, dress, or behaviour; any more than if they had never heard of an English nation.[1]

This is the fertile end of the Border, the end that was at one time laid waste because its land was rich, as well as simply because it lay between England and Edinburgh.

Until the Second World War, many of Berwickshire's big farms had big workforces. The Merse probably had a social structure that was in some ways more like that of parts of north-east Scotland than that of the hill farms and *herds' hooses*[2] further westwards along the Border line.

The birds sing this morning over a landscape as fertile and as farmed as ever, but largely without farmworkers.

I see Malc, ahead of me, trying to work out if a bull on the horizon is in our own clatchie field or in the one over the fence. The bull makes his general views loudly known, either to us or to his nearby field of cows and calves. We loosen our rucksacks, with the thought of jettisoning them if required. But the bull is indeed on the other side of the fence, and for that we smile at him, to his fury.

***

Past the steading at Woodhills, the view opens out, and beyond us lies much of the East March, like a huge marble table-top, veined with hedgerows and by-roads. All these lines are laid out till they knot together in a distant haze somewhere in the Lammermuirs or in history. Somewhere beyond that – above Athelstaneford[3] no doubt – the vapour trails of two planes today make a convenient saltire. To our west, the mist burns away to reveal the Cheviots.

We skirt round Mordington House, or its remnants, which are thought to be the burial place of 'Black Agnes', Countess of Dunbar and March. Agnes

---

[1] Daniel Defoe: *A tour thro' the whole island of Great Britain.*

[2] i.e. shepherds' houses. One of the most isolated of these once provoked the joke (in comparatively metropolitan Yetholm) that a shepherd's young daughter, on seeing the postman, had said to her mother, 'There's somethin the same shape's ma faither comin up the brae.'

[3] Athelstaneford near Haddington is where, according to (subsequent) traditional accounts, King Angus II of the Picts saw a vision of a white diagonal cross in the clouds on the eve of a battle with the Northumbrians in 832. He took this to represent the blessing of St Andrew on his enterprise, and so adopted it as his flag. The Danes saw a similar vision, but in their case at sunset, so accounting for their own red flag. So began the ongoing good-natured debate between Denmark and Scotland as to who has the world's oldest national flag.

is best remembered for her ferocious defence of Dunbar Castle in 1338, against a mammoth English army. After five months, the English forces gave up trying to defeat Agnes. According to one traditional rhyme, the English commander Salisbury desisted the experiment in despair, muttering of Agnes as he departed:

> She makes a stir in tower and trench,
> That brawling, boisterous, Scottish wench,
> Came I early, came I late,
> I found Agnes at the gate.[1]

Black Agnes is one of very few women whom Scotland's medieval chroniclers mention for a reason other than because of who her father or husband was. She was a formidable individual. Once, after a protracted attack on her by English siege engines, Agnes was seen sarcastically wiping marks off the side of the castle with her hankie. On another occasion, while she was in fact privately running very short of food herself, Agnes sent a single (and, again, sarcastic) loaf of bread and bottle of wine to the English camp and its (by then, probably, very hungry) commander.

***

We turn left onto a wee road towards one of the many ferm touns of the Merse, this one going by the name of Clappers. Writing in the 1950s, Rev Andrew Martin[2] offers an appealing explanation for the strange place-name. He quotes a local story that, when King James VI crossed the Border near here into his new kingdom in 1603, he was met with a particularly enthusiastic crowd who broke into applause. Many years later, on a much-postponed return visit to Scotland, James was asked by his courtiers which road he wanted to take north. He replied, 'By the clappers, I think'. While I very strongly suspect this is *not* how the place gets its name, the remark is nonetheless exactly the kind of thing James VI – with all his childish need for adulation – can be imagined saying.

In an earlier era, the priest of this parish was Bernard de Linton. He was long presumed to have been the same Bernard who became Abbot of Arbroath and (by a further assumption) the author in 1320 of the famous words of the Declaration of Arbroath. Evidence now suggests that these are two completely different people, but a pub-name in de Linton's honour in Arbroath gives him

---

[1] A traditional song, the words of which are attributed to Salisbury himself.
[2] *Third Statistical Account of Scotland.*

the credit, so I feel entitled to mention the Lamberton connection with Arbroath, at least as folklore, if not as history.

Whoever was indeed the author, this letter to the Pope from Scotland's barons gave elegant expression to sentiments such as limited kingship and national self-determination – a long time before it was common for anyone to voice them:

> *… Quia quamdiu Centum ex nobis vivi remanserint,*
> *nuncquam Anglorum dominio aliquatenus volumus*
> *subiugari. Non enim propter gloriam, diuicias aut*
> *honores pugnamus sed propter libertatem solummodo*
> *quam Nemo bonus nisi simul cum vita amittit.*

> (… For, as long as a hundred of us remain alive, never
> will we on any conditions be subjected to the lordship
> of the English. It is in truth not for glory, nor riches, nor
> honours that we are fighting, but for freedom alone,
> which no honest man gives up but with life itself.)[1]

If the village of Lamberton's connection with the Declaration is only folklore, then perhaps it can make a more solid local claim through William de Lamberton. As his name suggests, he may well have had his origins here. He became Bishop of St Andrews and Primate of the Scottish Church and had close ties to both Wallace and Bruce. De Lamberton had a major role in obtaining international recognition for Scotland's independence.

***

From Clappers down to the Tweed, the road itself becomes the Border for about two miles. In fact, this is virtually the only stretch of Border where the middle of a road (as opposed to the ditch on one or other side of it) is genuinely the frontier.[2]

The road and the nearby Bailies' Burn also mark part of the 'Berwick Bounds'. The burn's name refers to the practice of the Town Council of Berwick, who annually ride the Bounds here to mark the town's boundary with Scotland – a task that many of them may now, I understand, undertake by bus. More dramatically, it is here that Scott imagines English troops

---

[1] From the version published by the National Records of Scotland.
[2] Another very brief such stretch of road will be encountered near Wark Common, in a couple of days' time.

rallying before they make for Bannockburn:

> England was roused – on every side
> Courier and post and herald hied,
> To summon prince and peer,
> At Berwick-bounds to meet their Liege,
> Prepared to raise fair Stirling's siege.[1]

***

We pass a Scottish cemetery, where graves stretch to within a few feet of the Border, then a crossroads where England and Scotland are simultaneously announced on our left and right hands respectively. We soon see (on our right-hand, naturally) a crumbling Free Church being used as a shed. Abandoned for a century or more now, I think, it was built at the time of the Kirk's 1843 Disruption. It is tempting to wonder if the seismic events of that year, which split so many families across Scotland, resonated very much with the people on the left hand side of the road.

We eat our pieces at a clump of trees called Witches' Cleuch. In an article otherwise given over to his modish enthusiasm for turnips, George Fulton Knight,[2] the minister of Mordington in the 1790s, asserts that a nearby hillock is similarly called Witches' Knowe, because a witch was once burned there. I don't know if that is true.

Certainly, throughout the seventeenth century, people on the right-hand side of the road here were markedly more enthusiastic about witch trials than were people on the left. It has been suggested that the rate of such trials and executions in the Scottish Borders was ten-times that in Northumberland.[3] There seems to have been a particular outbreak of mania around here in the year 1629-30. Indeed, many of the places we will walk through on our expedition have their own sorry stories of witch trials and denunciations. Among such places, we could relevantly mention Lamberton, Foulden, Jedburgh, Kershopefoot and Stob Stanes at Yetholm (at which last place, the main witness for the prosecution gave his occupation as 'warlock').[4]

One of the more unusual local cases near today's walk is that of the unfortunate Margaret Lumsden, who in 1630 was convicted in Duns on the

---

[1] Sir Walter Scott: *Lord of the Isles.*
[2] *Statistical Account of Scotland.*
[3] Mary Craig: *The Border Burnings: The story of the witchcraft trials in the Scottish Borders 1600-1700.*
[4] Cited in Emma Carroll: *Witches.*

basis that she had allegedly been heard to speak Latin, despite being completely uneducated. It was decided that the only possible explanation for this was that she was possessed by someone who was better-read than she was.

By 1817, one local writer observes with a detectably genuine sense of relief that:

> ... such intolerant bigotry and enthusiasm have now happily lost their power, and the poor and aged are allowed to sink into the grave in peace, without suspicion of holding communion with the Prince of Darkness.[1]

Whether a witch burned here or not, Malc and I eat our pieces anyway. It is still not raining. Blessed, we conclude, are the piece-makers.

Malc points out that, if we follow the Border too literally here for much longer, we will need to swim across the Whiteadder.[2] So, we briefly leave the road-border and cut right, skiting down a muddy path near the vestiges of Edrington Castle. The castle is in fact now little more than one (possible) wall of a byre. The original castle was built when Malcolm Canmore was giving out land to those who had helped him defeat Macbeth at Birnham in 1054. We cross a footbridge here, over a hidden corner of the Whiteadder, whose high, steep banks fill the air today with the smell of wild garlic.

Not far from here, *Wilson's Tales of the Borders* reports a mysterious hiding-place:

> On the banks of the Tweed, and about half a mile from where the Whiteadder flows into it, on the opposite bank there is a small and singular cave. ...it is generally known by the name of the King's Cave, and the tradition runs that it was once the hiding place of a Scottish king, ...[or of] Sir William Wallace.[3]

In 1746, a solitary figure took up residence in the cave, generally understood to have been someone who had been 'out' with Prince Charles Edward Stuart. Given that the man wore 'a tall conical cap made of fox skins', it is also possible he was just a poor soul. In any case, he excited much speculation locally that he was conversant with evil spirits. Today, less

---

[1] Thomas Johnstone: *The History of Berwick on Tweed.*
[2] Pronounced '**Whitt**idder', with the emphasis on the first syllable, which rhymes with 'grit'. The first sound, needless to say, is as in 'whales', not as in 'Wales'.
[3] *Wilson's Tales of the Borders*, Vol. IV.

interestingly, the place is where the A1 road makes its way over the Tweed.

We note that it is, admittedly, starting to rain now.

***

This takes us into the village of Paxton, described in some versions of the song 'Robin Adair' as 'a wondrous couthie place'. As evidence of this claim, the Cross Inn here sells food and beer but, we note virtuously, we have had our pieces.

Paxton, founded by a Saxon family of that name, was in 1296 burned to the ground by Edward I of England, in an effort to get himself match-fit for the savagery he had in mind for Berwick a few days later. The siege of Berwick was in fact unspeakable, even by medieval standards.[1] Edward is known to have put thousands of men, women and children to the sword, and then prevented their corpses from being buried. Instead, he insisted that they be left lying in the streets, as a warning to those who remained alive.

According to Nigel Tranter's fictionalised account, Robert the Bruce first meets his future wife Elizabeth de Burgh in Paxton, while he is *en route* to Berwick to sign the Ragman Roll.[2] As for Paxton, it recovered from Longshanks' attentions, only to be burned again in 1482 and 1540.

In the *Statistical Account of Scotland,* the famous parish-by-parish record of the state of Scotland in the 1790s, Rev Adam Landels, the minister of Hutton, is given the task of describing Paxton. He does not seem entirely clear what kind of statistical information his editors are looking for. In one of his more random observations, he comments:

> The people are all of the ordinary size, except the parish school master, who is computed to be 7 feet 4 inches. His trunk is very large, his legs long, but not well made. There appears a weakness in them, and in his knee joints, so that he walks badly. He is very unwieldy, looks unhealthy and is only 25 years of age. He is very gentle in his manner, good humoured and obliging. He teaches Latin, mathematics, arithmetic, writing and English very well.[3]

As an information board now explains to us, Paxton is very proud of its connection with the athlete Eric Liddell (he was not born here – his mother

---

[1] Many estimates put the civilian casualties in excess of 15,000.
[2] Nigel Tranter: *The Bruce.*
[3] *Statistical Account of Scotland.*

was). Liddell won gold in the 400 metres at the Paris Olympics of 1924, despite this not being his favoured event. He famously refused to run his preferred 100 metres, because it was being held on a Sunday. Liddell, whose life is depicted in the film *Chariots of Fire,* died in 1945 in an internment camp in China where he was serving as a missionary.

***

Berwickshire has 'canting arms'. That is to say, the county coat of arms contains a pun. In Berwickshire's case, the pun comes in the form of a bear and a wych elm, although I was always brought up to believe that the tree depicted was an *aik* (oak). 'Bear-aik' seems a better pun to me. In either case, strangely enough, Paxton has become associated with an actual bear.

Wojtek was a Syrian brown bear cub, purchased in Iran by Polish soldiers during the Second World War. Wojtek (literally, 'Happy Warrior') grew to full size, achieved the rank of corporal in the Polish army, and helped move crates of munitions during the Battle of Monte Cassino in Italy. He also famously enjoyed wrestling, smoking and saluting officers. Along with the 22nd Company of the Polish Army, he found himself in Paxton at the end of the war, where he became a celebrity, and helped ensure the lasting affection which this stretch of the Border has had for Poland.

Wojtek is commemorated in numerous statues in both Scotland and Poland. He also, I like to think, helped ensure that when Poles started to arrive again in Berwickshire around the year 2004 (this time, initially, often to work the land), they found they had both a heritage and a welcome here.

We walk south, up the long drive of eighteenth-century Paxton House. It is raining properly now, and we decide to take shelter for a while. A sign offers us (in all apparent seriousness) the chance to play croquet. Instead, we head into the tearoom in the house's old stables. Voices from both countries are heard around us. We look out, hopefully, at the weather.

The neoclassical house, with its large collection of rare furniture and paintings, was built by Patrick Home, who (mistakenly) thought it would impress a wealthy German heiress[1] whom he fancied. It is possible she visited on a day like today. All he got was a pair of her gloves, which still hang as a forlorn souvenir on the wall. Paxton House, whose design is attributed to the eminent Scottish architect James Adam, was sold by Patrick to his cousin Ninian, whose descendent, the former Labour MP and MSP for East Lothian, John Home-Robertson, has now given its keeping over to a trust.

---

[1] The lady in question was actually an illegitimate daughter of Frederick the Great of Prussia.

The house's picture gallery, built in 1811, claims to be the oldest in Scotland, and is filled mainly with the things Patrick brought back from a grand tour of Italy. Any mystery in my mind about where the means suddenly came from to extend and furnish the house in such a lavish way is dispelled by learning the brutal fact that Ninian owned some 400 slaves in Grenada.[1]

We put on our jackets and head outside again. We try to get through the policies of Paxton House down to the Tweed, probably not by the route that anyone (including ourselves) intended us to. We clamber through the trees and undergrowth and slide down a greasy brae till we get to the high wall marking the edge of the house's gardens. Some tree-climbing takes us to the top of this wall. Jumping down from this point to the other side, however, would be quite an embarrassing way to die, not least as we can see now that there is a large hole in the wall only a few feet further along. Making use of this opening, we eventually find our way down to the Tweed.

The Border has got here before us, while we were having our tea.

***

On our way through the trees from Paxton House to the riverbank, we find ourselves on an old and seemingly forgotten stretch of road. The walls and bridges along its sides are slowly being taken over by moss and nettles, but the place briefly seems to give a ghostly glimpse of what a highway in Scotland might have looked like a couple of hundred years ago.

Our modest efforts to date mean we have now walked around the 'Liberties of Berwick',[2] the chunk of territory that Scotland lost in 1482.

For the bulk of its 97-mile length, both banks of Scotland's fourth-longest river are in Scotland. For the final three miles, both banks are in England. From here in Paxton however, and for around seventeen miles westwards,[3] the Tweed itself forms the Border. The Tweed Commissioners operate here under their own specific legislation, to ensure that there is an adequate legal

---

[1] Ninian was the British Governor of Grenada. Despite his various assertions that he (somehow) managed to be an enlightened or benevolent slave owner, most of those best qualified to judge took a different view. He was captured and executed during the great uprising of Grenada's slaves in 1795. For a literary account of Scottish slave owners, and of a similar uprising in Jamaica a few years earlier, see James Robertson's novel *Joseph Knight*.

[2] The Liberties of Berwick are coterminous with Berwick's Parish of Holy Trinity and St Mary, extending beyond the northern suburbs of the town, but not southwards into the settlement of Tweedmouth. Tweedmouth, though effectively almost part of Berwick now, lies on the southern bank of the Tweed and has therefore never been part of Berwick's national dilemma.

[3] Depending on how diligently we measure its various twists and turns.

framework in place to reassure salmon in this legally and politically complicated river.[1]

Around six miles to our west now, on the southern slopes of the Lammermuirs, is the village of Chirnside.[2] Chirnside is rightly remembered as the childhood home of racing driver Jim Clark, whose memorial commemorates his 25 Formula One Grand Prix victories, before he was killed in a Formula Two race in Germany in 1968.

Chirnside was also home, for much of his life, to the philosopher David Hume. Hume is generally claimed by Edinburgh as a son of her own, because of his birthplace there. In fact, he spent most of his childhood, and a great deal of his later life, at his family's small estate around Chirnside at Ninewells House. He was an *alumnus* of Chirnside's village school, from where he went more or less directly to Edinburgh University. The author of such monumental writings as *An Enquiry Concerning Human Understanding* and *An Enquiry Concerning the Principles of Morals*, Hume was, nevertheless, turned down for an academic post at Edinburgh University because of his reputation as an atheist. Certainly, all of his works were in 1761 added to the Vatican's *Index Librorum Prohibitorum*, its list of officially banned books. Hume is however said to have directly influenced the thinking of Charles Darwin, Adam Smith and Immanuel Kant.[3]

Famously, Hume felt he had to spend a great deal of time observing and editing out the 'scotticisms' from his work. It would probably surprise many now to know that, as the son of a minor eighteenth-century laird, Hume's boyhood language was in fact probably more like that of my grandfather (who, a couple of hundred years later, worked on the land at Ninewells) than it was like the speech of his own reading audience in England.

Chirnside, impressively, marked the tercentenary of Hume's birth by holding a philosophy festival in his honour in 2011.

We come to the Union Bridge, or the 'Chain Bridge' as it is more usually called,[4] which leads over to the little English village of Horncliffe. The bridge

---

[1] Much further west, similarly bespoke legislation also exists for the River Esk.

[2] Traditionally pronounced 'Chirsit' or 'Shirsit' locally, the village also has the unusual (for Scotland) distinction of having a Norman church, albeit one much altered in modern times.

[3] Sadly, as came to public prominence not long after our walk, Hume was also the author of some unworthy, ill-evidenced and (even allowing for the standards of the time) highly offensive comments about race.

[4] Any connection contrived by the present writer at this point between unions and chains would be forced, and will be avoided. The towers of the bridge bear the motto *vis unita fortior*. This, as was pointed out by someone in 2014, is the the Latin near-equivalent of the anti independence campaign slogan 'better together'. What is more certain is that the Latin tag has in fact been used as the heraldic motto for everything from the Retail Fruit Association to the Company of Scotland, the latter of which

was the longest wrought iron suspension bridge in the world when it was built in 1820. It is still impressive, with its commanding position over this broad section of the Tweed, which runs fast and red below us today through the broad and well-tilled landscape that lies on each side.

Over the bridge in Horncliffe, we hide from the rain at a sheltered park bench and seek whatever solace there is to be found in cold tea and melted caramel wafers.

My plan had not been to cross the bridge, but to keep walking along the Scottish riverbank. Malc, who reminds me he is a geography graduate, has persuaded me however that there would probably be long gaps in the Scottish footpath. He has pointed out that, without crossing the bridge, we would end up trudging aimlessly for two hours through sodden red Scottish clay. I have taken his advice. We have crossed the bridge. We find no footpath. We trudge aimlessly for two hours through sodden red English clay. My feet, I comment, are now sore. From across the Tweed in the Merse, my assembled ancestors audibly mock the remark.

***

Over there, under a long, grey sky, is Scotland. We cheer each other on by speculating about whether either natural dreichness or human dourness are potentially marketable energy sources for Scotland. They are certainly renewable. I hitch up my plastic trousers and pull the hood of my jacket over my face. About now, as we cross a stretch of fields marked on our fraying map as 'Hangman's Land', we both hit up against a slight loss of will. For what seems like a long time, we urge the walls of Norham Castle to blaze red now through the smirr. Eventually the castle – which provides the opening scenes of Scott's *Marmion* – does materialise, emerging with a dark authority out of distant, raven-infested black trees.

One slight disadvantage of walking along a border is that this inevitably involves jumping from one period of history to another, as the passing scenes dictate. Fortunately, however, Norham Castle makes so many appearances in Scotland's history, that passing it quite early on in our expedition provides a convenient opportunity to sort at least some events into chronological order.

The castle was first built in the twelfth century by the Bishop of Durham to defend himself against incursions by Scots. In 1136, nevertheless, King David I of Scotland made just such an incursion here at Norham and gained hold,

---

failed disastrously to establish a trading colony at Darien, in what is now Panama, in 1700. More happily, *Vis Unita Fortior* is also the name of a 2017 *Led Zeppelin* album of a concert in 1973.

for a while, of much of Northumberland. King William the Lion captured the castle again in 1174, and his son Alexander II had another go, besieging Norham for forty days without success.

On the other (i.e. Scottish) bank of the river from us now lies Holywell Haugh, where Robert de Brus and a dozen other competitors for the throne of Scotland gathered in June 1291, and where they appear to have given fealty to Edward of England as Overlord of Scotland.

Robert the Bruce (the above Robert's son), once he eventually became King of Scots, besieged Norham for almost a year without victory in 1318, and then again to no avail in 1319 and 1322. James IV tried in 1497 with the aid of Mons Meg (the mighty cannon that still looks out in this direction from the walls of Edinburgh Castle), and finally succeeded in 1513. Unduly emboldened, James then went on to nearby Flodden Field, where he was slain, along with several thousand more.[1]

Norham Castle at Sunrise, painted in 1798, is the work that Turner often credited as the picture that launched his career. When he returned to Norham in 1831, he reputedly observed:

> I made a painting of Norham several years since … and from that day to this I have had as much to do as my hands could execute.

I tell Malc this last fact. He is not presently interested.

***

Our first day's walk is coming to a close. Much as we have enjoyed it, we would be lying through our respective back teeth if we were to claim at this point that we could be doing with another mile more.

Even in the rain, Norham is a friendly-looking place, with its village green, its mercat cross (if they call them that in England), its butcher (who will make you a cup of tea for a pound) and its fine medieval church. Obscurely, and possibly not relevantly, until 1844 little Norhamshire here was an ancient exclave of County Durham, squeezed between Northumberland and the Tweed. Of more immediate interest is the fact that Norham is home to a very old pub, the Mason's Arms, behind whose bowed windows we now nurse

---

[1] It seems irreverent to record this, but I could not avoid noticing reports recently that the Royal Mid-Surrey Golf Course at Richmond has made a public claim that James IV's remains have ended up buried on their 14th tee. That story is too long and too unlikely to trouble the reader with further.

serious plans to eat and sleep.

Malc opens the door to the public bar and I follow him in. Concentrating on my sore feet for a moment, I forget to close the door behind me. Within ten seconds, a ferocious woman gets up from beside the bar's glowing open fire. She announces that she has been sitting there all day and doesn't now intend that the street should be heated by the establishment's efforts. She is a fellow guest.

I should have shut the door. But it is a knotty question whether you can be held to blame for something you did not really know much about. It has bothered theologians for centuries, and I have doubts about my own culpability on this score. I shut the door, and say I am sorry. The guest by the fire says, 'I'll make you sorry. We're not very subtle around these parts'.

Manners prevent me from agreeing. She smiles. Her accent places her somewhere in North Northumberland. First appearances and cross-border cultural misunderstandings can be deceiving. The Mason's Arms is in fact a very pleasant place to eat fish, chips and mushy peas, and drink cold beer by a warm fire. My feet recover. I sleep well. The weather forecast for tomorrow is not bad.

Day 2: From Norham to Coldstream

(Circa 7 miles)

Norham Church; Balliol and Bruce; Ladykirk and James IV; Both sides the Tweed; Ferm touns; John Duns Scotus; Twizel and the strange tale of Perkin Warbeck; Lennel, Polwarth and Coldstream; Flodden Field.

The friendly landlord of the Mason's Arms makes a good breakfast. My clothes have largely dried out overnight. We pack our bags and make our way through Norham, heading back for Scotland and, specifically, for our hotel in Coldstream. Or, as the fifteenth-century poet Blind Harry put it, when describing that very journey as made by Wallace:

> And out off it till Noram passit he.
>
> Quhen Wallace saw it mycht na bettir be,
>
> Till Caudstreym went and lugit him on Tweid.[1]

The tourist authority's leaflet says that Beatrix Potter was unduly unkind about Norham, describing it as 'a dirty town, where every tenth house is a public [house].' What the heck, I wonder inwardly, did Beatrix Potter know? Today, I am positively disposed towards Norham, and everything else. The sun is almost shining. Today's is a shorter day's walk than yesterday's, holding out the real prospect of our hitting the nightlife of Coldstream this evening.

The leaflet also describes Norham as 'England's most dangerous town', in fact paraphrasing the sixteenth-century historian John Leyland, who in more vividly wild-west terms said that Norham was 'the danngerest place in England'. Walking through Norham on a Sunday morning, this seems quite a bold claim. Thinking about it, however, I can see the point. Norham is only five minutes' walk from Scotland, as the SNP sticker on a car parked twenty yards inside England confirms.

We pass Norham's long, gold-coloured church, built near 'Ubbanford', the spot where according to tradition St Aidan crossed the Tweed in AD 635. Aidan was on his way from Iona to Lindisfarne to found a monastery there. Later, the coffin of another saint, Cuthbert (to whom Norham Church is now dedicated), was brought to Norham *from* Lindisfarne for a while, to keep it from the Vikings. Parts of the present church, including the chancel, date from as long ago as 1165.

In June 1291, the church was host to what was effectively a joint meeting of the Scottish and English parliaments. The outcome was that Edward I of

[1] Blind Harry: *The Wallace. Lugit:* 'lodged'.

65

England was asked to preside over a court to decide the identity of the new Scots king. This followed the dying out of the most direct Scottish royal line, after Alexander III fell from his horse at Kinghorn in Fife, and then his seven-year-old granddaughter, Margaret, the 'Maid of Norway', died in Orkney. These two deaths had created a scramble among Alexander's extended family, which Edward was able to exploit to the full.

Writing eighty years afterwards, in the Cathedral of Old Aberdeen, the Scots poet John Barbour rued the willingness of the Scots nobles to place themselves at Edward's mercy that day here in Norham:

> A! blynd folk full off all folly!
> Haid yhe umbethoucht yhow enkrely,
> Quhat perell to yhow mycht apper,
> Yhe had nocht wrocht on that maner.[1]

One tradition[2] is that part of this court's deliberations took place here, mid-Tweed on Blount Island, a tiny sliver of Scottish land lying in front of Norham Castle. Here, amid much cramped fanfare, according to this version of events, was announced a shortleit of two names: Robert de Brus and John Balliol.

Certainly, the court met again in Berwick in 1292, and chose Balliol, who did homage to Edward in Newcastle that Christmas. Perhaps he did homage to him at Norham too; it seems likely that Balliol took every such opportunity. Blind Harry certainly imagines such a scene at Norham, writing almost two hundred years after the event:

> He thocht till hym to mak it playn conquace.
> Till Noram kirk he come withoutyn mar;
> The consell than of Scotland mett hym thar.
> Full sutailly he chargit thaim in bandoune
> As thar ourlord till hald of hym the croun.[3]

Edward made bluntly clear to Balliol that he intended the Scottish king to become his vassal, ultimately gaining Balliol the humiliating name to posterity of 'Toom Tabard' or 'Empty Coat'. This is probably better more liberally

---

[1] John Barbour: *The Bruce. Enkrely*: 'seriously'.
[2] Cited by Eric Robson: *The Border Line,* among others.
[3] Blind Harry: *The Wallace.* 'He thought to make his conquest plain. To Norham church he came without delay. The representatives of Scotland then met him there. He fully commanded them into subjection, as their overlord, to hold of them the crown.'

translated as 'Stuffed Shirt'. These events, in due course, precipitated Scotland's Wars of Independence and the rise of Sir William Wallace.

On three occasions between 1318 and 1322, King Robert the Bruce used Norham Church as his headquarters (apparently using it to stable his horses) when he was besieging Norham Castle.

Today, the church contains, among other interesting things, a column built out of shattered carvings from different periods of the eighth, ninth and tenth centuries; a sort of scrambled jigsaw of Saxon saints and Celtic knots. Reputedly buried in the huge churchyard is St Ceolwulf, an eighth-century king of Northumbria, whose canonisation was perhaps not unrelated to the dispensation which he gave the monks of Lindisfarne to drink wine and beer (their order had previously allowed them only milk and water).

Also buried here is Corporal Daniel Laidlaw V.C. from just across the Border in Swinton. Laidlaw famously piped the King's Own Scottish Borderers out of their trench during the Battle of Loos in 1915 and kept playing until he was eventually wounded.

***

We pass the last school in England. It looks a nice wee place. The sign identifies it as the 'Norham Church of England First School (voluntary control)'. Although but a few paces inside England, there could be few clearer indications of how different the Scottish and English education systems are. We both scratch our Scottish heads. What is a first school? Is it a primary or a nursery? Do the Church of England get paid by the state to run it? Can anyone go, or is it restricted to the children of churchgoers? And if its classes are subject to voluntary control, does that mean the children have to agree to any requests made of them by teachers? I make a mental note to google all these perplexing English concepts.

We cross the fine nineteenth-century bridge over the Tweed to Ladykirk, and back into Scotland. The parish of Ladykirk was in fact two parishes up until the time of the reformation: Horndean and Upsettlington. By 1951, there were only 261 people living in Ladykirk, a decline which the minister at that time blamed in part on the fact that most houses in his parish still had no running water, and only three had electricity. He struggles to think of any particular sin or crime in Ladykirk, other than an undue interest in football pools.[1] These days, the population of the parish is barely 150.

Ladykirk is home to the Kirk of the Steill, built at the order of James IV

---

[1] *Third Statistical Account of Scotland.*

of Scotland. We look inside.

The church is believed to have been built in thanksgiving for a safe crossing of the Tweed by the king, after an accident of some kind at a nearby steill (pool), when he narrowly escaped drowning. Ladykirk is a remarkable survival of a substantial pre-reformation church, in a country where there are not all that many of those still in use. James IV certainly visited, and probably prayed where we sit now, on his way to disaster at Flodden Field.

The church was a frequent meeting place for Wardens of the Marches, on their formal 'days of truce'.[1] In 1559, this was where the Treaty of Upsettlington was signed between the Scottish and English governments, largely behind the back of Mary Queen of Scots, who was then still living at the French Court.[2] The treaty was a supplement to the Peace of Cateau-Cambrésis, which sought to end various Italian conflicts, but also guaranteed to maintain Scotland's Border as it stood, undertaking not to re-open the old Berwick question.

The Kirk of the Steill is imposing, solid and (despite the deceptive eighteenth-century top to its tower), very clearly old. It is vaulted within and roofed in stone without, and sits in a parted sea of red headstones. Inside, the kirk is a truly beautiful place. It announces loudly its royal and pre-Reformation origins; the French influence can be seen on its 'unbroken' style of stone vault. There is no wood in the roof, as James knew the dangerous location of the church, and stipulated that the building should be impervious to both fire and flood.

We sit for a while, and look up.

But the Kirk of the Steill, sadly, also feels very curiously like the *Mary Celeste*, or even the Flannan Isles lighthouse. It has an air of having been very recently and very suddenly abandoned. The Church of Scotland's website speaks in characteristically general terms. There is no mention of a minister, with only an unconvincing reference to its congregation 'generally' meeting on the second and fourth Sunday mornings of the month.[3] It is the second Sunday this morning. The flower rota on the wall has stopped around the same time as I understand the Mayan calendar did. The roll of baptisms ends mid-page, with the name of one infant who will now be fourteen. Dust is accumulating on the pews. The cushions in the better seats and in the pulpit

---

[1] See Day 5 for more on days of truce.
[2] There was, as another scarcely relevant aside, a brief campaign some years ago to have Mary Queen of Scots disinterred from Westminster Abbey and returned to Scotland, as if she were a human Stone of Destiny. Presumably, like the Stone, she would have been returned to Scotland in two bits. All this rather misses the point that Mary spent her whole latter career *trying* to get buried in Westminster Abbey. By that point, she saw herself as Elizabeth I of England's heir.
[3] I made enquiries, and they no longer do.

are slowly coming apart.

I remember a very evangelical-conservative preacher once triumphantly telling me that liberal ministers were what were to blame for Berwickshire having the lowest rate of church-attendance in Scotland. Possibly, but then not everything is a price worth paying for high church-attendance. The gentler side of the Church of Scotland has at times been vague, it has often been prone to political complacency. It is certainly now losing serious ground to harsher, U.S.-influenced theologies on the one front and to public religious indifference on its (much broader) other flank. But, for quite a long while now, it has been generally benign.

I hope that Ladykirk's church has a future, and that James IV's intention for prayers to be said here is not entirely in vain. I hope, at the very least, that someone is looking after the place. The Scottish Reformation may have made 'every man his own priest', but it also robbed most people of something else, something that people over the water in Norham probably still have. That is the idea that you can have a legitimate reason, other than fixing the heating, for going into a church on your own.

Yet, if I lived around here, I would certainly come to the Kirk of the Steill on Sundays, whether anyone else cared to join me or not.

***

In 1802 the English travel writer Richard Warner,[1] in one of his most ridiculous observations of all, had this to say of the path we are walking now:

> The Tweed, parallel to which our road to Coldstream lay, disappointed our expectations of picturesque beauty. Associated as the name of this river had hitherto been in our minds with poetical and pastoral ideas, we were prepared to admire its 'fringed banks' and 'sacred shades', the haunt of many a water nymph and sylvian deity; but alas... all was thrown upon the eye at once in its original nakedness.

We ignore Mr Warner, and find little to disappoint us in today's sunshine. We walk from the Ladykirk bridge, along the footpath that follows the

---

[1] One of Warner's more astute observations is on how (because of the much more widespread availability of schools in Scotland) working people here were much more likely to be able to read than their counterparts immediately over the Border. In Kelso, Warner is astonished to find '...a general taste for literature', and mentions that there was a 'universal diffusion of information among the lowest classes of its inhabitants'.

Scottish bank of the Tweed, upstream past the grounds of Upsettlington House. This is an easy walk. Daffodils and wild garlic line the path, and the broad river is contained behind lines of trees.

We mark our way from one angler's bothy to the next. I believe that the grander type of fishermen describe these as anglers' 'pavilions'. These formal little stone buildings are strung out along both river banks; sentry posts, if only ceremonial ones, along the Border.

This is the Tweed, not as John Buchan imagined it far upstream in the wilds of Tweedsmuir 'whaur Tweed rins wee', nor as Scott saw it running swift past his garden at Abbotsford. It is not even the industrious rivermouth we saw laid claim to yesterday by the people of Berwick. This is the stately length of the Tweed that is a national border, and which feels the need in consequence to maintain a certain air of dignity.

The song that surely best describes this part of the river is 'Both Sides the Tweed':

> What's the spring-breathing jess'mine and rose,
> What's the summer, with all its gay train,
> Or the plenty of autumn, to those
> Who've bartered their freedom for gain?
>
> Let the love of our king's sacred right
> To the love of our country succeed;
> Let friendship and honour unite,
> And flourish on both sides the Tweed.
>
> …Let virtue distinguish the brave,
> Place riches in lowest degree;
> Think him poorest who can be a slave,
> Him richest who dares to be free.[1]

I once heard this song introduced at a douce Edinburgh cèilidh by a very nervous hostess. She reassured her audience that 'Happily, this is at least one folk song that is not espousing Scottish independence.' I look back and wonder at her tone–deafness, if she really thought that. The references to bartering freedom for gain do not read like a ringing endorsement of the events of 1707.

---

[1] 'Both sides the Tweed' from James Hogg: *Jacobite Relics.* Gaughen's version replaces the Jacobite 'king' with 'land'.

In fact, this is probably the most dangerous type of Scottish folk song of all. It does not urge Scotland to get even with England, but rather seems to envisage a time when the two countries might co-exist on a basis of equality.

Dick Gaughan brought the song to a new audience shortly after the 1979 referendum, in which 51.6% of those voting voted for home-rule for Scotland.[1] Yet no Scottish Parliament came for another twenty years.

***

We walk on in spring sunshine past the big house at Milne Graden. At Milne Graden East Mains, we pass two wee islands in the river. According to the Ordnance Survey, the larger one – Dreeper Island – is in England. The smaller one – Kippie Island – is in Scotland, though changes in the current mean that the two islands have more or less joined now, at least physically. They are two of a series of curious little islands that lie along this stretch of the Tweed: low-lying specks of frontier scrubland, many with names of their own (and all with identified national attachments). The other names I know of are: St Thomas's Island (Scotland), Blount Island (Scotland), Canny Island (England) and the improbably-named Bendibus Island (in England and virtually joined now, it seems, to the English 'mainland').

In 1740, on the Scottish bank near here at Milne Graden, was born James Small. Although unlikely now ever to be a household name, Small transformed agriculture across the world by inventing the modern steel plough, a revolutionary change from the primitive, inefficiently-shaped wooden ploughs used before then. Small's generally uncelebrated contribution to the world's economic growth is not easily calculated but is almost certainly huge.

Even a century ago, however, work on the land here, though improved, was still arduous. One Border village bard records the life of farm workers like himself, explaining here the task of 'singling' turnips:

> Up and doon the dreels they gae
> Jock and Tam thegither,
> Knockin oot the neeps aa day;
> Hinnae time tae blether.[2]

---

[1] The result of the 1979 referendum was set aside by the UK Government, as the relevant legislation required 40% of *all* those on the electoral roll – a total which included non-voters and the recently dead – to vote 'yes' in order for a 'yes' to have any effect. No equivalent stipulation applied in the event of a 'no' vote. I was eight at the time. My first, and no doubt scarring, political memory is of my father explaining that *'The deid folk votit "no"'*.

[2] Ronald D.M. Kerr, 'The turnip singlers', from Walter Elliot: *The New Minstrelsy*

Four or five miles westwards now, across the flat countryside from here, are the villages of Swinton and Leitholm. This is the little stretch of Scotland's edge where my paternal grandparents, a ploughman and a domestic servant, both grew up in the years before the Great War.

My grandmother, who lived to be 101, endured into the twenty-first century as an impressively thrawn survivor from another world – the rural Lowlands of a whole century before.[1] The society of which she was a product would probably have been fairly recognisable to Robert Burns, in many respects. It was a place where – incredibly – bonded servitude still existed for a few of the very poorest, and where moral anxiety was voiced about how the increased availability of bicycles was allowing some farm servants to stray as much as fifteen miles in a day.

Like most people working on the land in the Lowlands, my own family flitted at regular term-days from fee to fee around their own corner of Scotland. The many places they lived and worked – places like Kaimes West Mains, Linton Bankhead, the Hirsel – had in my mind (as in reality) always been as self-evidently Scottish as Falkirk or Portree or my father. It is only when I look at them now on my map, all circled in my father's hand, that I fully realise that Kaimes West Mains is in fact only four miles from England. Linton Bankhead is five miles. The Hirsel is a mile-and-a-half.

My grandmother spent much of her long retirement in the nearby town of Duns, cheerfully making tattie soup, playing the fiddle, holding and explaining inflexible opinions, and washing her clothes with a bath, stick and wringer. If one story is to be believed, she maintained until well after the dawn of the internet a boycott of German goods in Berwick's shops, a policy which apparently extended as far back as the latter part of the First World War.

I have also heard it said that she once wrote a particularly forthright letter to the owner of one estate on which my grandfather had not long previously been employed, telling the laird to pay more attention to the good management of his farms, and less to affairs of state. The recipient was the Earl of Home, who was I believe Foreign Secretary[2] at the time.

I do not profess that getting up in a cold house in the winter to light a fire represents a rural idyll. Nor does having to leave school to work in the fields of a man who reaps where he does not sow. But it is very definitely a world

---

of the Scottish Border. Singling is the unpopular and back-breaking task of thinning out seedlings with a hoe, so that the plants have room to grow to full size.

[1] This ancientness in my grandmother first impressed itself on me when, on lifting up her kitchen lino at a flitting around 1980, I saw that the newspapers lining it underneath were from the 1890s.

[2] Despite this reprimand, Home shortly afterwards became UK Prime Minister.

worth learning something about. I thank my grandparents if I have.

***

Somewhere across the fields to our right now – as far as anyone can tell – was born one of the giants of thought in the medieval world. The philosopher and theologian John Duns Scotus[1] was by tradition born on the estate of Grueldykes near Duns, nine miles north of here, around the year 1266. He taught in Oxford, Paris and finally Cologne, where he died in 1308.

It is a strange thought that, while Wallace was ravaging his way westwards along the Border here and Longshanks burned Berwick, John Duns was grappling with the question of whether God's actions are good because He is God, or whether God is good because of His actions.

The 'Subtle Doctor', as he was nicknamed, has perhaps proved to be rather too subtle to make for easy reading down the centuries. I admit to a longing for him to pause, just occasionally, to produce examples from the world of everyday life as he proceeds at breakneck speed through his metaphysical conclusions:

> Conclusion 15: Plurality must never be assumed without necessity... Conclusion 16: Everything ordered to an end is excelled.[2]

, John Duns' detractors succeeded in making his name a byword for stupidity – a dunce. This is in fact still the traditional local pronunciation of the town's name – Dunse – although, a hundred years ago, the 'e' was officially taken off the end in an effort to try to encourage Berwickshire folk to make 'Duns' rhyme with 'guns' instead.[3]

In fact, John Duns is now recognised as having made a huge impression on metaphysics, on the arguments around the existence of God, and on the Catholic doctrine of the Immaculate Conception. He came to rather different conclusions on all of these fronts to those reached by the Merse's other great philosopher, David Hume (upon whom we stumbled just yesterday).

In 1993, the Blessed John Duns Scotus was at last beatified by Pope John Paul II.

---

[1] The last part of his name simply refers to his nationality, i.e. 'John Duns, the Scot'.
[2] From Scotus's *Sentences*.
[3] The unjust association with the word 'dunce' may or may not also explain why it was decided to name the town's secondary school Berwickshire High School, rather than Dunse High School.

***

Near Milne Graden, we climb up from the riverbank through the trees and onto the road, which then more or less follows the river from here past the farm of Tweedmill. On the English riverbank opposite us now is the mouth of the Till. Not quite visible through the trees is the village of Twizel, and the ruined castle in which James IV of Scotland convened a council or parliament in 1513. Parts of both armies crossed the Till here that year, on their respective ways to Flodden Field, over the newly-built Twizel Bridge.

In *Marmion*,[1] Scott visualises the Scots army on the bridge, a scene which is very easy to imagine if the reader has ever walked on the other side of the Tweed here:

> Upon the eastern bank you see;
> Still pouring down the rocky den,
> Where flows the sullen Till,
> And rising from the dim-wood glen
> Standards on standards, men on men,
> In slow succession still.
> And sweeping o'er the Gothic arch,
> And pressing on, in ceaseless march,
> To gain the opposing hill.[2]

For three centuries, this bridge remained the longest stone span in England and, amazingly, it stands intact today. *Marmion* also reports that there was, at some distant point in time, a nine-foot stone coffin near the church at Twizel. In this, the remains of St Cuthbert are said to have floated by themselves down the Tweed from Melrose:

> In his stone-coffin forth he rides,
> A ponderous bark, for river tides;
> Yet light as gossamer it glides,
> Downward to Tilmouth cell.

---

[1] It is difficult now to realise fully the impact which this one long poem had on the world. When Scott published it in 1808, *Marmion* created a Border literary landscape whose place-names and characters were suddenly as widely known as those in *Lord of the Rings* or *Star Wars* are now. One of those places was Twizel.
[2] Sir Walter Scott: *Marmion*.

Unfortunately, it is now impossible to verify this story, as a local farmer long ago announced that he wanted the coffin for a trough, causing the saint then to appear and smash it up in a fit of pique.

The banks of the Till were also – according to one long and melancholy tale – where a woman called Barbara Moor once had seven sons, all of whom met grisly ends.[1]

A much better-attested story concerns how the castle at Twizel was a casualty of the memorably-strange affair of Perkin Warbeck. Warbeck emerged from obscurity to make the claim, throughout most of the 1490s, that he was in fact Richard Duke of York, one of the two young 'Princes in the Tower'. These were the two boys who had been imprisoned and then 'disappeared' in the Tower of London in 1483. Warbeck made a very public claim that, on this basis, he was the rightful heir to the English throne. He subsequently recanted these claims – under some considerable pressure – but in the meantime provided some sport for the natural enemies of the King of England in the royal courts of Spain and Scotland.

James IV of Scotland was encouraged by the Spanish ambassador to support this odd cause, and so a Scottish army came through Twizel in 1497 for this purpose. James IV enjoyed the massive disruption which Warbeck briefly caused Henry VII of England, but tired of him in the end, and eventually sent him to Ireland on a ship which was significantly named the *Cuckoo*. These events led directly or indirectly to the Treaty of Ayton of 1497, resulting in a seven-year truce between Scotland and England.[2]

***

A few miles to our north now lies a settlement so small as barely to be there at all: Polwarth, (or *Polart*, as that name is traditionally said locally). Polwarth merits an uncommon number of mentions in Scottish literature.

At the end of the sixteenth century, both Alexander Hume and his elder brother Patrick were poets here. Alexander's poetry gives an insight into the mind of post-Reformation Scotland. Often using a metre that is shared very recognisably with the Scottish Psalter, Hume regularly dips in and out of religious language to describe the Border landscape:

> O then it were a seemly thing,

---

[1] *Wilson's Tales of the Borders*, Vol. III.
[2] The treaty also included an undertaking not to destroy the fish garth at Kirkandrews on Esk. We will eventually encounter this very long and involved story near the end of our journey.

While all is still and calme,
The praise of God to play and sing,
With cornet and with shalme.[1]

Meanwhile, the very different image of dancing at 'Polwart on the Green'
is a traditional theme employed by, among others, Allan Ramsay:

Let dorty dames say na,
As lang as e'er they please,
Seem caulder than the sna',
While inwardly they bleeze;
But I will frankly shaw my mind,
And yield my heart to thee;
Be ever to the captive kind,
That langs na to be free.
At Polwart on the green.[2]

The road takes us up the Tweed now as far as Lennel's ruined kirk, which
was in use from the twelfth to eighteenth centuries. Until 1716, Lennel lent
its own name to the parish now called after the nearby town of Coldstream.
Here, in Scott's poem, Lord Marmion rests on his way to Flodden, and here
Malc and I rest on our way to the pub. We lie map-reading for a while among
long, course grass and skull-and-crossbone-seared headstones.

From Lennel, it is not long now till we reach Coldstream (population,
2,100). This is a veritable Mexico City of activity, compared to any other
settlement we will walk through on our whole journey until its very end.[3]
Coldstream has a museum, pubs, shops, hotels – the whole jing-bang.

We check into our hotel, not far from Coldstream's own castle, the Hirsel.
In my upstairs room, I prop open the window with the bit of spare skirting-
board which has helpfully been supplied for the purpose. I look out along the
town's douce but lively High Street, which forms the high road from England.

Coldstream is as Scottish as Norham is English. Its long and solid main
street of respectable shops, with equally respectable houses above them, its

---

[1] Alexander Hume 'Of the Day Estivall' in Bawcutt and Riddy (eds): *Longer Scottish Poems Volume I, 1375-1650.*
[2] Allan Ramsay: 'Polwart on the Green' from *The Tea-Time Miscellany.*
[3] Discounting metropolitan Berwick (with a population of around 12,000), which we only really saw from a bus, Coldstream is the biggest place we will pass through directly on our walk until Gretna (population 2,700).

pubs, its castle, and its two kirks (including the redundant *kirk we dinna gang tae,* if the reader gets that rather aged joke[1]). All these proclaim to the world – and to England in particular – Coldstream's sense of sonsie self-assurance and general pleasedness. Commercial traffic rumbles out of the town, and so out of Scotland. In an otherwise green landscape, the Cheviots shine incongruously snow-covered today, as if we were at the foot of a range of little Pyrenees, while the Tweed boils black with the spring's rain and thaw.

Coldstream – whose name means what it sounds like – was where Edward I invaded Scotland in 1296. The town much later played a role in the restoration of Charles II in 1660, when General Monck (having changed sides), marched south from here. He led what had originally been a Roundhead regiment and is now called the Coldstream Guards. The Guards now come here once a year, having been granted the freedom of the town in 1968.[2]

Malc is looking to place his annual bet on a horse and is encouraged to find a street near the Coldstream Guards Museum called Bookie Lane. The book is not the one he was thinking of however, and the name commemorates the Bible factory set up here in the 1840s by Rev Adam Thomson. A plaque reminds us that Thomson managed to break the monopoly on the printing and selling of all Bibles. Somehow, at that point, the copyright was held by a private individual who had managed also to ban the import of Bibles from England.[3] Thomson slashed the sales-price until repeated efforts to put him out of business by the commercial publishers were eventually successful. At one point, however, the Coldstream Bible factory employed some three-hundred people.

***

The town of Coldstream bristles, unambiguously Scottish, right up to the very bank of the Tweed. Proving the point is the monument to the Battle of Flodden Field (1513) which stands, near the site of Coldstream Priory,[4]

---

[1] This reference to one of Coldstream's redundant kirks (a museum now) is an allusion to an old joke, once in circulation in England, about the Scottish tendency towards religious schism. If the reader has not heard it in recent decades, it goes something like this: 'A Scotchman was shipwrecked on a desert island all alone. After ten years, he was rescued by a passing vessel whose sailors were amazed to find that the Scotchman had, in the ensuing time, built not one but *two* places of worship. *"This",* the Scotchman explained, *"is the kirk A gang tae. An thon's the kirk A dinna gang tae."'*

[2] That said, the Coldstream Guards do not recruit in Coldstream or anywhere else in Scotland. By a parallel anomaly, the KOSB, despite their base in Berwick, don't generally recruit in Berwick.

[3] Another motivation for the Bible factory was to remove a host of typos from several editions of the Bible then on sale. One of these included among the Commandments the troubling words, 'Know ye not that the righteous shall not inherit the earth?'

[4] Coldstream Priory is said to be where many of the nobles killed at Flodden were buried.

at the water's edge. A saltire flies in the evening light, and a sword-shaped sculpture points over the river in the direction of the battlefield.

On the day itself, James IV, egged on by the Queen of France and others, had the advantage in numbers. The Earl of Surrey was an astute general, however, and managed to encircle the Scottish forces at Flodden Ridge, cutting off any prospect of retreat back over the Border:

> What checks the fiery soul of James?
> Why sits that champion of the dames
> Inactive on his steed,
> And sees, between him and his land,
> Between him and Tweed's southern strand,
> His host Lord Surrey lead?
> …O for one hour of Wallace wight,
> Or well-skill'd Bruce, to rule the fight,
> And cry-'Saint Andrew and our right!'
> Another sight had seen that morn,
> From Fate's dark book a leaf been torn,
> And Flodden had been Bannockbourne![1]

Estimates suggest that perhaps 10,000 Scots died and 1,500 English. Both countries had relied on their Borderers and, in Scotland's case, the consequences of that were devastating. The impact of Flodden psychologically on Scotland, and in particular on the Scottish Borders, cannot be exaggerated. It was a sentiment captured over two-hundred years afterwards by Jean Elliot in her famous lament, 'The Flowers of the Forest', which she set to a much older tune of that name:

> I've heard the lilting, at the yowe-milking,
> Lasses a-lilting before dawn o' day;
> But now they are moaning on ilka green loaning;
> 'The Flowers of the Forest are a' wede away.'[2]

Writing at the end of the nineteenth century, J.B. Selkirk imagined the battle's aftermath in these terms:

---

[1] Sir Walter Scott: *Marmion.*
[2] The only known work of Jean Elliot, published around 1776.

Noo we've naether haunds nor hairt-
In oor grief, the wark's forgotten,
Tho it's wantit every airt
And the craps are lyin rotten.
War's awesome blast's gane by,
And left the land forlorn;
In daith's dool hairst they lie
The shearers and the shorn.
O Flodden Field.[1]

In Selkirk (if I may stray a little from our path for a moment), a folk-memory still exists that only one of the eighty or so men sent from that town to Flodden ever returned. His name, it is held, was Fletcher. He came home with a captured English standard, which he threw down in the town's market place, an action remembered each year in a powerful part of Selkirk's Common Riding ritual. Selkirk, however, is not the only place in the Borders where Flodden is still on many people's lips. Here in Coldstream, there is a ride-out to Flodden every August. In nearby Swinton, the bell on the village kirk reputedly tolled disaster in 1513 and is still known locally as the 'Flodden Bell'.

It is possible that the Scottish Border never again experienced a sorrow quite like Flodden until the onset of the First World War.

***

We walk to the pub at the other end of the town, the Besom,[2] for some food and beer (both of which turn out to be good) and to plan out tomorrow's journey. Today's has been a short walk along the Tweed, and tomorrow we will do the same, until we eventually leave the river behind us.

In the Besom, a friendly Coldstream man strikes up conversation, mentioning how house prices are getting pushed up unhelpfully by people selling houses in the cities to retire here. It doesn't make things ideal for families like his, he remarks.

Other Scottish voices at the next table beyond him raise the subject of the Battle of Flodden, and complain that they never learned anything about it at school. Indeed, I hear one of them say, they learned very little about Scotland

---

[1] J.B. Selkirk: 'Selkirk after Flodden', from *The Complete Poems of J.B. Selkirk (James Brown)*.
[2] This is a good name for a pub. As well as its basic meaning of a broom or brush, in Scotland a besom is also a cheeky, slightly disreputable woman.

at all. It is ironically reassuring sometimes to know that it's not just Malc and I who go on about all this. The pair of us compare notes.

To be fair, we did actually get told about a fair bit of Scottish history and literature at primary school. Anything more, however, we learned from our families, from our own reading, or from hearing folk songs. It certainly did not come from anything on the curriculum of Scottish secondary schools in the 1980s.

But that is something to talk about another day. Malc and I don't need to rehearse our views about all this with the table next to us. We are sleepy, and in agreement, and generally anticipate each others' thoughts anyway, if we have any new ones.

As we walk back up through Coldstream, I am able to give Malc some good news. Tomorrow, it is promised, is actually to be warm.

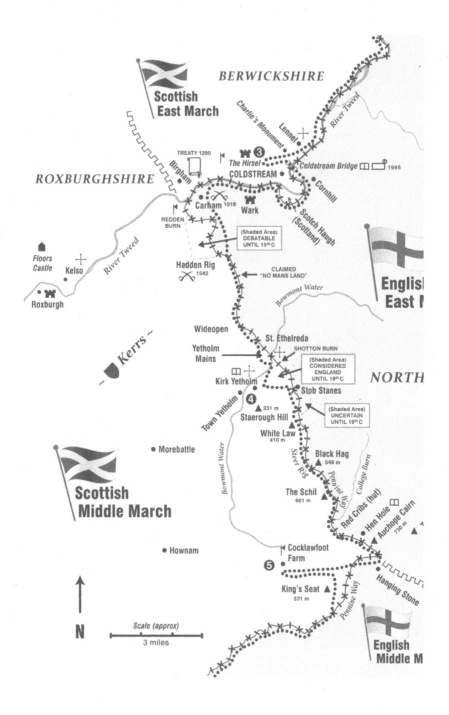

Map 3. The Scottish Middle March, from where the Border leaves the Tweed.

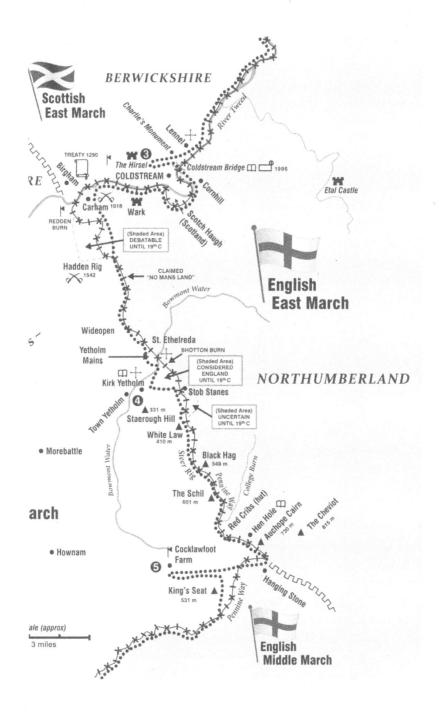

BERWICKSHIRE

Scottish
East March

RE

TREATY 1290

Birgham

Charlie's Monument

Lennel

River Tweed

The Hirsel W ❸
COLDSTREAM ●

Coldstream Bridge 📖 🏠 1996

Cornhill

Etal Castle W

Carham ✗ 1018
Wark W

REDDEN
BURN

Scotch Haugh
(Scotland)

(Shaded Area)
DEBATABLE
UNTIL 19th C

Hadden Rig
✗ 1542

CLAIMED
"NO MANS LAND"

Bowmont Water

English
East March

Wideopen

St. Ethelreda

Yetholm
Mains

SHOTTON BURN

(Shaded Area)
CONSIDERED
ENGLAND
UNTIL 19th C

NORTHUMBERLAND

Kirk Yetholm 📖 ✝

Stob Stanes

(Shaded Area)
UNCERTAIN
UNTIL 19th C

Town Yetholm

❹ ▲ 331 m
Staerough Hill

White Law
410 m

● Morebattle

Steer Rig

Bowmont Water

Black Hag
▲ 549 m

College Burn

Pennine Way

arch

The Schil
▲ 601 m

Red Cribs (hut)

Hen Hole 📖

● Hownam

Cocklawfoot
Farm

Auchope Cairn
730 m

The Cheviot
▲ 815 m

❺

King's Seat ▲
531 m

Hanging Stone

Pennine Way

English
Middle March

ale (approx)

3 miles

Day 3: From Coldstream to Yetholm
(Circa 13 miles)

'Charlie's Monument'; Robert Burns in the Borders; The Stone of Destiny passes through; The Reivers; The False Alarm; A sudden linguistic boundary; Cornhill and Scotch Haugh; Wark and Carham; Roxburgh and the Kerrs; Fergus of Galloway; Hoselaw and Wark Common; 'Get tae Birgham'; Yetholm.

The weather forecast was right. It is a nice day, and high-time to be up. Malc is not at breakfast by eight, so I go to knock on his room. There is no response. I turn round and see him emerge from a room three doors down the corridor. I am, Malc points out dryly, knocking at my own door. In defence, I explain that I am fine with a map and a compass, just not in confined spaces, and when presented with a row of identical doors. Sadly this is not the first incident of its kind. Malc notes it, for the purposes of future casting up.

***

The most obvious thing which anyone visiting Coldstream sees is the massive seventy-foot column standing near the bridge. Its sheer scale suggests that the person atop it is perhaps going to be George III, Nelson, Wellington or Burns. In fact, somewhat incredibly, this is a vastly over-the-top monument to the area's local MP. More incredible still is that this was not only put up within the MP's own lifetime, but simply marks his first and only local election victory.

The monument's inscription explains that Charles Marjoribanks MP[1] was the son of the local laird, and had 'high talents and amiable qualities'. These qualities must have been striking indeed, if his constituents built him this. He immediately afterwards died, after only one year as a backbench Liberal MP. The monument says a lot more about the respect in which lairdly families were held at this time than about anything else. That respect is summed up in rather condescending terms by Rev John Edgar, minister of the nearby parish of Hutton around this period, when he says of his flock that:

> Few of them intermeddle with the irritating subject of politics
> …knowing that their superiors are interested in their welfare.[2]

[1] Pronounced 'Marshbanks'. Despite this, the family name derives (it is claimed) from a connection with Marjory, daughter of Robert the Bruce. Most people in fact see the family as reiving Johnstones who went 'legit'.

[2] *New Statistical Account of Scotland*, 1845. Mr Edgar's remarks go a long way to illustrating why the Great Disruption had taken place, two years earlier, over the issue

However, if I am to be more generous for a second about 'Charlie's Monument' (as it is often called) it does mark an important moment, when elections had at last become something like worthy of the name. Marjoribanks was elected at the first elections after the Scottish Reform Act of 1832.[1] This legislation expanded the number of people in Scotland who enjoyed the right to vote from a miniscule and highly privileged 5,000 to about 65,000. The increased figure now represented something like 13% of adult males in Scotland.

Not that long prior to this, in 1820, a number of those who had campaigned too loudly for the vote were either executed or transported.[2] Even after 1832, the franchise continued to be limited to males who were the heads of households, and who either owned a property worth £10 or rented one with a rental value above £50. It was to be a long time before the UK made any claim whatsoever to be a democracy. Indeed, as late as 1867, Prime Minister Benjamin Disraeli warned the House of Commons:

> We do not live – and I trust it will never be the fate of this country to live – under a democracy.[3]

Even later, at the outbreak of the First World War, not only did no woman have a vote, but neither did well over a third of men, including most of those then fighting in the trenches.

The reader should remember all that, either when they next see Charlie's Monument, or perhaps just when they next hear the UK describing itself to the world as the ancient inventor of democratic values.

***

We come to the stately Union Bridge over the Tweed, the second of that name we have crossed. This one was built under its own specific Act of Parliament in 1759. In a house at the Scottish end was formerly a wedding venue for eloping couples. Three Lords Chancellor of England apparently

---

of the undue influence which local lairds had appropriated for themselves in appointing ministers to local charges.

[1] Passed alongside the parallel legislation for England and Wales which is remembered as the Great Reform Act. Prior to this, in 1788, Berwickshire had only 153 voters and Roxburghshire a mere 105.

[2] The leaders of the 1820 agitation were hanged, then decapitated to make sure. Sir Walter Scott was visibly on the wrong side of all this. He visited Jedburgh during the later political unrest of 1831, and made some speeches which went down very badly indeed with the crowd.

[3] Benjamin Disraeli: Speech to the House of Commons, 1 March 1867.

took advantage of it. However, like the similar establishment at Lamberton Toll, Coldstream's wedding industry was latterly eclipsed by that of Gretna.[1]

The English half of the bridge is a Grade II listed building. The other half is Grade A, according to the different scale used for these things in Scotland. Right in the middle, a plaque marks where Robert Burns embarked on his only trip furth of Scotland. We discover that, appropriately enough, if you want to read the plaque properly, you have to kneel on the road:

> ROBERT BURNS crossed this bridge, entering England for the first time, 7th May 1787, and kneeling, prayed for a blessing on his native land in the words:
>
> 'O Scotia! my dear, my native soil!
> For whom my warmest wish to Heaven is sent!
> Long may thy hardy sons of rustic toil
> Be blest with health, and peace, and sweet content!'

The lines come from 'The Cottar's Saturday Night', which continues (as a rebuke to many an establishment-minded Burns Supper speaker):

> O Thou! who pour'd the patriotic tide,
> That stream'd thro great unhappy Wallace' heart,
> Who dar'd to, nobly, stem tyrannic pride,
> Or nobly die, the second glorious part:
> (The patriot's God, peculiarly Thou art,
> His friend, inspirer, guardian, and reward!)
> O never, never Scotia's realm desert;
> But still the patriot, and the patriot-bard
> In bright succession raise, her ornament and guard!

It feels like a very deliberate act for Burns to have recited these words on the Border. This was a time, it should be remembered, when Scotland was officially 'North Britain' and the Border was held by many to have little further meaningful existence.

As Burns was crossing the Border here, some of his most quoted (and most disquieting) lines were in fact almost certainly taking shape in his mind. It seems likely that, only the previous day, he had attended church in Duns, where

[1] Coldstream weddings merit a mention in Smollet's *Expedition of Humphry Clinker*.

he had seen a louse crawling over the fine bonnet of the young lady sitting in front of him:

> Ha! whare ye gaun, ye crowlan ferlie?
> Your impudence protects you sairly:
> I canna say but ye strunt rarely
> Owre gauze and lace;
> Tho' faith! I fear ye dine but sparely
> On sic a place.

> ...O wad some Pow'r the giftie gie us
> To see oursells as ithers see us![1]

***

Coldstream Bridge was reputedly celebrated in the middle of the nineteenth century, when a legal test-case tried to establish whether a man who threw a stone from the bridge at a boy swimming underneath it should be tried under Scots or English law. One of the contentions advanced was that the criminal intention took place in the brain of the perpetrator, and therefore happened in the country from which the stone was thrown. Another argument was that the crime itself actually occurred in the country where the stone landed. I defer to the reader on that point, if the reader is a lawyer.

The bridge is also where a bigger stone, the Stone of Destiny (Scotland's ancient coronation stone), came home in 1996. This was following the Stone's seven-hundred-year detention in Westminster Abbey, where it had been taken to from Scone by Edward I of England. Writing in the fifteenth century, Blind Harry summarises the situation:

> This jowell he gert turss in till Ingland;
> In Lwnd it sett till witnes of this thing;
> Be conquest than of Scotland cald hym king.
> Quhar that stayne is Scottis suld mastir be.[2]

---

[1] Robert Burns: 'To a Louse'. It was also, very possibly, from this same sermon in Duns that Burns was distracted when he passed a note along the pew to another lady: 'Fair maid, you need not take the hint / Nor idle texts pursue / 'Twas guilty sinners that he meant, / Not Angels such as you.' ('Epigram to Miss Ainslie in Church').

[2] Blind Harry: *The Wallace*. 'He made this jewel travel to England. In London he set it to witness of this thing; by conquest of Scotland he called himself king. Where that stone is, the Scots should masters be.' The last words here refer to the prophecies

By 1996, the UK Government was keen to head off growing demands for parliamentary democracy in Scotland, and came up with the idea of sending the Stone home instead, amid much ceremony, to Edinburgh Castle. It duly arrived there via Coldstream, in an open-top Landrover, sitting in perspex-covered splendour as if it were perhaps the head of state of a poor but newly-independent Commonwealth country reviewing a parade of his bodyguards.

When the Stone reached Edinburgh, Malc and I, kilted, stood at each end of a political banner in the Royal Mile, waiting for the Land Rover and pretending not to be affected by the underlying, (and unintended) symbolism of what was of itself a fairly contrived event.[1]

Matters did not quite work out as the UK Government intended, although perhaps cèrtain prophecies[2] about the Stone did. Within three years, a parliament was sitting a matter of yards from the Stone's new home, just as it had been in its previous location further south. I forget whether it was our own banner or someone else's nearby that day which read: 'Thanks for the stone – now can we have the oil revenues?'

There was of course another, unofficial, but more impressive time that the Stone came back to Scotland, for a few heady weeks in 1951. That, however, was a lot further west. I will return to that subject if I get that far on my way.

***

Up to now, it has been conveniently possible to make sweeping statements about the character of whole sections of the Border, but unfortunately I cannot do so today. Today's walk takes in several radically different versions of the Border in the space of a few miles.

Coldstream nestles physically nearer to (and possibly culturally further from) England than any other place of any size on our journey. On leaving

---

mentioned below.

[1] Looking back, it is very difficult not to see parallels between this 1996 event and the 1822 visit of George IV to Edinburgh, the first time a reigning British monarch had bothered to come to Scotland in over a century and a half. Scott and others saw this event as a very necessary way to head off the demands for parliamentary reform which had been expressed in the disturbances of 1820. For the occasion, George IV wore the kilt (which, until not that long previously, had been illegal). He infamously wore pink tights underneath.

[2] *'In fallat fatum Scoti quotumque in locatum invenient lapidem, regnare tenentur ibidem'*, (Wyntoun Chronykyl). This is a prophecy subject to various interpretations, but most usually translated by saying that 'if destiny prove true', the Scots would reign wherever the Stone was found. Perhaps a more accurate prophecy might have been to say that, wherever the Stone was found, at least an attempt to govern Scotland would be made by a parliament sitting in that place.

Coldstream, our route today will take us through the fertile fields of the Tweed's English bank, with views at different stages of both the Cheviots and the wide sweep of the Merse. Finally though, we will cut away from the Tweed completely, climbing through a gentle upland landscape and on towards twin Border villages with a history so exotic that, until recently, the people of nearby Kelso referred to them as 'Little Egypt.'

Looking over into Scotland now is Hume Castle, (built by the ancestors of the Earl of Home whom my grandmother rebuked). The eye is drawn to it, for miles on each side, along the long indistinct skyline over to our west. Its silhouette stands out, black and ragged: not so much like a sore thumb, as a thumbnail hit by a hammer. It perceptibly watches the Merse.[1]

Somewhere buried under the eighteenth-century folly which we see now are the remnants of a medieval fortress. In this, the Humes generally held out against anyone who interfered with their business model. The castle was, however, captured by English forces during the time of the 'Rough Wooing', Henry VIII of England's unsuccessful effort to ensure that his son (later Edward VI) might be married to the infant Mary Queen of Scots.[2]

Hume Castle hints at much more than the political history between Scotland and England though. It introduces for us the subject of the reiving times.

Until now, I have concentrated largely on what the Border has meant for Scotland's national sense of itself. I will offer a view on that more than once again. Already, I have discerned the reader's howls of impatient protest that I might be going to simplify the Border's history down to a series of historic 'fights between the Scots and the English'.[3] Certainly there were plenty of those.

However it was not wars, ultimately, that the 1603 union brought to an end; there was plenty of blood still to be shed in Scotland over political and religious questions in the century-and-a-half that followed. What ended was the *reiving*, if I can use that word as shorthand for a whole social system of organised family hatreds – and still more organised crime – that flourished along this line from the fourteenth to early seventeenth centuries. Primarily,

---

[1] I seem to remember one of my father's aunties saying that she had lived on various Berwickshire farms in her long life, but had never been out of sight of Hume Castle. This remark seemed strangely to reinforce the idea that the castle was watching the landscape, at least as much as the other way around.

[2] Between August 1543 and December 1544, English forces laid waste to much of the Borders, and recorded the destruction of 192 towns, towers, farms, churches and bastle houses, killing some 400 people.

[3] That last phrase is sometimes smugly used to describe everything which the 1707 Union is held to have put a stop to, as if the Union were a teacher intervening in a playground fight, (rather than the larger of the two combatants announcing that he himself was now the teacher).

the reivers' business on both sides of the Border was the theft of cattle and the gathering in of related protection moneys. The latter brings into our language the word 'blackmail'.

The Border reiver's headquarters were his peel tower, a distinctive type of highly-fortified farmhouse. We will pass near a number of these on our way. The Border line itself provided a useful means for people to run between the (locally) fairly weak authoriy of one king and another. As often as not, theft and violence were perpetrated by Scot on Scot, and by Englishman on Englishman. The Border regions were a lawless place, probably like no other in Scotland (and certainly like no other in England). Both governments attempted at least to contain this carnage to the very edges of their respective countries.

A walk along the Border takes us through these tribes' former spheres of bloodthirsty influence. The families arguably get wilder, the further west we go: Humes, Kerrs, Scotts, Elliots, Armstrongs and Grahams, to name only the major ones, in east-to-west order. The last two of these families are found in large numbers on both sides of the Border, and in the reiving era had somewhat negotiable national loyalties. As for the inter-family hatreds, these are probably more easily explained in a diagram[1] (below) than in continuous prose.

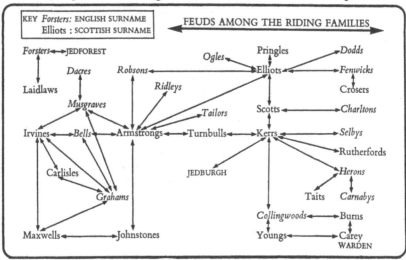

The story of the reivers cautions even me to look at the Border simply as a frontier between two national identities. Although it is certainly that too.

***

Hume Castle stands hollow now. The Homes[2] have long since moved to the

---

[1] Diagram taken from G.M. Fraser: *The Steel Bonnets*. Used here by kind permission of Harper Collins Publishers.

Hirsel, near Coldstream. Long after it was deserted, however, Hume Castle did briefly enjoy an unlikely and infamous revival of one role it had formerly had in the reiving days. Then, families had warned each other of night-raids by their rivals by means of a system of beacons. At the start of the nineteenth century, the castle again hosted such a beacon, this time set up to warn against Napoleonic invasion.

On the night of January 31 1804, the Berwickshire Volunteers who were stationed at Hume Castle unfortunately mistook charcoal burners on Dirrington Great Law for the lighting of the next beacon in the chain to the east, lit their own beacon, and instantly caused what became known as the 'False Alarm'.[1] Within minutes, all the beacons to the west of Hume Castle as far as Cumberland were lit. There was briefly a massive panic across much of southern Scotland, and some three thousand troops were mobilised in the firm belief that the French had landed in Berwick.

A fictionalised version of this incident[2] tells of how people at Hownam Law see a party in full swing at a house in Preston, and take this to be the beacon on Duns Law. Word reaches nearby Duns, causing the Duns volunteers to march *Dad's Army*-style through Longformacus to Haddington where, it is naturally assumed, Napoleon will be keen to head first.

***

We need to be on the English side of the river for a while now, as the Border will soon turn southwards, away from the Tweed.

Following the B6350 road, which is never more than a field away from the river, we see over in Scotland the remnants of Lees House, the former home of the Marjoribanks family. Our road takes us along the English riverbank now through the village of Cornhill. The weather is promising, the going is flat, and we can hear the Border as it runs now along the other side of a hedgerow.

The writer Billy Kay came here during his pioneering TV series on the Scots language, *The Mither Tongue,* in the early 1980s, when he featured a comparison in the vocabulary available to children on each side of the Tweed in Coldstream and Cornhill. Many viewers in Scotland were amazed to find how suddenly much of that vocabulary changed on either side of the Union

[2] 'Home' is how the Earls of Home and some other Berwickshire Humes spell their name. They still pronounce it 'Hume' though, and this illogicality irritated the philosopher David Hume so much that he changed his own name from 'Home' to the more obvious spelling.
[1] Also sometimes called the 'Great Alarm'.
[2] *Wilson's Tales of the Borders,* Vol. XVII.

Bridge. Many were also astounded to learn that Scotland had a literature, a fact which had been assiduously kept from them in school.

One thing that the Border continues to mark is a very definite and sudden linguistic boundary. A number of travel writers, desperately seeking evidence of the Border's non-existence, have been both confused and disappointed to discover all this. Graham Robb, for example, describes moving house to the Border and making the:

> ... arresting discovery that Scottish accents do not fade gradually into English ones, in the way that the regional accents of different parts of England do.[1]

Much of the distinctive vocabulary traditionally available to a Lowland Scot does seem to stop, in the main, fairly exactly at the Border. What we think of as Scots shibboleths, (though, in reality, many of these were once also used in Northumberland) are generally absent from the vocabulary of someone born south of the line.

That may be to overstate things a little, but in terms of accent, whether they are speaking Scots or Scottish Standard English, a Border Scot sounds much more like someone born a hundred miles north of the Border than they do like someone born five miles south of it.

All that said, if the reader is from the Borders, they will be aware of the distinctive spoken form which Scots takes in this part of Scotland. For example, the numbers *ane, twa* and *echt* (to use the spellings most often used in written Scots) are pronounced *yin, twae* and *eyt* respectively, in much of the Borders. The form of *ane* traditionally used before nouns – *ae* – becomes *yae,* and in many places the pronouns *we* and *ye* become *oo* and *ee*.[2]

I am not quite naïve enough to think that any future *Linguistic Atlas of Scotland*[3] will again be able to set out the subtelties of dialect differences between the Roxburghshire villages of Eckford, Denholm and Oxnam. However, I trust the reader will not think me overly carmudgeonly if I express a hope that people in Scotland will continue to be able to distinguish between the words *loch* and *lock,*[4] or between *whales* and *Wales*.[5] I certainly hope Scots

---

[1] Graham Robb: *The Debatable Land.* Rory Stewart in *The Marches* likewise observes how 'One forty year old [in England] described his complete bafflement at recently seeing his first Burns night supper, although he lived only ten miles from the border'.
[2] Pronouns in the town of Hawick are a whole other story, and several miles outwith my scope.
[3] J.Y. Mather and H.H. Speitel (eds): *The Linguistic Atlas of Scotland* (Croom Helm Ltd, Beckenham, 1986)
[4] I have met some younger Scots who cannot.

will not come to utter such a culturally valuable word as *dour* as if it rhymed with *cower,* or say Oor Wullie's name as if it had two 'i's in it (so depriving it of a 'dark' 'l' sound). If even the tendency of some self-proclaimedly 'aspirational' Scots to say the word 'go' as if it had a diphthong in it can be arrested, I will be a happy man. Scotland will have done its wee bit to stop the world's linguistic Amazon burning.[1]

I bumped into the present Duke of Buccleuch a couple of years back. Trying to keep the conversation on safe ground, we had a pleasant enough talk about Sir Walter Scott. This led to the revealing insight that most of the Duke's friends read Scott in French, as they find that easier than following the Scots in which many of Scott's characters speak. I am not sure what that says about the social chasm between the Duke and his still largely Scots-speaking tenants. To be fair, it also says something about the paucity of opportunities more generally in Scotland for people to read Scots and become aware that it might have any value.

Although much of Scott's dialogue may be in Scots, his narrative is of course in English. Taken together with the Reformers' decision to circulate English rather than Scots translations of the Bible, this has contributed to the lack of a widely-developed or standardised prose literature in Scots.

It is as well from time to time, therefore, to reverse Scott's own polarities, and to write in Scots prose, with quotations in English if required. I have been prevailed on not to write the whole book like this. Reading Scots may well be an uncomfortable experience for the reader. If so, then, like so many uncomfortable experiences, it is doubtless good for them.[2]

---

[5] This is a distinction which made President Trump's tweet about meeting the 'Prince of Whales' even funnier in Scotland than it was in the rest of the world.

[1] Half of the world's 7,000 or so languages (including Scottish Gaelic) are now considered endangered. My complaints here are not about language change – all languages change – but about the undue pressures in the last couple of hundred years on people in Scotland to change in one direction, and one direction only.

[2] It wad be fair tae say at no near sae monie fowk reads Scott as uised tae a hunner year syne. But it's likely a hantle mair nor read him *forty* year syne, whan the last o Scott's faimly at Abbotsford wes black affrontit mair nor aince bi tourists speirin at them *'Where can we see the Antarctic stuff?'* (an thaim thinkin on the Polar explorer Robert Scott). There is things aboot Scott, richt aneuch, at hinners modren readers. The ten pages in *Waverley* at Scott gies ower tae the settin o ae table for denner is sic an example. Scott disna haud wi the proverb at 'guid gear comes i smaw bouk.' Nor is his wark 'aw ae oo', as can be seen frae the hinneren o his life, whan he wes screivin nicht an day tae keep up wi the mortgage on his muckle new hoose at Abbotsford. There is romantic nories i Scott, forby, at no awbodie can haud wi. Mark Twain gaed the lenth o pittin the wyte o the American Ceivil War on Scott, because Scott's beuks hed smittit the American Sooth wi the *'disease'* o chivalry. It is true at the suthren states hed an unco likin for Scott, but Twain threipin at Scott *'did more real and lasting harm perhaps than any individual who ever wrote'* disna soon lik an awthegither fair assessment. It isna.

***

We head on through Cornhill to a field marked on old maps as 'Scotch Haugh'.[1] It is so-called because, very strangely, this one little field on the English riverbank is actually in Scotland. It is not at all clear why this single speck of arable land has always been a tiny foothold of Scotland.[2] Along the whole stretch of the Tweed that forms the Border, there is no other Scottish soil anywhere on the southern bank. It perhaps forms its own little opposite (though not equal) reaction to the Berwick question further downstream on the other bank.

Another name for this place, 'Dry Tweed', initially seems to suggest that the river has changed course here, but J.L. Mack and other writers specifically reject this idea. The field is sometimes also known as the Baa Green, probably simply because, when not planted with crops, it made a good playing-field. This has grown into a tale locally that the nationality of the field was at one time decided annually by a game of handba' between the peoples of Coldstream and Cornhill. Eventually, this story goes, after a string of Coldstream victories the Cornhill folk gave up, and (working on the same principle as the Jules Rimet Cup) the Baa Green was handed over to Coldstream permanantly.[3] Whatever the real reason for it being Scottish, Scotch Haugh is a magnificent little Border oddity. An effort by Northumberland County Council to annex it into England towards the end of the nineteenth century was happily unsuccessful.

We continue along the road to Wark, where a motte and bailey poke out from behind someone's back garden. These are the remnants of Wark Castle, which was attacked by David I of Scotland in 1133. Blind Harry later imagines Edward Longshanks pausing here to consider what local helpers he might find for the task of sacking Berwick:

> King Eduuard than it tuk in gret grevuance.
> His ost he rasd and come to Werk on Twede;
> Bot for to fecht as than he had gret drede.[4]

---

[1] As with all haughs, the 'gh' is pronounced as the 'ch' in 'loch'.
[2] Scotch Haugh is marked out as Scottish at least as far back as a map of 1771 by Andrew Armstrong.
[3] The story of the annual handba' game, if true, means Scotch Haugh once alternated nationality in (almost) the same way as a tiny, uninhabited island does today in the Bodasoa river on the border between France and Spain. The nationality of this island has been exchanged between the two countries every six months since a seventeenth-century treaty.
[4] Blind Harry: *The Wallace. Ost:*host

Legend also has it that the Order of the Garter was founded here in the middle of the fourteenth century, when, during a ball at the castle, a garter worn by the Countess of Salisbury slipped down her leg, and Edward III thought it would be funny to wear it himself. There is an admittedly high chance that all this is nonsense. Another, less glamorous, story that Wark Castle was once recaptured by English forces crawling up a sewer from the Tweed into the castle kitchen, has more of the grim ring of medieval truth about it.

***

The hills blaze now in spring sunshine. I realise that, peelly wally as we are after a long Scottish winter, we will now be getting a tan. I had promised Malc that the Black Bull pub here would be a place to stop for some lunchtime refreshment. Google did not lie to me on this point; there is indeed a Black Bull in Wark, but unfortunately it is another Northumbrian village of the same name near Hexham.[1] Malc sighs. I don't know this side of the Border very well.

We keep going for the next village, which is Carham. Once home to a priory of Black Friars, burned by Wallace, and now home to a phone box, Carham was where Malcolm II won his victory exactly a thousand years ago.[2] The battle was forewarned by a comet which appeared for thirty successive nights.[3] This seems only appropriate; Carham played a crucial role in determining where the Border eventually ended up.[4]

The likely battle-site is today a prime field of prime cattle. We would not know that a victorious Scottish army had once marched this way, but for the noticeably regular presence of old irn–bru bottles in the ditches beside us. Indeed there is nothing to announce the battlefield at all, unless you look very hard. A paper notice pinned to a fence-post gives warning that an open-air bar licence has been applied for in time for a planned re-enactment to celebrate the anniversary here in July 2018. It's good to see that someone else has remembered.[5]

---

[1] Incidentally, Nigel Tranter, in *The Illustrated Portrait of the Border Country*, (and indeed in his fictional trilogy *The Bruce*) comments on the periodic claims made by Scotland on parts of North Tynedale around the village of Hexham between 1159 and 1295. These are probably not claims that many people in Hexham would find very compelling today.

[2] We walked past Carham in April 2018. A minority view among historians is that the date of the battle was really some two years earlier than 1018.

[3] It seems that there was indeed a comet, reported on around Europe, in July 1018.

[4] See Chapter 4.

[5] A commemoration at Carham in July 2018 included, according to its programme, a 'skirmish', a 'last man standing one-on-one fighting competition' and a 'musical interlude'.

If we had walked a couple of hundred yards further on down the road here, we would in fact have seen a small plaque at the gate of Carham's St Cuthbert's Church, which gives a good summary of the battle's importance:

> The result of the battle irretrievably split the ancient Patrimony of St Cuthbert ... The Kingdom of Northumbria, which had once stretched from the Humber to the Forth, was finally broken. The process of creating a border between the newly emergent kingdoms of Scotland and England had begun.

The English border-surveyors of 1222 stopped in Carham to negotiate. First, six knights from each country were chosen, then twelve each, before any exact line could be agreed on around here. The English knights wrote home to describe wearily the Scots' tendency to moan and quibble about the established (i.e. English) order of things. Later, when further committees of knights were given the task of mapping out the detail of the Border in 1245 and 1246, they again hit up against numerous heated challenges and disputes when they got to Carham, to the extent, it seems, that they gave up.

Alistair Moffat makes a persuasive argument that the consequences of this episode can still be seen in the strange wanderings of the Border line here, which alternates between natural features of the landscape and a series of very brief, officious-looking straight lines across farmland. An alternative explanation for some of these zig-zags might be that much later disputes about access to common land eventually led the Ordnance Survey, Solomon-like, to lay its official ruler over the middle of the fields in question.[1]

Certainly, disputes over these fields seem to have been fairly continuous. Bowes' surveys of 1542 and 1550 record that the English tenants of Wark and Carham were increasingly infuriated at the Scots about this issue. Bowes says that there was a mutual acceptance of both nations pasturing the land but complains that the Scots were now sowing it too for their own use. Later still, according to Rev Robert Turnbull,[2] minister of Sprouston, Wark Common was the scene of at least one violent dispute in the 1730s over whether 'Scotch farmers' had the right to graze animals there. Turnbull reports that clubs were used and heads were broken.

It is, by a Scot's standards, now a warm day, and we pause for a rest. The Border cuts south here at the mouth of the Redden Burn,[3] one of several places

---

[1] In fact, Bowes' Survey records that inconclusive attempts were made at formal international negotiations between Scottish and English commissioners over various small parcels of land here around Haddon Rig in the mid sixteenth century.

[2] *Statistical Account of Scotland.*

appointed for days of truce in the times of the Wardens of the Marches. Its name comes indeed from 'riding-burn', (referring to the practice of riding a march). Here, at last, the Border leaves the Tweed.

One of the most appealing uses made in literature of the section of the Border line we have just walked is provided by James Hogg. In this, he imagines an ingenious medieval technology being devised by the commander of one English-held castle (Berwick) for feeding the English garrison then holding another (Roxburgh). Hogg visualises a system of underwater pullies being operated along the Border, dragging provisions up this stretch of the Tweed and then over the line here at Carham towards Roxburgh. He describes how a fisherman on the Tweed one night thinks he has encountered something truly supernatural:

> He struck at it with his barbed spear… and in a moment he had it in his boat. It was an excellent sirloin of beef. The man was in utter amazement, for it was dead, and lay without moving, like other butcher meat; yet he was sure he saw it running up the water at full speed.[1]

I had proposed following the Border pedantically south now over the hillside from here, in search of an old hawthorn border marker-hedge which I had heard might still exist. Malc prefers, however, to stick to the road that cuts just inside England for a mile or two through Wark Common. After the hotel room door incident and the phantom pub in Wark, I decide against pressing home my argument on this, and so we take Malc's preferred route.

***

For anyone interested in lines on maps – and surely all are – Carham is an interesting place. It marks not only the border between Scotland's ancient East and Middle Marches, but is also where the old counties of Berwickshire and Roxburghshire meet each other at the English Border.[2] Strangely enough, we are crossing from a county whose eponymous city was long-ago annexed by England, into a county named after a city which was deserted equally long-ago.

The town of Roxburgh (six miles west of Carham, up the Tweed near

---

[3] Actually, to use the names found on modern maps, the Redden Burn runs very briefly into Hadden Stank, and then equally briefly into the Carham Burn, before meeting the Tweed.

[1] James Hogg: *The Three Perils of Man: War, Women and Witchcraft.*

[2] Both these former counties are now part of the Scottish Borders local authority area.

Kelso) was one of Scotland's most important half-dozen cities in the middle ages, and was often struggled over by both countries. Perhaps Roxburgh's most surprising appearances in Scotland's literature are in French – in the *Roman de Fergus* by Guaillaume le Clerc. This was probably composed by William Malveisin, a Frenchman who latterly became Bishop of Glasgow.[1]

It is a curious thought that Norman ladies sat by castle firesides across medieval Europe and listened to this account of a hapless young knight called Fergus of Galloway. Because of its language, *Fergus* has never really been accepted into the canon of Scottish literature, yet he deserves to be. We see Fergus rampaging his way from technicolour battle scene to battle scene, chasing a white stag through some places along the Border that are very recognisable from our walk, from Liddel Castle to Jedburgh, to here at Roxburgh:

> *Par un jor est montes as estres*
> *Et mist son cief par les fenestres;*
> *Vois les terres et les lairis*
> *Et tot environ le pais*
> *Et la terre de Lodien.*
> *Et Roceborc vois tot de plain*
> *La u s'amie asisse estoit.*

(One day, he climbed to the upper floor, and put his head out of the windows. He can see the tilled and the uncultivated land and, all around, the country and territory of Lothian. And quite clearly he sees Roxburgh, where his beloved is besieged.)[2]

Fergus is not quite as unsubtle a parody of the Arthurian romance as Austin Powers is of James Bond, but his listeners would have been equally conscious of the joke.

The poem was written around the year 1200, just when the Border as we now know it was solidifying. It looks back though into an unspecified period, perhaps a couple of hundred years earlier, when the emerging Scotland was a land of component and largely independent parts. Lothian, Galloway, Alba, Strathclyde, and the Kingdom of the Isles[3] all get a mention in *Fergus*.

In the Roxburgh of history, rather than fiction, James II of Scotland made the mistake of standing beside a cannon which exploded while he was besieging

---

[1] This is the contention of D.D.R. Owen in *Fergus of Galloway*.
[2] Text and translation from D.D.R. Owen, *op cit.* Original French taken from *Fergus: Roman von Guillaume le Clerc*, Ernst Martin (ed).
[3] See Chapter 4 for more on these places.

the town in 1460, causing his widow to hurry their young son to nearby Kelso Abbey, where he was crowned James III.

Around this time, probably following a downturn in the wool trade, Roxburgh went into a decline and nothing is now visible on the site but a few stumps of the city's walls, poking out of their defensive hillock. Roxburgh, or the little that remains of it, looks bemusedly today over the Tweed towards the three hundred or so windows of Scotland's largest inhabited house, the palatial Floors Castle. Ruined Roxburgh seems out of place and time here now, as if Fergus of Galloway had, for reasons unknown, woken up with a hangover in Versailles.

***

Industrial reiving accounts, at least in part, for how the Ker[1] family (now the Dukes of Roxburghe) came eventually to build Floors.

In an earlier time, most peel towers here had spiral staircases that went clockwise when looking upwards, to allow those running downstairs to have their right hand free to hold a sword. The Kerrs, according to well-known legend, built their stairs the other way round as, like the Benjaminites of the Old Testament, they were all said to be left-handed:

> But the Kerrs were aye the deadliest foes
> That e'er to Englishmen were known.
> For they were all bred left-handed men
> And fence against them there was none.[2]

The story brings to mind the traditional tale that reivers kept their sons' right hands covered when they were being baptised:

> And at the sacred fount, the priest
> Through ages left the master hand unblest,
> To urge with keener aim, the blood-encrusted spear.[3]

Whatever the hand might do in the future with any sharp instrument, it was not to be held accountable to any Christian standards. Presumably, on

---

[1] This particular branch of the family spell their name with only one 'r'.
[2] James Hogg: 'The Raid of the Kerrs', first published in *Blackwoods Magazine*, Edinburgh, November 1830.
[3] John Leyden: 'Ode on visiting Flodden', from *Poetic Remains of the late Dr John Leyden*.

this basis, the Kerrs covered their babies' left hands.[1]

***

We walk over Wark Common. Near here is Threep Cairn, a name which no doubt reflects the disputed nature of this piece of land.[2] On the other bank of the Tweed from us now sits the Scottish hamlet of Birgham.[3] The name means 'bridge village', but there has been no bridge over the Border here for centuries, so today we can only look over at Birgham from England.

In 1188, Henry II of England allegedly sent the Bishop of Durham here to levy taxes in this part of Scotland, with a view to funding his latest crusade. Scotland's king, William the Lion, came to meet him in Birgham. No taxes were forthcoming.

Birgham is yet another tiny settlement on the Border that gives its name improbably to an international treaty, this time in the midst of events that led ultimately to Scotland's Wars of Independence. In 1290, the Treaty of Birgham was authorised at a meeting of the Scottish Parliament which was held in the village. This agreed that Scotland's young queen, Margaret the 'Maid of Norway', would be married to Edward, the heir of Edward I of England. Margaret was six years old and Edward was five. There were weak assurances in the Treaty about this match not compromising Scottish independence, but these never came to be tested, as Margaret died on her way from Norway shortly after the treaty was signed.

These events have, according to folklore, lent Birgham's name to an unkind turn of phrase, best explained by this nineteenth-century writer:

> Everyone has heard the phrase 'Go to Birgham', which signifies much the same as bidding you to go to a worse place. The phrase is familiar not only on the Borders, but throughout all Scotland, and has been in use for more than five hundred years, having taken its rise from Birgham being the place where the Scottish nobility were when they dastardly betrayed their country into the hands of the first Edward; and the people, despising the conduct and the

---

[1] It is often suggested that the Scots word *corrie-fistit* or *kerr-fistit*, meaning 'left-handed' (probably from *ceàrr*, the Gaelic word for 'left' or 'wrong') accounts for the family surname, though there is little evidence for this.

[2] J.L. Mack cites the use of the name Threep Cairn here from *A Companion to Capt. Armstrong's Map of Northumberland*, 1769. *Threap* is a Scots word meaning to dispute or generally go on about something.

[3] Pronounced '**Birj**-am'.

cowardice of the nobles have rendered the saying 'Go to Birgham' an expression of contempt to this day.[1]

There is something about 'Go to Birgham' that for some reason reminds me of the Fifer's curse 'Awa tae Freuchie an fry mice'. I treasure the phrase away mentally, as I walk past. The Treaty of Birgham did come to prominence again briefly recently when, for a while, the pub in Birgham took the name 'The Treaty'. Since becoming Scotland's first community-owned pub, it has happily reverted to its old name of the Fisherman's Arms.

***

On Wark Common, we eat our pieces near the bridge over the old Kelso-to-Coldstream railway which once ran here just south of the English bank of the Tweed. A short section of the old line, lying just to our west, follows the Border itself. J.L. Mack notes that, a century ago, trains could be seen cutting in and out of a line of hawthorns near here which had been planted as border-markers long before the railway.

A friend has told me that, somewhere around here, there still stands a rusting sign on the old railway, announcing the Border to passengers. This does seem to be a more than sentimental staking of claims by the Victorian rail network. In 1849, the North British (that is to say, Scottish) Railway Company was incensed that the (English) North Eastern Railway was so bold as to build one solitary railway station of its own in Scotland. This was at the hamlet of Sprouston, four miles west of us here, over the Border. It is said the North British viewed this as a hostile act for many years thereafter, and the incursion was not repeated.

Malc and I debate what might represent a fair division of the sandwiches, and I explain to him the origin of the phrase 'Nottman's bit'. I say that as if there is some reason why he or the reader should have heard of it. In fact nobody who is less related to me than my cousins uses the phrase, but I give him the derivation anyway, as if it were in a dictionary.

When my grandmother was very young, a local minister called Mr Nottman visited the house, I think at Swinton, not far from here. Her mother, putting a cake on the table, cut a single, normal-sized slice, and jokingly offered Mr Nottman 'onie bit o't ye like.' Mr Nottman, taking my great-grandmother at her word, took (and ate) the other slice, which encompassed something like 300 degrees of the whole. This made a lasting impression on the family. This 'majority share' of a cake, not previously having had a name,

[1] *Wilson's Tales of the Borders*, Vol. VIII.

is therefore Nottman's bit. I reflect that poor Mr Nottman, as the result of one moment of madness around 1910, is now remembered, probably, for nothing else he ever said or did. It is a sobering idea, but a very useful phrase. I commend it to the reader.

The sun is at its height. Peewits cry. Rising peewits once famously betrayed the presence of reivers and, later, of their covenanting descendents along the Border, causing both to get up and break for cover. But, for ourselves, it takes a bit of an effort to get going today after a rest. Malc has gathered some static inertia, and it is admittedly comfortable lying in the sun. Bees drone.

Malc tries to get me to tell the story of Nottman's bit again from first principles, without showing strong signs that he was listening first time around. This represents a clear sign that he does not want to move. We move in the end.

***

A couple of miles to the west from here, just into Scotland, is the site of the Battle of Haddon Rig. Originally the venue for march meetings, it eventually became a battlefield, where Scottish forces were victorious in 1542, during a series of reprisals and counter-reprisals along the Border. A factor in Scotland's victory was possibly the fact that the English participants were mainly from Redesdale, and therefore primarily interested in establishing the whereabouts of local cattle. It was a victory that was quickly overshadowed by Scotland's disaster at Solway Moss (which I will mention again, if we eventually get that far west).

The road is, again, very briefly the Border itself now. We walk down the white line – just for the strange international sensation of it – before the Border falls into the ditch on our right. The road comes to Pressen Hill, a farm steading which is just – and only just – inside England. Pressen Hill may actually be the nearest there exists anywhere to a house that straddles the Border.[1] Eric Robson reports that the farmhouse here is in England, but that its garden has been extended over the Border, so that the farmer's greenhouse is now in Scotland.[2] Near the farm is a little copse that J.L. Mack and other authors say has been disputed into modern times. They cite stories of fox-hunters and others who have long given it the name 'No Man's Land'. The Ordnance Survey does not express any such hesitation about where the Border lies here, but it is a nice story, and obviously founded on real, if miniscule, boundary questions of the past.[3]

---

[1] See Day 5 for the story of just such a fictional house.
[2] Eric Robson: *The Border Line*.
[3] Certainly, Bowes' survey of 1542 records numerous disputes about which country

It was near the neighbouring farm of Pressen, a mile to our east and inside England, that Sir Alexander Ramsay of Dalhousie surprised English supply chains, and so assisted the redoubtable Black Agnes (whom we met a day or two ago) in her defence of Dunbar Castle.

We come to the farm of Hoselaw Mains, a couple of fields inside Scotland. A mile or two further into Scotland, another farm appears on the map as Hoselaw, but is often known as Hoselaw Bank. In the ferm raw here is the second house that my mother lived in as a child. I had not quite realised, until now, that her home was only five or six houses from the Border.

We follow the Border along a jagged line of trees just on our left. In 1385, Richard II of England camped near here with his army. Immediately over the Border from Hoselaw Mains, there is indeed a hill called Camp Hill, if that has any bearing on the matter. It was somewhere here, of all places, that Richard chose to create his uncles Dukes of Cambridge and Buckingham. He was on his way to burn Melrose and Jedburgh Abbeys.

The fig-leaf for this last action was probably the fact that Scotland and England, at this point, acknowledged two different Popes. Scotland (like France) supported the Pope in Avignon, Clement VII, while England (like most other places) recognised Urban VI in Rome. Many Scots are aware of the thrawn story of Scotland's willingness to split theological hairs with her neighbour (and, ideally, with herself) over the 'ideal' form of Protestantism. It comes as little surprise to hear of seventeenth-century violence waged over such vexed questions as whether Protestants should sit or kneel to pray, or of later factionalism around the scarcely perceptable differences between such groups as the 'lifters' and the 'anti-lifters'.[1] To learn, however, that even *before* the Reformation Scots would not agree with England on even such a basic point as the identity of the Pope, suggests a stubbornness borne out of something more viscerally innate than organised religion.

But Richard II would probably have burned the Border abbeys, in any event.

***

We decide there is no obvious path now, so we might as well just head into the trees at Hoselaw Mains and follow the Border itself over Wideopen. The

---

had the right to plough and sow certain fields around Pressen. Bowes destroyed the fields in question (having taken the view that they had been illegally occupied by Scots).

[1] This last was a doctrinal difference based on whether or not it was felt right for a minister to lift up the communion cup in front of the congregation when it was blessed. This is a debate worthy of the war between the Big-enders and Little-enders in Jonathan Swift's *Gulliver's Travels* (these being two groups who argued about which end boiled eggs should be eaten from).

map says 'Wideopen Moor', but for people here, the place name Wideopen is a noun, not an adjective.

As an aside, assuming we are dealing with the same place here, Wideopen seems to have a connection to one of the more sarcastic recorded remarks from the reiving times. A certain Jock Dalgliesh of Wideopen had his bloodthirsty behaviour justified (if we can take the writer entirely seriously) in a letter from the Deputy Governor of Berwick, John Carey in 1596:

> It was not so barbarouslie nor butcherlie don as you thinck it to be. It should seeme your honor hath bene wrongfullie enformed in sayinge he was cutt in many peeces… for if he had bene cutt in *many* peces he could not a lived til the next morning, which themselves reported he did – which shewes he was not cutt in *verie* many peces.[1]

A new lamb follows me for a while up the hill, bores of the task, and turns back. We are on a different kind of Border now, a whole world away from the Tweed. The Border is a fence, and then a fence beside a burn, and then a dyke. We keep to the Scottish side here and climb alongside a line of old trees that eventually marks the boundary. Near the top of Castle Law here, the border dyke carries a plaque marking where the Kelsae Laddie (the principal of the annual Kelso civic week) rides out to each year with his followers. The plaque quotes a song perhaps more associated with the Border than any other:

> March, march, Ettrick and Teviotdale,
> Why the deil dinna ye march forward in order?
> March, march, Eskdale and Liddesdale,
> All the Blue Bonnets are bound for the Border.
> Many a banner spread
> Flutters above your head,
> Many a crest that is famous in story.
>
> …Trumpets are sounding,
> War-steeds are bounding,
> Stand to your arms then, and march in good order;
> England shall many a day
> Tell of the bloody fray,

---

[1] Letter from John Carey to Lord Burleigh.

When the Blue Bonnets came over the Border.[1]

The lines, needless to say, are by Sir Walter Scott, and give a fiery summary of his own romantic view of the reivers. The song is now also associated with the King's Own Scottish Borderers Battalion.

We had promised ourselves to stop for a drink of water when we got to the brow of the hill, but the view makes us forget. At once, the Bowmont Valley opens out in front of us, in sunlit splendour. A deer runs close in front of us and leaps into Scotland. The Bowmont lies quiet before us, its whins burning yellow up into the hills. In the distance, the kirk of Kirk Yetholm can be heard chapping five.

Town Yetholm and Kirk Yetholm[2] are twin villages on either side of the Bowmont, and both are very much – if only narrowly – inside Scotland. From Castle Hill today, the two Yetholms seem to lie in a red bed, squeezed together into some warm fireside alcove between Staerough and Yetholm Law. If so, they appear to be coorying in from the draughts, but making a point of not lying too close to each other.

We follow the Border dyke down the brae and onto the Town Yetholm road at Venchen. Here a 'Welcome to Scotland' sign awaits, as does another sign further down the road, welcoming us to Town Yetholm. I can't quite see from here, but I wonder if that sign continues '... twinned with Kirk Yetholm'.

We cross the road and the bridge over the Bowmont Water, and make for the farm at Yetholm Mains. The farm sits right up against the Border, which here takes the form of the Shotton Burn, trickling into the Bowmont.[3] My grandfather was born in the ferm raw of workers' houses here. Later, my mother was born there too. That house has long since been pulled down and replaced by a row of modern houses,[4] though the original pig sty remains.

If my mother's second house at Hoselaw looked to me, earlier today, like it was very near the Border, then the sight of her first home here dispels that idea from my mind. When compared with Yetholm Mains, Hoselaw looks now to have as much claim to being in the Borders as Midlothian does. In fact, here is now literally the first house in Scotland (or the last, depending how you look at it). I had forgotten that the back garden of the house actually comes right up to the Border itself at the Shotton Burn. The house is a few paces into

---

[1] 'Blue Bonnets over the Border'. The song probably has older, possibly Jacobite, origins but it appears in Sir Walter Scott's 'The Monastery'.
[2] Pronounced 'Yett-um'.
[3] Actually, the Ordnance Survey seems to have settled the Border here on a straight nineteenth-century line of trees a few yards onto the 'English' side of the Shotton Burn.
[4] By a strange coincidence, in more recent times, Malc points out to me that his own grandfather lived in exactly the same little row of houses beside the Border here.

Scotland, just beyond where the surface of the road officially changes colour. It is empty. The last tenant has decorated their wheelie-bin with saltire stickers.

I wonder whether the Australian poet Les Murray was thinking of here at Yetholm Mains, when he recalled his ancestors:

> Isabella Scott, born eighteen-oh-two,
>
> grows gaunt in a cottage on Cheviot side,
>
> the first and last house in Scotland, its view
>
> like a vast Scottish flag, worn linen and blue.[1]

Just twenty minutes' walk over the Border from here is the farm of Shotton,[2] where I remember visiting relatives as a very young child. I recall coming away from these visits having mentally stamped this pleasant – and I felt very creditably cosmopolitan – experience onto my passport.

***

After a couple of miles, we come into Kirk Yetholm, where an old lady cutting her hedge smiles and congratulates us. We realise as we pass that she almost certainly thinks we have walked along the whole Pennine Way, all the way from Edale, which is somewhere near Manchester, and some ridiculous 286 miles to the south. We accept her congratulations, entirely fraudulently.

For the moment, the expedition for Malc and me is at an end, though I nurse hopes of getting him to do another stretch of the walk at some later stage. We have covered the whole East March of Scotland, and made a very small start on the more challenging – but much more easily defensible – Middle March.

We arrive at Kirk Yetholm's village green, with its monument to the Romany[3] community, and see at last the thatched Border Hotel. My mother comes to visit us, to check that we are OK. This is very welcome, even if writing it down makes our adventure sound less adventurous than it really was.

---

[1] Les Murray: 'My ancestress and the secret ballot, 1848 and 1851'.

[2] When the English official Bowes made his survey in 1542, he took the opportunity officially to lay waste a six-acre field of corn between Shotton and the English village of Mindrum, as it had been unauthorisedly planted by Scots.

[3] I realise that the issue of what name to use for the Roma or Romany people is a sensitive one. I will generally say 'Romany', though will also include some (mainly historic) uses of the word 'Gypsy'. In any event, I will always capitalise this latter name, which has often unfairly – and perhaps almost uniquely among names for any ethnic group – not been given such a distinction in the past.

CHAPTER 6
The Middle March
Day 4: From Yetholm to Cocklawfoot
(Circa 12 miles)

The Romany monarchy of Kirk Yetholm; Yetholm Kirk; The Pennine Way; A curse on the reivers – and on all our rival towns; The Cheviots; Hen Hole and the legend of Black Adam; The ballads and Scott's 'Minstrelsy'; Cocklawfoot.

We have been in the Middle March since Carham, though not as yet in the Middle March *stern and wild.* Hour by hour though, the walk increasingly takes us whole landscapes away from the fertile haughs of the Merse. Internally, I begin to rifle more through my mother's family's anecdotes now than my father's.

Our starting point today is Kirk Yetholm, an interesting wee place by any standards. This is not just because of its situation at the meeting point of two kingdoms, but also – not a little mysteriously – because of its former status as the seat of a recognised monarchy all of its own.

Yetholm's own colourful Romany royals descended, probably, from the 'John Faw, Lord and Earl of Little Egypt' whom James V of Scotland acknowledged in 1540. This is most likely the same Johnnie Faa whose alleged wife-stealing tendencies are recorded in the ballad 'The Gypsy Laddie':

> I'll mak a hap to my Johnny Faa,
> And I'll mak a hap to my deary;
> And he's get a' the coat gaes round,
> And my lord shall nae mair come near me.
> And when our lord came hame at een,
> And speir'd for his fair lady,
> The tane she cry'd, and the other reply'd,
> 'She's away with the gypsie laddie.'[1]

As we have seen, there are two Yetholms, each lying thatched round its own green.[2] Of the two villages, it is Kirk Yetholm that has the strong

---

[1] *Child Ballads,* 200.

[2] That sentence perhaps leaves an unduly quaint impression. Nice as the two Yetholms certainly are, it is worth remembering that, until relatively recently, visitors commented on Yetholm's thatched houses (among the very last in Lowland Scotland) as evidence of the area's then lack of economic development, rather than of its

connection with Scotland's Romany heritage. Writing two centuries ago, John Leyden describes the village's Romany (in terms that make me wince more than a little):

> On Yeta's banks[1] the vagrant gypsies place
> Their turf-built cots; a sun-burn'd swarthy race!
> From Nubian realms their tawny line they bring.
> And their brown chieftain vaunts the name of King.[2]

Leyden calls the Romany people 'Nubians'; the word 'Gypsy' is itself of course a contraction of 'Egyptian'. This is what they were generally misunderstood to be, when they first came to Scotland (ultimately from somewhere in northern India), most likely towards the end of the fifteenth century. The Romany had mixed fortunes in Scotland. While James IV, James V and Mary all took a broadly tolerant view, James VI nursed near-genocidal sentiments towards them. Despite this, the Yetholm Gypsies regularly claimed that they were nothing less than the fulfilment of the words in Ezekiel:

> I will scatter the Egyptians among the nations and will disperse them throughout the countries.[3]

The Romany royals went a step further and said that their dynastic surname Faa was a corruption of 'Pharaoh'.[4]

The Romany people were said to have been granted houses in Kirk Yetholm after the Second Siege of Namur (a battle in what is today Belgium) in 1695, when the Laird of Yetholm, Captain David Bennet, had his life saved by a Gypsy. Whether this is the case or not, the Romany were very probably in Kirk Yetholm before this date, and the presence of the Border (convenient for a people who were not always welcomed by the authorities in one country or the other) was likely a factor in their choice.

In 1835, a well-known assessment of the Yetholm Gypsies was made by Yetholm's minister, John Baird:

---

potential for second homes.
[1] Leyden has, for his own poetic reasons, decided here to re-christen the Bowmont Water the 'Yeta'.
[2] John Leyden.
[3] *Ezekiel:* Ch. 30 v. 26 (Revised Standard Version)
[4] Fall (often pronounced Faa) is in fact a widespread name in and around East Lothian, with no obvious Egyptian connection. Romanies often adopted local surnames in the areas they settled.

They are much less distinguishable as a peculiar race now …Still their language, their predatory and erratic propensities and in general their dark or dusky complexion, black piercing eyes and Hindoo features sufficiently betray the original of this despised and neglected race. …the language spoken by the Yetholm Gypsies corresponds very nearly with that spoken by the English and Turkish Gypsies, and most of these have also been traced to an Indian origin. On this subject however, they observe a profound secrecy …At home they are normally peaceable. Their quarrels, which do not often take place, and are only among themselves, are very violent while they continue, and the subject or ground of quarrel is seldom known but to themselves. On these occasions they are much addicted to profane swearing.[1]

Like Leyden's comments, Baird's make uncomfortable reading for any modern audience. To be fair, Baird does go on to speak fairly kindly of the Yetholm Romany, praising their interest in education. He mentions the increasing tendency of parents who are out on the road to leave their children in the village so that they can attend school. This was a development which ensured that the Romany people of Kirk Yetholm long ago ceased to be a recognisable group. However, they have left their mark on Scotland's folklore, as well as on local vocabulary. I think I can (just about) recall my grandfather once reciting the following shibboleth to make the latter point:

A gadgie when he is a chor,
A jugal always fears.
For jugals as a rule are kept
By gadgies with big keirs.

Which is to say, 'A man, when he is a thief, always fears a dog, because dogs are kept, as a rule, by men in big houses.'[2]

**

The Pennine Way starts off at the little street that one guide book calls

---

[1] *New Statistical Account of Scotland*, 1845.
[2] In *The New Minstrelsy of the Scottish Border*, Walter Elliot traces this local rhyme at least as far as a poem published by Thomas Grey in the *Berwick Advertiser* in 1910.

'Gypsy Row', another (more judgementally) calls 'Tinkers' Row', and Yetholm folk themselves call Muggers' Raw.[1] Here, a wee two-room house (self-catering holiday accommodation now) announces itself as 'Gypsy Palace'. 'The Pailace', as it was always known, was where my great-grandfather lived for a while, and its impressive name is owed to the people who lived in the house immediately before him.

Here was where Charles II Faa Blythe, the last king of the Yetholm Gypsies, died in 1902.[2] The royal line expired with him, as Charles's brother, Prince Robert, was held to be of doubtful character. He was allegedly caught trying to pass off wild rhubarb as the garden variety, and his royal reputation was further undermined when he was then accused of selling spectacles to old ladies – glasses which turned out to have no glass in them at all.

The Romany monarchy is a strange part of the Border's history, and the Yetholm kings enjoyed a real power and standing among the Romany of the south-east of Scotland. It is perhaps easiest to explain going backwards. King Charles II was a hawker, crowned before a great crowd in 1898, fifteen years after the death of his mother Queen Esther, who lived in an older palace on the other side of the road.

Queen Esther famously won the Romany crown after a spirited fight with her sister, Princess Helen (who declared herself 'weil lickit'), and was for long a kenspeckle figure on her pony and trap, in her scarlet gown and elastic-sided boots, smoking on a long clay pipe. Her father, Charles I reigned from 1847 to 1861. Two King Wulls before him both descended from Jean Gordon (c1670-1746) and her husband, Patrick Faa.[3]

Jean Gordon is almost certainly the original for one of Sir Walter Scott's maddest but most interesting characters, Madge Wildfire. In *The Heart of Midlothian*, Madge meets a sorry end at the hands of what is effectively a lynch mob in Carlisle. This is largely because of the supposed sins of her mother. In reality, it seems it is largely because Madge's own demented behaviour simply annoys people. And, no doubt, because she is a Gypsy:

> …they heard the hoarse roar with which the mob preface
> acts of riot or cruelty, yet even above that deep and dire note,
> they could discern the screams of the unfortunate victim.

---

[1] 'Muggers' became a name for the Romany people, because of the trade which many of them pursued in making or selling mugs and pans. Many of my own Yetholm forebears were what one census gently calls 'itinerant manufacturers of horn spoons'.
[2] Charles II, by way of contrast with his Stuart namesake, ended his days running a boarding-house in Muggers' Raw.
[3] The fact that Patrick Faa seems to have used the title King did not prevent a court from transporting him to America.

...When they came to the muddy pool, in which the mob were ducking her, according to their favourite mode of punishment, the magistrate succeeded in rescuing her from their hands, but in a state of insensibility, owing to the cruel treatment which she had received.

The real Jean Gordon died in Carlisle too, not long after being similarly stoned and half drowned by an angry crowd, though in her case her crime seems to have been her politics, not her mental health. When she expressed her sympathies for Prince Charles Edward Stuart, she was thrown into the River Eden, and it is said that every time her head came up, she shouted 'Chairlie yet'.

It is another Gypsy, Meg Merrilies, who provides perhaps the most fascinating character in Scott's novel *Guy Mannering*. It is very likely that Meg too is based either on Jean Gordon, or perhaps on her grand-daughter Madge:[1]

But at this moment, the door opened, and Meg Merrilies entered. Her appearance made Mannering start. She was full six feet high, wore a man's great-coat over the rest of her dress, had in her hand a goodly sloe-thorn cudgel, and in all points of equipment, except her petticoats, seemed rather masculine than feminine. Her dark elf-locks shot out like the snakes of the gorgon, between an old-fashioned bonnet called a bongrace, heightening the singular effect of her strong and weather-beaten features, which they partly shadowed, while her eye had a wild roll that indicated something like real or affected insanity.[2]

There are people today, of course, who are less comfortable about Gypsies as soon as they step off the pages of literature. In an online interview in 2017, Douglas Ross MP (afterwards leader of the Scottish Conservative Party), was asked what he would do in the troubling circumstances in which he became Prime Minister, and if, for some reason, he were able to act 'without repercussions.' Other people might have said something general at this point about solving world hunger. Mr Ross's instant response was: 'tougher

---

[1] There seems little doubt that Scott had one of the Yetholm royals in mind as his model. Meg is described as a 'sovereign' and she has a nephew by the name of Faa.
[2] The local emblem of the sloe-thorn cudgel is a fairly clear sign that Meg hails from Yetholm. I notice one of these hangs above the bar in Kirk Yetholm's Border Hotel.

enforcement against Gypsy Travellers'. Not action against any alleged crimes by Gypsy Travellers, be it noted – just action against Gypsy Travellers *per se*.

At least some of my own Yetholm ancestors would certainly have fallen under Mr Ross's cold glare.[1]

***

Before I set out walking today, I look in on the black whinstone kirk in Kirk Yetholm.

It was built in 1836 on the site of much older churches, starting with one in the twelfth century. Peace talks were held here between the representatives of Henry IV of England and Robert III of Scotland in October 1401, following an attempt by the former to land troops in Leith. The talks came to little, due to the English negotiators' familiar preoccupation with seeking to claim overlordship over Scotland. So, sadly, there is no Treaty of Yetholm. Later, in 1513 (according to one story) many of the dead of Flodden were buried here.

Behind its flinty walls, Yetholm Kirk is bright, cheery and lit with two windows entitled 'Jesus the Good Shepherd' and 'Jesus Light of the World', which were put there in memory of a Yetholm Gypsy called Andrew Blythe who, interestingly, came to be a teacher.

My grandfather, who worked on the land around Yetholm his whole life, was an elder here for over fifty years. When I first arrived at Glasgow University, I told someone that my grandfather was 'one of the elders in his village', a remark which I remember being told brought 'a very African picture' to my more sophisticated classmate's mind. Another student in the class was then dumbfounded to be told that my grandfather was a Celtic fan. Fifty miles to the north-west of Yetholm, I learned, the coexistence of these two things in one person (kirk elder and Celtic fan) was apparently against several laws of nature. Like most Scots from outside the four or five counties surrounding Glasgow, I had not even considered such a question before.[2] I was (to use a very good phrase) *fresh in frae faur oot*.

***

<hr>

[1] I was speaking not long ago to a member of the Roma community in Glasgow (who had come there from Eastern Europe) and mentioned cheerfully that I was probably at least 12.5% Romany myself. He was more than surprised to find anyone in my line of work owning up to the possibility of having Romany people in even their distant family background. The discrimination which Romany and other travelling people still face is very real.

[2] I can only compare my sense of confusion here to that experienced by one Celtic fan I know, my friend Humza Yousaf MSP. He recalls how a man once angrily confronted him in Glasgow about what Humza was told was his 'Irish heritage'.

112

When Malc and I made our start on the Scottish Middle March, the Cheviots were white. It is August now, but my thoughts still turn to how I can avoid the need to carry a tent. I think I have worked this out. This is just as well, as today I am walking with another old pal, and I see little prospect of this one agreeing to camp. He is a solicitor these days. He has met me in Kirk Yetholm wearing a suit, something which does not bode entirely well. This is the sardonic Mr Grant McLennnan.[1]

Grant's view regarding the suffering of fools is perhaps modelled on the one employed by the central character in the second, third and fourth series of *Blackadder*. He changes his clothes for today's walk, but not his grim predictions about our prospects of survival under my stewardship. He asks me if he will get back in time to iron his shirts tomorrow night. I seek to manage his expectations.

Grant and I set out from the hotel, and walk up Muggers' Raw past the Palace. We make a start on the Pennine Way from its official finishing point here, climbing up out of the village and onto the Cheviot ridge. There is a good path ahead of us for most of today, but we are now onto the long section of the Border line which is uninhabited. The Carter Bar (two days' walk ahead of us) is the only road that the Border crosses between here and Deadwater Farm, near Kielder. Deadwater is some thirty miles over the Cheviots from here and will be the last inhabited house beside the Border for another couple of days after that.

I have, however, worked out an elaborate system of car convoys to ensure a means of escape each evening. I have left my own car at Cocklawfoot, a farm seven miles up a single-track road on the Bowmont Water. The plan today is to walk from Kirk Yetholm to Cocklawfoot.

Different people have formed different impressions of the Cheviots. In this morning's mist they loom impressively enough, though for me their familiarity is their main attraction. The American writer Washington Irving, by contrast, when he first saw them, did so 'with mute surprise, I may say disappointment',[2] after what he had imagined of them from reading Scott. Daniel Defoe, on the other hand, was more excited, penning perhaps the most inaccurate description ever of the Cheviot, and comparing its height to that of the Merrick in Galloway, 'which they say is two miles high.'

A much fairer description than either of these comes from the mouth of Frank Osbaldstone, the central character in Scott's *Rob Roy*:

---

[1] Like Malc, Grant was my flatmate at Aberdeen University. The neighbours called the house a 'nationalist commune', but it was just a political cell really.
[2] Quoted by F.R. Banks: *The Borders*.

The Cheviots rose before me in frowning majesty; not, indeed, with the sublime variety of rock and cliff which characterises mountains of the primary class but huge, round-headed, and clothed with a dark robe of russet, gaining, by their extent and desolate appearance, an influence upon the imagination, as a desert district possessing a character of its own.

In any event, the Cheviots are a clear *natural* boundary, if the reader requires such a thing of Scotland to take her existence seriously. That said, of course, many of the same writers who have dismissed the very *lack* of natural features along some other more populated parts of the Border have then – noticeably changing tack – sought to argue that the lack of *people* in the Cheviots means that boundaries here are an irrelevant concept anyway.[1]

You can't win with some people.

***

We can't go much further along the Cheviots now without talking about the reivers again. The reader may want to look for modern parallels for the reiver, perhaps in Chicago, or in parts of rural Albania or Afghanistan. Scott suggested (without evidence) looking somewhere 'beyond New Holland'.[2]

To give some idea of what Scotland's government thought of the reivers, we need only look at the much-quoted official curse on them which Gavin Dunbar, Archbishop of Glasgow, ordered to be read from all Border pulpits in 1525. This must surely rank as one of the longest, most official and most comprehensive curses of all time, as even a short excerpt of it indicates:

> ...I CURSE thair heid, and al the haris of their heid. I CURSE thair face, their ene, thair mouth, thair neise, thair tung, their teith, their crag, thair shulderis, thair breast, thair hert, ...and everilk part of thair body frae the top of thair heid to the soill of their feit. ...I CURSE thaim gangand and I CURSE thaim rydand. ...I CURSE thaim etand and I CURSE them drinkand. I CURSE thaim walkand and I

---

[1] Curiously, the very same people who argue this about the Cheviots rarely seem to argue that the lack of people living in the English Channel makes *it* irrelevant as a border.

[2] i.e. Australia.

CURSE thaim slepand. ...I CURSE them at hame. I
CURSE them fra hame. I CURSE thaim within the house,
I CURSE thaim without the house. I CURSE thair wiffis,
thair barnis...I WARY thair cornys, thair catales, thair woll,
thair scheip, thair horse, thair swyne, thair geise, thair hen-
nys, and all thair quyk gude. I WARY...thair barnys, thair
biris, thair bernyardis, thair cailyardis, thair plewis, thair
harrowis, and the gudis and housis that is necessair for their
sustentatioun and weilfair. ...and finally I CONDEMN
them perpetualie to the deip pit of hell, to remain with
Lucifer.[1]

The reivers possibly had some hand in the creation of a network of
ferocious inter-district suspicions which survives still in the rivalry between
the Border towns today. 'Rivalry' is actually perhaps too gentle a word,
implying that there might be a tongue somewhere near a cheek.

I think of the town motto that 'Dunse dings aw',[2] as well as one of the
most-sung songs in Selkirk, which commits the Merse, and particularly the
Earl of Home, to the care of the Prince of Darkness.[3] I think of the woman
in Selkirk in the 1970s who apocryphally wrote in outraged terms to the local
paper to complain that the road to Galashiels had been straightened, thus
unhappily bringing that town two minutes closer to her. I think too of the
outbreak of panic in Selkirk during World War One about a German
Zeppelin, which was said to be coming to rain death on the town. The panic
was instantly calmed by a second telegram bearing the reassuring news that
the airship had 'only gotten the lenth o Hawick'. I think of the people in
Hawick who still maintain that 'A day oot o Hawick's a day wastit', or who
vow they would 'raither be a lampost in Hawick than the Provost o Selkirk';
I think of the mutual suspicion traditionally existing between Morebattle and
Yetholm, and the suspicion which the people of Hawick (according to their
neighbouring detractors) nurse for the rest of humanity. While I do not want
to fuel that last unkind stereotype, I can but note that the final verse of one

---

[1] In 2001, these words were engraved by an artist on a boulder in Carlisle Castle.
Shortly thereafter, via a series of bizarre misunderstandings, this artwork became a
political issue, after it was held by some people locally to have unleashed supernatural
forces. These forces were in turn then held responsible for various events including
the Foot and Mouth outbreak that year and a number of redundancies at a local
bakery. *Ene*: eyes; *crag*: neck; *gangand*: going; *rydand*: lit. riding, but here meaning
specifically reiving; *wary*: curse; *quyk gudis*: moveable possessions.
[2] 'Duns beats everyone else.' *Ding* can imply doing so violently.
[3] This is possibly because of Home's ancestor's open-to-question role at the battle of
Flodden. From 'The Souters o Selkirk' (traditional song, collected by Burns and
others).

song, sung at Hawick common riding, does (on the face of it) seem to speak fairly approvingly of the idea of the entire population of Galashiels being hanged from trees.[1]

And I think[2] of those people in Selkirk who refer to the people of Galashiels as 'Pail-merks'. This last is because – still triumphantly casting up the fact that Selkirk got modern sanitation a couple of years before Galashiels did in 1915 – they hold that the inhabitants of Gala to this day bear indented on them hereditarily from birth the marks of sitting on buckets.

Perhaps modern communications have softened all these feelings since I was at Selkirk High School thirty-five years ago. Perhaps the advent of social media has inflamed them again.

***

Pippa Little hails from Tanzania, was brought up in Scotland, and now lives in Northumberland. She offers a rare perspective on the Cheviots and the reivers, as imagined from the viewpoint of a woman of that time:

> The Cheviots
>
> Are a long darkening room, unswept
>
> As if men who came hungry
>
> Cleaved its hearthstone with their axes
>
> Tore cloth from skin, skin from bone
>
> Departed bloody handed.[3]

The Cheviots stretch out ahead of us now, along the Border and into the clouds, fading away into ever-fainter silhouettes and ever-rougher grazings. With Kirk Yetholm behind us, the top of Staerough[4] is on our right now.

I had thought that the gathering in of genuine folklore might now be a dead art.[5] However, in the course of writing this book, a story was passed

[1] 'The Border Queen'.
[2] Fondly.
[3] Pippa Little: 'The Cheviots', from *Foray: Border Reiver Women*.
[4] Pronunciation '**Steer**-uff', though I have also heard the last consonant sound pronounced 'ch', as in 'loch'.
[5] In the 1950s, the folklorist Hamish Henderson was still able to say that he could go around Scotland collecting songs from the oral tradition and feel that he was merely 'holding a tin can under the Niagara Falls'. It is not unreasonable to ask whether the same could really be done now, or whether very much of this folk tradition is still being passed on to new generations. I once met a lady who told me how strongly she believed in the (oft-quoted but well-founded) African proverb that it 'takes a village to raise a child'. I asked her if her own children ever spoke to any other adult in their village. She

surreptitiously to me about Staerough. It sounds like something passed down, until now, strictly within the society of women. It is said that there is a cave somewhere on Staerough that makes eerie noises. Until more recently than I suspect my source wished to admit, it was believed by some that these noises were the sounds of souls seeking to be born into this world. Yetholm women hoping to become pregnant would go to Staerough alone, and hope that a new soul would find them.

Soon, there is a fork in the Pennine Way in front of us. We take the left side of it over the Halter Burn, and up the Shieldknowe Burn. In centuries past, the Halter Burn was the Border. The line once ran down the burn to our left until it met the Shotton Burn at the ruins of St Ethelreda's Chapel.[1] A survey of 1542 seems to confirm this, speaking of English efforts to restrain what looks like an ingenious (if modest) attempt at national territorial expansion by the good folk of Yetholm. They had tried to move the Halter Burn – and with it the Scottish Border – a whole field or two to the east:

> Remember that near the foot of Halterburn, the Scots had
> dammed the water, of intent to make it to alter the course
> and river towards England so that thereby they might win
> the haughs along that burn side. And Sir Robert Ellerker
> had broken the damming and set the water again in its right
> course.[2]

Ultimately, Scotland won more of this hillside from the map-makers than she could ever have scratched out by damming burns. At the start of the nineteenth century, the march here moved to the watershed a mile or so to the east of the Halter Burn, bringing – for reasons unknown – the hills of Green Humbleton and Burnt Humbleton into Scotland. As it has turned out, our small detour into Kirk Yetholm for the night has taken us nearer to this older Border (a slightly more modest one, from a Scottish point of view) than it has to the modern line. Today, that line runs up the Shotton Burn, along old earthworks at the Countrup Sike and then southwards by means of some straight-ish lines to the point where we re-join it now.

We pass the turn-off which leads onto St Cuthbert's Way, the 62 miles of walk that lie between the abbeys of Melrose and Lindisfarne. We keep on instead to the Stob Stanes, two standing-stones which the Scottish and English kings decided should mark the March after the border survey of 1222. Today,

---

could not think of one. This was pre-lockdown.
[1] St Ethelreda was the wife of King Ecgfrith of Northumbria.
[2] *Bowes Survey and Reports* (1542). Given here in the form quoted by J.L. Mack.

the stones actually lie a hundred yards inside Scotland, and the Border takes the form of a nearby dry-stane dyke. Dykes and fences mark most of the Border here, though J.L. Mack says an older turf march-dyke runs near the stones too.

We make sure we turn right here, again following the Border. For a few miles now, the Border line is the watershed from which the rain runs down into Scotland and England. Our way along that ridge is often found for us today along a path made up of huge stone slabs (helicoptered in from the ruins of Yorkshire mills), and punctuated by wooden stiles and sign-posts. We enjoy the modern comforts of this hillwalking motorway while they last. The Pennine Way will more or less follow the Border for all of today's walk.

This takes us over White Law, named, most likely, after its white grass. A straight line[1] in the Border, running southwards here for almost a mile, probably reflects a slight doubt at some point in the mind of the Ordnance Survey. Straight sections of the Border (rare for more than a couple of hundred yards at a time), usually indicate such previous uncertainties. Indeed, the O.S. Map of 1859 put the eastern slopes of White Law inside Scotland, but the Border came back to the top of it again in their map of 1896, where it has since remained.

Perhaps contributing to those slight uncertainties, the thirteenth-century knights who were given the job of delineating the Border turned back here on their road from Berwick. Beyond White Law, they decided, there was little point in plodding further into the Cheviots. Nobody lived out here then, and nobody lives here now.

But Grant and I are made of harder, more doctrinaire stuff. We keep walking.

***

For a short while, a determined breeze keeps the clouds away, but then we are in or above the cloud line for much of the rest of the day. From time to time though, the sun breaks doubtfully through, and several square miles of both countries flash briefly beneath us through holes in the mist, in sudden map-like detail.

We make our way along Steer Rig to the Black Hag, which looks into Scotland over the Curr, and walk on to the Schil. We follow the Border on to a 'mountain refuge hut' at Red Cribs, just below the Cheviot itself[2] and look down towards Sourhope.[3] The hut would be a fine place to get out of any storm, or even put by the night if need be. We step into the hut to eat. When

---

[1] See Day 8 for a discussion of these and other very rare straight sections of the Border.

[2] By the Cheviot (singular) is meant the 'Muckle Cheviot', the highest of the range.

[3] Pronounced 'Soor-up'.

we step out again, we can now see the little burn that runs down eventually to Mounthooly Farm in England, and the red sides of the little cleuch that we assume gives Red Cribs its name. No sooner is all this seen, than it disappears again into the mist.

We keep on the Pennine Way, along the Border and over Auchope Cairn. From here, it is said, can be seen Lochnagar on a bright day. I take that claim on faith alone. Then we walk on past Hen Hole, a sharp gulley that falls down into England on our left. I have heard tell of this place getting the name of 'Hell's Hole' too, and today it does have something of the sulphurous loch about it. Cloud rises up from it, as if this were the crater of some volcano. Grant and I see enough of the edge to give us every desire to stay clear.

This is a place with an uncommon number of legends to its name. One of these is that somewhere or other down among the scree is home to the 'snow egg', a mysterious spot beyond the light of day where one little lump of winter's snow never melts in summer. More convincing[1] is the story that here was a 'beef tub', that is to say a place for hiding stolen cattle. Still another tale is that eldritch-sounding sirens sing men and women to their deaths over the edge here. One version says that a group of hunters were once lured into a ravine, where they still sleep, waiting to be awakened by a pure soul blowing on a hunting horn. We hear neither sirens nor hunting horns today through the fog, and make a point of not listening overly hard.

More widely circulated than any of these stories is the brutal legend of Black Adam. He lived, it is said, here at Hen Hole, in a cave whose mouth could only be reached by a huge leap. On the morning of a wedding at Wooperton,[2] while the groom was out collecting the priest, Black Adam raped and murdered the bride, before going on to rob the guests. The groom, Wight Fletcher, chased Black Adam back to Hen Hole, where the pair of them locked together in a fight, and fell here, like Moriarty and Holmes, to their deaths in the College Burn below:

> Slowly right owre, then they fell,
> For Fletcher his hold did keep;
> A minute and their twa bodies
> Went crashing doun the steep.

---

[1] This is probably more impressive than the tale of the snow egg, particularly to a modern audience who have fridges.

[2] Wooperton is over the hills, near Wooler. Incidentally, at the time of writing, there was a superhero film in production called *Black Adam*. It is unclear whether Wooler features in this.

Loud and lang, Black Adam shrieked,
And naething Fletcher said;
And there was neither twig nor branch
Upon their rocky bed.[1]

We come to a point where both our path and the Border take a sharp bend to the west. Here, a wee road leads off our own, up to the viewpoint on the top of the Cheviot. It gets there by way of Scotsman's Cairn, not far from Scotsman's Knowe.[2] We stick to the main path though, not taking this detour. The Cheviot, like most of the other high peaks in the Cheviot range, has its top just inside England. The remains of nineteen aircraft from the Second World War lie on its slopes.

Through the mist, we can just see on our left now the Hanging Stone, a natural gathering of stone slabs marking the point where the English East and Middle Marches meet.[3] The Hanging Stone was right on the Border itself until that moved marginally to the watershed in the sixteenth century. The Stone has been a hundred yards inside England since then. It is an eerie place. The name led to a story (not the other way about) that a hawker had by accident hanged himself by his backpack here. Elements of that story, and of this place, bring to mind certain lines of 'Tam o Shanter'. In today's weather, this looks like just the kind of uneasy spot that Tam would have crept carefully by on his way home:

And past the birks and meikle stane,
Where drunken Chairlie brak 's neck-bane;
And thro' the whins, and by the cairn,
Whare hunters fand the murder'd bairn.

***

We know the world of the reivers best through the literature which it produced – the Border Ballads. It was however Sir Walter Scott (and his researchers[4]), in his *Minstrelsy of the Scottish Border,* who brought those

---

[1] 'Black Adam of Cheviot', from Frederick Sheldon, (ed): *The Minstrelsy of the English Border.*
[2] Both places are actually just inside England.
[3] The East and Middle Marches of *Scotland* meet further east, as we have seen, at Carham.
[4] These included James Hogg and John Leyden.

ballads to world attention. Many ballads are not specifically local in theme, and represent survivors of an ancient corpus of 'land-lowping' ballads that appear in many places in many forms. A great number of them however deal very recognisably with the reiving times and, as we will see, with a number of very specific places on our route.

Quite how Scott managed to sell the *Minstrelsy* remains a mystery, considering the weight of introductions and footnotes under which he re-buried these treasures. It has taken later editors to scrape away this, as well as some of the irrelevant (and sometimes bad) new poems with which Scott further padded out the book.

Yet, stripped back of all this, we see that Scott has collected some genuinely old ballads that burn fierce, succinct, un-chivalric pictures of what the reiving times were like as human experience. Consider these brutal words, from the beaks of two corbies,[1] overheard surveying a slaughtered man whom they have found lying behind a fail (i.e. turf) dyke:

> In behint yon auld fail dyke,
> I wot there lies a new-slain knight:
> And naebodie kens that he lies there,
> But his hawk, his hound and lady fair.
>
> His hound is to the hunting gane,
> His hawk, to fetch the wild-fowl hame,
> His lady's taen another mate,
> Sa we may mak our dinner sweet.[2]

Scott reshaped this, as he did the other old ballads that he heard. For all his many talents, however, I suggest Scott could not have *invented* this one. This one looks grimly genuine.[3]

***

We are out of Yetholm now, and into the straggling parish of Morebattle.[4]

---

[1] i.e. crows.

[2] 'The Twa Corbies', from Scott's *Minstrelsy of the Scottish Border*.

[3] An English version of this ballad 'The Three Ravens' is considerably more reassuring about the assumed loyal tendencies of dogs, hawks and widows (and indeed about the manners of corbies), than is this merciless Scottish version.

[4] The lonely southern part of this parish was – a very long time ago – a parish of its own. The parish of Mow or Moll had a kirk at what is now the farm of Mowhaugh.

In 1791 the minister here gave a half-hearted explanation for the place-name, saying that there had once been a battle here, but he didn't know which one.[1]

White grass and heather and scree fall away from our path now, down to the snow egg, to the stolen cattle, to banshees and Black Adam. Dry-stane dykes from both countries reach up to us today from unseen villages, staking a claim over the clouds on behalf of agriculture and (it feels today), of forgotten kings.

From here on, for a few miles, various cairns mark our progress along the Border. We make our way over Score Head, and King's Seat, looking down into England's Murder Cleugh, a place-name to bring reivers to mind if ever there was one. We see a sign to our right hand, pointing down an old road called Clennell Street. This takes us to Cocklawfoot, a farm once known for its drovers' inn. This was a howf, used for meetings of the Wardens of the Middle Marches, in the days when the place went by the name of Hexpethgate. These days, Cocklawfoot Farm has a nice-sounding Bed and Breakfast that gives you your tea, makes you your next day's pieces and is famous for its scones.

Be not deceived, I warn Grant. We must put the scones from our minds, and think of this sign-post as nothing but a mirage, put here *tae caw the feet frae ablo forfauchen pilgrims, an pit them aff their stott*. Something nearer reality is that the B and B is booked out for months.

So we walk down the brae from here and along the burn. Ahead of us, the Curr and White Law are already distorted by an evening light that squeezes blues into reds, like a 1970s photograph. Just beyond the farm, we find our car again. We ford the burn once more, as we make our way back to Kirk Yetholm. Grant says he is glad we are not trying to put up a tent tonight. He is more than aware of the 'roundabout incident' that dogs my hillwalking reputation. The story seems to be on the lips of everybody I meet. It appears to be part of the folk tradition now. I dwell on the injustice of all this, briefly.

Grant and I will tell anybody who asks us that we camped beside a burn among the Cheviots.

---

[1] *Statistical Account of Scotland.* In fact, the name is probably the Old English *botl* ('house'), plus either the Old English *mor* ('moor') or the Gaelic *mòr* ('big').

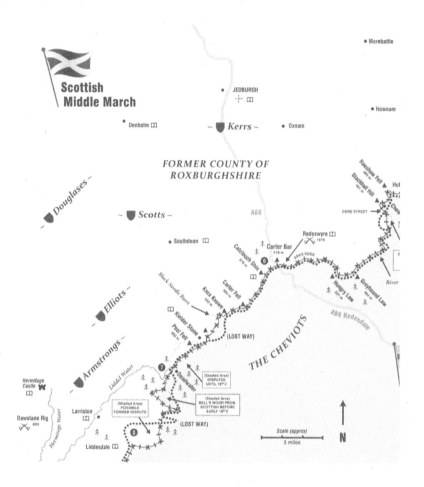

Map 4: The Scottish and English Middle Marches, as they run along the Cheviots.

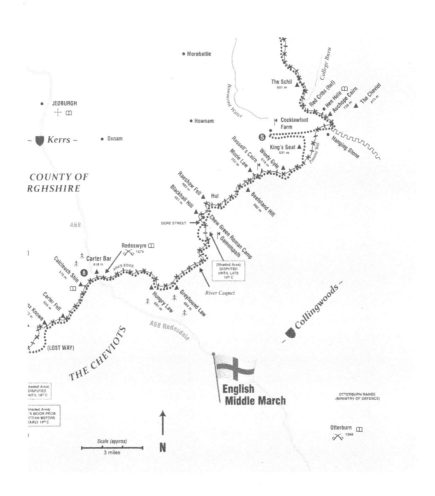

● Morebattle

● JEDBURGH
✠ ☐

~ 🛡 Kerrs ~   ● Oxnam

COUNTY OF
RGHSHIRE

A68

The Schil
501 m

Red Cribs (bui)
Hen Hole ☐
Auchope Cairn 726 m   The Cheviot 815 m

● Hownam

Cocklawfoot
Farm

⑤ King's Seat

Hanging Stone

Russell's Cairn 469 m
Windy Gyle 531 m
Mozie Law 552 m

Raeshaw Fell 460 m
Blackhall Hill 451 m

Hut

Beefstand Hill 560 m

DERE STREET

Chew Green Roman Camp
Gamelspath

Redeswyre ☐
1575

Carter Bar
418 m

Calcleuch Shin 519 m   ⑥

(Shaded Area)
DISPUTED
UNTIL LATE
18th C

~ Collingwoods ~

JINK'S EDGE

River Coquet

Carter Fell 500 m

☐

z Knowe

Hungry Law 399 m

Greyhound Law 400 m

•••• (LOST WAY)

A68 Redesdale

THE CHEVIOTS

✚
English
Middle March

OTTERBURN RANGE
(MINISTRY OF DEFENCE)

haded Area)
DISPUTED
NTIL 18th C

naded Area)
'N MOOR PROB.
'TTISH BEFORE
ARLY 18th C

Otterburn ☐
1388

Scale (approx)
3 miles

N ↑

Day 5: From Cocklawfoot to the Carter Bar

(Circa 17 miles)

*A mythical house straddling the Border; Lord Russell's Cairn; Morebattle,
Hownam and the Covenanters; On undue aristocratic influence; Romans in the
gloamin at Chew Green; The Battle of Otterburn and the Raid of the Redeswire;
Border laws and lawlessness; The Carter Bar.*

'The Vacant Chair' is a couthie Victorian tale, set in the hypothetical
farmhouse of Marchlaw, somewhere up here in the Cheviots. The story is a
wry take on the predicament that is the Border. It is, however, worth
reassuring the reader that (after having made a thorough investigation of the
matter on foot) I can find no house like Marchlaw here or anywhere else:

> Peter was placed in very unpleasant circumstances, owing to
> the situation of Marchlaw House, which, unfortunately, was
> built immediately across the 'ideal line' dividing the two
> kingdoms; and his misfortune was that, being born within it,
> he knew not whether he was an Englishman or a Scotchman.
> …The parlour was distinctly acknowledged to be in Scotland,
> and two-thirds of the kitchen were as certainly allowed to be
> in England: his three ancestors were born in the room over
> the parlour, and, therefore, were Scotchmen beyond question;
> but Peter, unluckily, being brought into the world before the
> death of his grandfather, his parents occupied a room
> immediately over the debatable boundary line which crossed
> the kitchen. The room, though scarcely eight feet square, was
> evidently situated between the two countries; but, no one
> being able to ascertain what portion belonged to each, Peter,
> after many arguments and altercations upon the subject, was
> driven to the disagreeable alternative of confessing he knew
> not what countryman he was. What rendered the confession
> the more painful was, that it was Peter's highest ambition to
> be thought a Scotchman.[1]

---

[1] *Wilson's Tales of the Borders,* Vol. I. The same story tells of this house's cross-border
Christmas dinner table, one end of which bears a haggis and the other a sirloin steak.
Peter hesitates about whether to observe Christmas, so giving away his real nationality.
It is now virtually forgotten that, from the Reformation onwards, Christmas went very
largely uncelebrated in Scotland. Only in 1958 did it become a public holiday
(although it had been acknowledged in a cursory way for a good while before that). I
remember hearing my grandfather in Yetholm recalling his bafflement and disdain
when, in the 1940s, his Northumbrian wife put up a Christmas tree in the house.

I would happily have given Peter a passport, which of course in any *normal* country would have been the simple answer.

***

Although my walk has now taken me into the hills of the Middle March, it has so far always done so within walking distance of farms and villages I know. Soon I will be heading into the wilds, and beyond my ancestral comfort zone. Later today, I will leave even the path itself behind me, and plough on along the Border through the heather.

Our journey brings Grant McLennan and me over from Kirk Yetholm by car, and back up to the top of the Bowmont Water. By the time we get as far as Cocklawfoot, the Bowmont is just a burn, and one too small to justify a bridge. We ford it in the car, with a spray of water rising behind us, and pheasants fleeing across the path ahead. The air here today is a strangely reassuring mixture of damp and glaur.

We look up at the ridge of the Cheviots. A low line of cloud keeps from us any indication of how high the hills that form the Border here might really be. I think of the comment, sometimes heard muttered, that Scotland needed the Himalayas, but God gave us the Cheviots. Himalayas they might be, for all we can tell today, under their low blanket, but in places the clouds soon part for long enough to see a long, gnarled spine of modest hills: Auchope Cairn, Score Head, King's Seat, Windy Gyle. Some of the hillsides are of a grass so white that the shadow of a cloud is visible as it inches over them. Others are dark and lit up only by the searing yellow of the whins.

Grant and I are met here by another old friend who has agreed to humour me on the next section of my way. This is Stuart Rivans from Rutherglen. Grant worms from Stuart the information that he and I were, as students, both party to the much-recounted 'roundabout incident'. The reader will feel that an explanation is soon required. Suffice to say, for the moment, that Grant feels that in Stuart he has found the final piece of evidence in his case against my hillwalking abilities, and my abilities in general. Grant treasures the new eye-witness account of the incident with the joy of a man who has just discovered in a long-buried ancient text the authority for a long-held personal prejudice.

Stuart is now a Modern Studies teacher – I strongly suspect, a popular one. As such, I do not seek to implicate him in the politics of this book. However, I hope it can now safely be said that, as students, Stuart and I together organised an incident which strained my own relationship with the authorities of Glasgow University for some time. I would not do it now, but it is the kind of thing absolutely everyone should do when they are twenty.

At that time, George Younger, the former Secretary of State for Scotland, remained one of the most immovable (if most polite) advocates of the position that no matter how many people in Scotland wanted a Scottish Parliament, they weren't getting one.[1]

Despite this, Younger was to receive an honorary degree from the University. Stuart and I, plus two or three others including the Rector of the University,[2] decided that the ceremony should be modified. My memory is of leading a group of students out of the graduation hall, while Stuart and other friends, disguised (unconvincingly) in the gallery as journalists, silently unfurled an enormous banner over the top of proceedings which read simply 'Democracy for Scotland'. One of these infant 'journalists' ran from a pursuing janitor and television crew, offering the hurriedly-thought-up excuse that he had to go, because his wife was – suddenly – having a baby. He got away.

Despite our efforts, it was another eight years before the Scottish Parliament was eventually reconvened.

***

Stuart, Grant and I walk up the burn again from Cocklawfoot to re-join the Pennine Way. The three of us head south-west now over Windy Gyle, which at 619 metres is the highest point above sea-level on the whole Border. Today, we will be on the Border and in the clouds all day, so we will see only occasional dramatic intimations of the countries to either side. Yet we will see enough to make the trip worthwhile. The contrasting views north and south from here often leave the impression (if one were to judge by today's isolated evidence alone) that Scotland is a more fertile country than England.

One thing we do see through the mist on Windy Gyle is Lord Russell's Cairn. This is actually a series of much more ancient cairns than the name suggests, but the story is that, at a march-meeting here on 27 July 1585, a disturbance broke out over a claim that an Englishman had disrupted the day of truce by stealing a pair of spurs. Lord Russell got up from his seat to investigate the matter and was promptly shot by a Scot for his pains. This is probably as vivid an illustration as any that the system of march laws and days of truce did not quite work.[3]

---

[1] The number of Scottish voters who voted at elections for parties supporting the formation of a Scottish Parliament was by then running at 75%.

[2] The lead singer of *Hue and Cry*, Pat Kane.

Here, a nick in the Border to our south is called, tantalisingly, Split the Deil. The fence over the top of Windy Gyle marks the Border line and, looking into England from here, some more striking names jump out from the map, including Scotchman's Ford and (another) Murder Cleugh. We cross a path going off to our right northwards called 'The Street', an old drove road that runs from Hownam and crosses the Border between Windy Gyle and Mozie Law. General Roy's military map of 1755 calls this the 'Clattering Path'. It is probably one of the roads used by the enormous traffic of Highland cattle that came south via Falkirk to English markets from the seventeenth to nineteenth centuries.

Hownam,[1] into whose out-of-the-way parish we are now crossing, is a place I seem to recall Yetholm people speaking of as if it were beyond the dark side of the moon. This was possibly simply because it was beyond Morebattle, but perhaps also because of the reputation that the Hownam and Morebattle areas once had for Covenanters. Some of these seem to have lingered on in the hills here with the tenacity of Scott's 'Old Mortality'. Open-air conventicles were held at Gateshaw near the Kale Water on a piece of land that became known as the 'singing braes'. These meetings began again anew in 1725, when the Duke of Roxburghe exerted his newly-won right to appoint a minister to the charge of Morebattle. A heated dispute took place in Morebattle kirkyard, which resulted in many people worshipping in the fields for some years afterwards, rather than accept the premise that their landowner enjoyed any right to run a kirk. Gateshaw, lying between the villages of Hownam and Morebattle, founded a secessionist church in 1739, and for long afterwards the area around here nursed organised opposition to the system of landed patronage to which the established Kirk was succumbing.

There are not many people permanently resident in the parish of Hownam these days, under a hundred possibly. Probably very few of those would now see themselves, in any sense, as Covenanters.

***

We follow the Border through a hazy landscape which, today, is worthy of *The Hound of the Baskervilles*. Picking our way along the ridge, we keep an eye on the map, reassured frequently by a solid path, and still more constantly by the border fence, which we never let leave our very limited sight.

We come to Plea Knowe, an interesting name that reflects ancient litigation over who this summit belonged to. The matter looks settled now, as today

---

[3] Lord Russell had, nine years before this incident, been involved in the 'Raid of Redeswire', on which we will hear more very shortly.

[1] Pronuncuation '**Hoo**-nam'.

the Border goes right over the top of it. Our path takes us briefly into England, bypassing a zig-zag in the Border at the ominously-named Foul Step. Then we head to Mozie Law and Beefstand Hill, (the last of these being named, I am going to take it, after the activities of cattle reivers). J.L. Mack writes a century ago that there were visible traces of a great turf dyke running up the Border to Mozie Law all the way from Windy Gyle, though this is not obvious today, either from the landscape or the map.

Once we are over the top of Lamb Hill, there is another mountain refuge hut at the wild-west-sounding Yearning Saddle, and we stop here for a rest. On our north side here, just beyond the hut, and up along Raeshaw Fell[1] are some ancient earthworks. These more or less coincide with the Border for a stretch. The present Border follows the nearby watershed line that was set in the sixteenth century, so the correspondence is not quite exact, but it is tempting to think that this earthwork did indeed act as a national border marker before then. J.L. Mack certainly contends that this is a section of a ditch dug to mark the Border in the thirteenth or fourteenth century.

Whatever exact Border line you draw here is a fairly strange shape. Some, including J.L. Mack, have accounted for this by arguing that there may once have been a royal deer park marked out here. There is certainly evidence of royal hunts in this area. Records exist from the twelfth century of a legal requirement that all dogs around here should have one foot shortened, so they could not compete with the royal pack.

The Pennine Way continues, short-cutting some further jaggy corners in the Border by avoiding the summits of Raeshaw Fell and Blackhall Hill, skirting instead round their eastern (English) sides.

***

As the three of us make our way through the clouds, I begin to wonder on whose land it is we now tread.

I make no inflexible argument against old families quietly running small estates and keeping up houses but, in the modern world, their right to special influence should go little further than that.[2] And yet, I know of few places in Scotland today where the views of local aristocrats are still given such serious consideration as they are in the Borders.

I recall how the Laird of Gala, in 2014, used his annual reception for the Gala Braw Lad to lecture people on the dangers of voting for independence.[3]

---

[1] Or Rushy Fell, as it is sometimes called.
[2] They should not, for hypothetical example, enjoy any great over-representation among politicians.

I think also of one of hundreds of doors I knocked on during that year's independence referendum, a door which I found up a very long and well-tended drive. Before I could say anything, the elderly dowager who answered the door, looked at my 'Yes' badge, and shook her head at me, more in sorrow than in anger. Addressing me as if I were a naughty servant – possibly, I imagined, one she had earlier chastised in Kenya – she said simply, 'After all we have done for you people,' and closed the door.

I think too of the late ninth Duke of Buccleuch, who during a previous referendum – the devolution referendum of 1997 – gave a speech of great preposterousness in Kelso, in which he warned of grave calamity, should Scotland ever have her own parliament. He said that he foresaw 'a tartan curtain descending over the United Kingdom'. I remember thinking how unthreatening the image sounded. He was opening a bridge at the time, in his supposedly impartial capacity as the Queen's local Lord Lieutenant.

And I remember, very suddenly as I climb now over Windy Gyle, about a forgotten walk in the Border hills with my family when I was about fifteen. A local titled individual was officially opening a new footpath that crossed his land. I am not clear quite how my father was prevailed upon to come to such an event.

The laird, I recall was giving a braying account of the great personal trials to him involved in owning land, keeping horses and paying taxes. I became increasingly aware of the sound of my father slowly but steadily kicking one of the back tyres of our car. Facing away from the speaker, he kicked very audibly indeed for the whole duration of the speech. People around me, including the speech-maker, noticed.

I had not read much then, nor looked into my family history. I was embarrassed. I am not now.

***

The Border now leads us briefly into an even older world. For a short distance now, the Border and the path both more or less follow the old Roman Road, Dere Street. This is the Saxon name for the road which the Romans built (conceivably during their gloamings[1]) around 150 AD. It

[3] This reminds me of stories I have heard from around Scotland of general elections in the 1950s and before. Then, farmworkers were often invited to the *big hoose*, to be told of the awful consequences for them of not voting Tory. These homilies typically mentioned casually the dangers that might come if any hike in the Laird's taxes were to lead to the workers on his estate losing their jobs and tied houses.
[1] 'Roman in the Gloaming' is, as the reader doubtless knows, a version of Harry Lauder's 'Roaming in the Gloaming', rendered into Latin, and begins *'Sub noctem*

runs from York to both Hadrian and Antonine's walls. It is possibly also the route that Julius Agricola travelled on his way to Scotland in 80 AD, in his efforts to bring the place under proper Roman control.

The road we walk now is noticeably straight. It takes us just off the Border and into the remains of the Roman camp at Chew Green. The camp's square form rises suddenly, and very visibly man-made, out of the people-forsaken landscape around it. It is said to have been big enough to hold 16,000 men. Sometimes called Makendon Camp, after the estate it is on, it sits a few yards inside what is now England.

It is difficult to imagine what an Italian sodger would have made of being posted here. Perhaps, however, we do not have to rely completely on imagination; this area is still part of a military installation today, the Otterburn Ranges. We have therefore perhaps some insight into the possible views of the Roman legionaries by looking at one plaintive exchange, posted recently on the 'Army Rumour Service' website (arrse.co.uk):

> Hello, I am in the ACF and my first camp has been to Okehampton and I didn't really like it. ...it was a very long drive as well. I was pondering if I should go to this camp [Otterburn]. So, what's it like? Is it any good? What are the billets like, etc.?

Which provoked the response:

> It is a very long way and I didn't like it. There was rain, then more rain. Then I went again and it rained again. Next time I went, it rained and then it rained some more. I got very wet and it rained some more. The next time I went, it rained and rained. Sometimes it rained some more. Sometimes I heard it doesn't rain, but I can't tell you about such an event.

I raise my phone to take a photo – Stuart laughs aloud – and I realise that I am taking a photo of mist. Chew Green really is the middle of nowhere, a fact reflected in the more Roman-sounding name it is sometimes given – *Ad Fines*.[1] There is no evidence the Romans ever called it this, but they should have.

Later, there was a medieval village on the site, called Kemylpethe or Gamelspath, just inside England.[2] This border-crossing was once a place

vagare praeter Clutha litora'. It deserves a wider popularity than it currently enjoys.
[1] Meaning 'On the Edge' or (appropriately, given that the Border has come to run almost exactly through the camp) 'On the Border'.

designated for the trial by hand-to-hand combat of any Scot accused of a crime in England. In one such case, recorded in the fifteenth century, there was a famous duel between England's sixteen-year-old Robert Snowdon and the celebrated Scottish champion, John Grieve. Greatly to the crowd's surprise, Snowdon killed Grieve. Another even bloodier incident was in 1511, when Sir Robert Ker of Caverton attended a day of truce here as a representative of the Scottish Crown, only to be killed by a group of Englishmen. One of those responsible was a certain John Heron, apparently better known locally by his nickname, which was Bastard.

Around a mile south of the camp is a once-disputed area of ground called Plea Shank. Marked on maps as late as 1840 with a short apologetic gap in the Border line, this little piece of hillside had for long (as its name suggests) been subject to litigation. It was half-agreed at some stage that the Scots should graze one half of it and the English the other, but successive Ordnance Survey maps (amid some controversy between local landowners) have marked it variously as Scottish, Disputed and (for the last century and more) English.

This was almost certainly the very last[1] (and probably the most physically out-of-the-way) genuine dispute over any section of the Border line.

***

At the southern end of the Roman camp, the path turns right and follows the River Coquet westwards. We keep this little border burn on our left. After a couple of hundred yards in Scotland, we can see that we are crossing back into England again. No sign tells us this, in as many words, but a notice does warn hillwalkers not to expect any more of Scotland's liberal laws on the right to roam. These have briefly let us wander virtually anywhere without any fear of encountering the English concept of trespass. A second, larger, signpost reminds us of the other danger we face, now that we are back on England's Otterburn Range – that of being shelled by the Army.

Where we cross the burn again, we see the corner of a large English plantation on the horizon at the ominously-named Ogre Hill. This is our cue, finally, to leave the Pennine Way behind us and cut across the countryside to the west. This, as also crosses my mind, is our first real opportunity on the whole walk to get lost. One of the great benefits of having an internal compass of limited power is that one gets to see lots of new places. I don't think that this is to be recommended this late in the afternoon, however, and so I study

---

[2] Bowes' Survey of 1550 suggests that it was far from undisputed as to which country Gamelspath was actually in.

[1] Last, with the exception of the one on the Solway Firth (see Chapter 8).

the map with some care.

The going has been easy until now, but from here on it becomes hard work underfoot, as we make our way round the northern edge of the forest that marks the Border. Usefully, each country's division of the Forestry Commission here (as in most other places along the Border) has planted up to, but not over, the edge of its own respective jurisdiction. So the tree-line is a clear border-marker to follow. We have gone thirteen miles today on a reasonably good path. Now we have to walk another four or five through some much rougher terrain, and before it gets dark.

We skirt round the Heart's Toe[1] and Greyhound Law, still hugging the border fence, and head on to the appropriately-named Hungry Law. The latter, we conclude, is so-named after travellers who have no more dry matches for their camping stoves. Here the forest comes to an end, and we come down out of our cloudy Olympus long enough to see both countries lying below us in a series of deepening shades of blue. Looking into Scotland, we can see Ruberslaw, the Moorfoot Hills and the three peaks of the Eildons.[2] To the east of them, at varying distances along the dimming horizon, stands the lighthouse-like monument to the battle of Waterloo at Peniel Heugh, and then the Lammermuirs and Hownam Law.

The Border cuts across open land here over Catcleugh Hill for half a mile or so. Following this, we find the southern edge of Scotland's Leithhope Forest. Again, the tree line exactly marks the Border, this time along Arks Edge. We start to get tired. We have a couple of false dawns as to when the walk might actually be going to end. It is gloaming now and our feet are sore. Like Beckett, I blame on my boots the fault of my feet.

Somewhere, away ahead of me now, Grant (who, when he is not being a solicitor, has an unlikely double life as a human karaoke machine) is working his way through a number of Scottish songs made popular again by the *Corries*. These are presently interspersed (I think I now hear drifting over the heather in the evening calm) with *My baby just loves to dance,* and possibly even *Ruby, don't take your love to town.*

***

Along this section of the Border, it is wisest to keep to the Scottish side as much as possible. I am not advocating this merely as some point of jaundiced principle, but for the practical reason that to our south now, as mentioned, is the vast

---

[1] I am assuming that for 'heart' here, we should read 'hart' (i.e. a deer).
[2] As the reader will be aware, the Eildons were carefully divided into three by the wizard Michael Scott.

Ministry of Defence property at the Otterburn Range, where there are regularly live firing exercises. Since 1911, huge tracts of this landscape have at times been out of bounds. At points during the Cold War, these moors were shrouded in some mystery, not least when Otterburn was involved in the development of the UK's 'Blue Streak' missile-launching system.

Otterburn is of course also famous for much older and less potentially-total wars, namely the battle here between Scots and English forces in 1388. An English record of the battle, a poem called 'Chevy Chase',[1] exists, but a sparser, more compelling account from Scotland survives in 'The Battle of Otterburn.' Ahead of me, Grant is making good progress through his repertoire, and – incredibly – has now reached this very ballad:

> It fell about the Lammas tide,
> When the muir-men win their hay,
> The doughty Douglas bound him to ride
> Into England to drive a prey.

The Battle of Otterburn was genuinely national warfare, falling as it did not long after the wresting back of southern Scotland from the hands of Edward III. The ballad describes something of the enmity between the Douglases and the Percies too, and recounts the capture of a Douglas pennant in the course of the battle. Yet the ballad is just as arresting as a song as it is as history, and famously contains these eerie, uncomfortable lines:

> But I hae dream'd a dreary dream
> Beyond the Isle of Sky;
> I saw a dead man win a fight,
> And I think that man was I.[2]

The sun is beginning to set now.

***

Eventually, the trees on our right hand come to an end, and we can at last peer down to the view that the tourists see from the Carter Bar. The cars

---

[1] 'Chevy Chase' contrives a long back-story to the battle, about a Percy going out to provoke a Douglas during a hunt in the Cheviots (in a place nowhere near the actual battle).

[2] 'The Battle of Otterbourn', from *Minstrelsy of the Scottish Border* (I have altered a couple of words here to fit more with the *Child Ballads* version – which is better).

have their headlights on now, as they wind their way from Jedburgh to the frontier. It is still easy enough for us to see our feet though, and the border fence. It is a short walk now along Wooplaw Edge, so named (we idly conclude) onomatopoeiacally after our own ironic cries of delight at nearing the end of today's route-march.

In 1375, the Carter Bar (or Redeswire, to use its other name) is mentioned by John Barbour as a byword for the extremities of the country, describing Bruce's recapture of Scotland 'fra Redis Swyr till Orkynnay'.[1]

Here on our right somewhere now was the scene of the 'Raid of the Redeswire' in 1575. A stone near here, and a ballad, mark the event:

> The seventh of July, the suith to say,
> At the Reidswire the tryst was set;
> Our Wardens they affixed the day,
> And as they promised, so they met.
>
> Alas! that day I'll ne'er forgett!
> Was sure sae feard and then sae faine –
> They came theare justice for to gett,
> Will never green to come again.[2]

The raid is often described as the last great battle between the Scots and the English. In fact, it is probably better to think of it as yet another day of truce that went very badly wrong, probably after an accusation was made against the English Warden Sir John Forster.

However the dispute began, it ended up in a large and violent skirmish. Both Sir John Carmichael, Keeper of Liddesdale, and Forster himself became involved in a drink-fuelled fight. This eventually drew in large groups of bystanders and caused a number of people including the Keeper of Tynedale, Sir George Heron, to be killed. In any event, the Raid of the Redeswire is still celebrated as part of the Jethart Callants' Festival every year. The Scots took three hundred English cattle, to make the whole exercise feel worthwhile. From such unlikely heroic material are great ballads made.

The wider legacy of the Raid of the Redeswire, however, was as a significant diplomatic incident which threatened to disrupt warming relations between the two governments. By way of reaction to the skirmish, there circulated in

---

[1] John Barbour: *The Bruce*.
[2] From early editions of Scott's *Minstrelsy*. The ballad had earlier appeared in Allan Ramsay's *The Evergreen*. *Green*: to long for.

Scotland a bizarre fake papal bull, 'Ane bull of our haly fader the paip, qu-hairby it is leesum to everie man to haif tua wyffis'.[1]

On the face of it, this very odd document is simply a piece of rather virulent propaganda, directed at those in Scotland who had not subscribed to the Reformation. It puts the story about that the Pope has given his flock permission to practice polygamy. However, the publication's references to the Bartholomew's Day Massacre (during which many French Protestants had been slain) mark it out as a seemingly serious attempt to influence opinion. It essentially argues that Scots should identify Catholics as their enemies, not the (Protestant) Queen of England. This piece of fake news, weird as it undoubtedly is, was a very direct response to the instability which pro-English Scots feared might result from the Raid of the Redeswire, the bloodshed that took place here on the slope we are walking over now.

It is the hour now for the midges to make their appearance. We keep walking.

***

The abnormal situation of the Border during the reiving times created an imperative for the development of a concept of international law, even if one of its own lawless and blood-spattered kind.

This situation was borne out of a mutual realisation in both countries that it was pointless trying to apply the normal rules of anything to the Borders. This was recognised in the *Leges Marchiarum*,[2] created at conferences in 1248 and 1249. These set out thirteen articles of such law to govern life along the Border,[3] among the most extreme (and most flouted) of which involved the death penalty for Scotsmen who married Englishwomen. Most laws dealt, however, with the issue of theft. George MacDonald Fraser explains the three options available to an aggrieved party:

> If he was a weak or friendless man, his recourse would be a
> complaint to his Warden, and a demand for justice under
> the international law the Marches. If he were a man of

---

[1] See 'A Scottish Anti-Catholic Satire Crossing the Border', in *English Historical Review*, Vol. 129.

[2] To use a name much later given to them.

[3] The author of the sixteenth-century *Complaynt of Scotland* complains *inter alia* about the breaking of these Border laws. He also warns that for Scots and English people to live together under one government in future would be 'as it is on possibil that tua sonnis and tua munis can be at one tyme to giddir'. Allowing for the sometimes hysterical tone of all this propaganda, it is as well to remember its context, which was Henry VIII's brutal 'rough wooing' along the Border.

his hands, and most were, he might decide to wait and plan for the day when he could raid the robbers in his turn and get his revenge illegally with interest. Or he could decide on a pursuit, across the frontier if necessary.[1]

This last option is 'hot trod': that is to say, the right to recover one's property by force up to six days after the theft.

'Days of truce' were ordained at specified times and places along the Border. These events were held, as we have seen, with mixed results, but they provided the opportunity for complaints to be formally heard. Cases could be decided by means as varied as trial by a jury in the other party's country; or 'on the Warden's honour' (he had to take responsibility if his gut instinct was wrong). Many questions were settled via duel or trial by combat on the Border itself. The question of evidence does not seem to have been a major consideration.

Just as common was the practice of *bauchling*, which was to ride through an assembled crowd, shouting detailed abuse at an alleged offender and challenging him either to pay compensation or to fight the matter out. Bauchling was outlawed, except by official licence, in 1553.[2]

***

Of all the Border laws, the one that seems most relevant to ourselves now tonight is the one allowing animals to be pastured on the other side of the Border only as long as they come home by sunset. We are wanting home now, and it is dark. We fall the last few yards to the car park at the Carter Bar.

The burger van I had half-hoped for is not here, and the childhood memories of a piper standing here on the Border are not realised. Sadly, we are 150 years too late for the pub that once was here, but we don't overly mind. We head away to retrieve cars left at distant Cocklawfoot, and make our own respective ways northwards to eat and wash.

I mentally search out someone tolerant enough to come with me on the next stretch of my border-walk, probably the wildest and least-walked stretch of all.

---

[1] George MacDonald Fraser: *The Steel Bonnets.*
[2] The concept of bauchling by licence perhaps has something to commend itself to the producers of mid-morning television programmes.

Day 6: From the Carter Bar to Deadwater

(Circa 9 miles of Border. Circa 12 miles walk, when the detours mentioned are included)

Jethart tales and snails; The Carter Bar; Border signposts and the Scottish Cringe; Border beacons and Brexit; James Thomson, the dead poet; Trudging through heather to Duntae Edge; The Justified Sinner crosses our path; John Leyden in 36 languages; The Kielder Stane and Peel Fell; Deadwater.

So begins my next attack on the Border – if that does not sound unduly hostile – this time from the Carter Bar to Deadwater Farm, near Kielder.

I meet up with Grant, but another and much less sarcastic Grant this time. This is my former colleague Grant Moncur,[1] who was for five years my private secretary when I was a government minister, and who is a past master at saving me from myself. I do not know how the civil service assign private secretaries to ministers, but in Grant's case, they put some thought into matching our respective temperaments.

Given the time that I know Grant spent in the Territorial Army, I am judging that he will probably be able to read a map at least as well as I can. Some of Grant's T.A. time was in fact relevantly spent driving lorries here at the Otterburn Training Camp.

Today, as we make our way west from the Carter Bar, we will be heading into the wilds. Neither of us has ever tried to walk the route we will take today. I doubt if all that many people do.

***

Since a tiny stretch of the parish of Jedburgh runs along the Border, I feel just-ified in mentioning the town of Jedburgh itself, some twelve miles to our north.[2]

Jethart,[3] as Jedburgh is known to its people, is famed for its Augustinian abbey and for the house where Mary Queen of Scots once stayed while she was ill.[4] In 1285, King Alexander III married his French Queen, Yolande de Dreux at the Abbey, an event which was gatecrashed by none other than Death himself, as a fifteenth-century Latin history records:

---

[1] Grant is a civil servant and is, I should therefore say, not commenting on any of the more political observations made in this book.

[2] I am marginally breaking my 'ten-miles from the Border' rule for a moment. In fact, the parish of Jedburgh was for long bisected into two completely detached parts until, in 1891, boundary commissioners created a land-corridor through the village of Dolphinston.

[3] 83 spellings of Jedburgh's name have been recorded; 'Jethart' reflects the local pronunciation.

[4] Later events gave her good cause to remark 'Would God I had dee'd in Jethart'.

Eventually in the procession came a mysterious figure… It apparently floated like a ghost rather than walked on its feet. Just as it seemed to be disappearing from everyone's sight, the whole joyous procession came to a halt, the music faded, and the dancers all suddenly froze.[1]

Jedburgh today is known for its serious rugby, and for its even more physical games of handba held at Candlemas and Fastern's Een,[2] when each end of the town – the Uppies and the Doonies – join in a free-for-all game.[3] Jedburgh is also home to the Jeddart axe (a four-foot-long weapon favoured by reivers); 'Jedburgh justice' (a sardonic term for summary execution anywhere); and Jethart snails. The last is a type of boiled sweetie whose recipe was apparently provided by a Napoleonic prisoner of war who (it is to be presumed) missed eating actual snails.[4]

James Hutton (1726-97), one of the fathers of modern geology, made studies of rock formations at Inchbonny near Jedburgh, which first demonstrated the impossibility of the world being only six thousand years old.[5] However, the most significant scientific figure who actually hailed from Jedburgh was Mary Fairfax Somerville, born in the town in 1780. The world was not ready for a woman of Somerville's talents. Her parents could not quite believe that they had a daughter who wished to learn Latin and mathematics, rather than the proposed needlework. She was in time the author of a book called *Molecular and Microscopic Science*, and became a fellow of the American Philosophical Society. Said to have influenced James Clerk Maxwell, she has belatedly been recognised by having both a crater of the Moon and an Oxford College named after her.

---

[1] Walter Bower: *Scotichronicon* (author's translation).

[2] 2 February and Shrove Tuesday respectively.

[3] This sport was (according to one unsubstantiated legend I have heard), originally played with an Englishman's head. 'Until the 1960s', as a friend from another Border town once dryly finished that sentence, when the story was put to him.

[4] A friend of mine was disappointed to find recently that a sweetie shop in Jedburgh was not stocking Jethart snails. Scotland is an immeasurably more self-confident place than it was thirty years ago. And yet, I reflect, we also live in an era when the football sticker albums circulating among Scotland's schoolchildren have now ceased to make any reference to the existence of Scottish football teams. Some Scottish pubs no longer stock any Scottish beers.

[5] No doubt Hutton's studies at Inchbonny (as well as at Siccar Point on the Berwickshire coast) earn him a place in an *Index Librorum Prohibitorum* in some states of the U.S.A. today. Meanwhile, one or two Scots geologists today make a great deal (light-heartedly) out of the fact that the 'Whin Sill' lies roughly along the Border (indeed parts of Hadrian's Wall are built on it). This scar marks where, relatively late on, Scotland has attached itself to the Eurasian Plate – and therefore to England. The reader should not read too much into my mentioning this.

Nearer to Jethart than either of these two places is the committee room of the Scottish Parliament which now also bears her name.

***

Just to our west now lies the far-flung parish of Southdean, where it is said Robert III and James, Earl of Douglas met at the kirk in 1388 to plan the battle of Otterburn. It was also there that the Scots reputedly returned to bury their dead.

We are at the Carter Bar. This far west along the Border, I am now entering exotic and relatively unknown territory, for me. So the reader will feel a sense of relief that my last relevant personal anecdote of its type relates to a school trip in primary one, when I bought a '99' cone at the Carter Bar, despite having actually asked for an ice lolly. This was because the friendly Geordie selling it and I could not understand anything each other was saying. Perhaps the same man will be alive and available to sell Grant and me a bacon roll. We have had our breakfasts elsewhere *en route*, to cope with the eventuality that he is not.

The Carter Bar is probably the most iconic way to arrive in Scotland, and the only way to do so by road through the Cheviots. One evening in 1928, the travel writer H.V. Morton stopped his car here:

> There are certain views in all countries which must quicken the heart of the man who sees them again after an absence – such is the sight of Scotland from the Carter Bar ... Here is something as definite and unmistakable to a Scotsman as the white cliffs of Dover are to an Englishman. The heathery moors slope down to a distant valley. The sun is setting. The sky above the Lammermuirs is red and troubled. The wind drops. The autumn mists far below are creeping from wood to wood... I can hear a dog barking miles off in the valley. I am all alone at the Border, one foot in England, the other in Scotland. There is a metal post with 'Scotland' written on it. It is a superfluous post. You do not need to be told that you have come to the end of England.[1]

The minister of Southdean in 1845 similarly writes about the magnificent view of Scotland awaiting the tourists here:

---

[1] H.V. Morton: *In Search of Scotland*.

This view is no doubt greatly enhanced by the uninteresting country which must be traversed before entering into Scotland.[1]

It is unclear whether this unduly unkind remark is intended to extend to the whole of England, or merely to the last few miles of it.

***

Today, at the Carter Bar, the signs welcoming drivers into each country take the form of large inscribed boulders. I have heard this is because previous, smaller, signposts were regularly being taken away as souvenirs.

Twenty years ago, probably half of the 24 roads that cross the Border displayed nothing at all, beyond a tell-tale slight change in the colour of the road surface, to indicate that a line was being crossed. Now, thanks partly to a campaign by the St Andrew Society, few entry points remain unmarked. At the main ones, there now stand big blue signs bidding motorists:

Welcome to Scotland Fàilte gu Alba

It is amazing to see the incandescent reaction that three words – even in a small font – can ignite in some people.[2] So, in 2015, Tory MSP Jackson Carlaw tweeted sarcastically:

> Our education system is failing … but at least the SNP spent £26m on Gaelic roadsigns.[3]

The most curious reactions of all come from people who seem to think that such road signs prove (in the face of all evidence) that the idea of promoting Gaelic has been invented by the pro-independence lobby. Rory Stewart (not altogether unsurprisingly) reacts in pretty much this way to just such a border signpost:

---

[1] *New Statistical Account of Scotland.*

[2] As someone who now uses Gaelic often in daily life, these reactions are, incidentally, also fairly offensive.

[3] This remark, as well as being a fairly full-frontal attack on Scotland's teachers, overstates by a factor of at least ten what was actually spent on bilingual road signs. The figure quoted reflects the sum spent on all public services delivered through Gaelic that year. The figure spent on all public services delivered through *English* would make instructive comparison.

The people who lived on this spot today, like 99 percent of Scots, spoke English[1] ...they had never spoken Scottish Gaelic ...but this arbitrary line had ...created a new heritage in its place ...an invented nation had triumphed. *Fàilte gu Alba.*[2]

Such cultural paranoia by no means confines itself to Gaelic. Scotland has not yet quite developed immunity to the Scottish Cringe.[3]

The Cringe may not be as systemic an ailment as it was in Boswell's day, two centuries ago. It is not even so real as it was in the 1990s when, as students, we all received an official leaflet from Aberdeen University's careers office advising us on how to write a C.V. for a job application. This warned us *on no account* to describe our nationality to potential employers as 'Scottish'.

Yet the Scottish Cringe does still break out on Scotland's skin from time to time. There are still those in Scotland, it seems, who have nothing to fear but hope itself. Extending even beyond the shadow of Orangeism and its seedy penumbra, some do politically embrace the condition as a way of life. It is difficult to see other explanations for those few firms which now loyally produce Union-Jack-clad 'British Whisky' and 'The Great British Haggis'. It is similarly difficult to see what else but the deepest of cringes could produce such anxious political reactions as this one, made in response to the shocking proposal that Scots sitting their Higher English exam should have to have learned something about at least *one* Scottish writer:

> Will the Minister ensure that Scottish Studies is taught objectively?...Will the Minister give a cast-iron guarantee that those things will be impartially taught, and will not support a particular point of view? ...Internationalism must be preserved.[4]

Scotland is not superior to anyone. Any claims of such a kind by any nation are self-evidently ridiculous and dangerous. So too, I would merely add to

---

[1] This comment is somewhat at odds with the remark which one south of Scotland Tory once snorted to me in a corridor at Holyrood that 'half' of their constituents in the Borders could 'barely speak English'.
[2] Rory Stewart: *The Marches.* Mr Stewart does not seem to see any invented qualities in Britishness.
[3] Generally defined as feelings of low self-worth which cause some Scots to feel embarassed by seeing or hearing expressions of Scottishness. One scholarly diagnosis of the condition is contained in Craig Beveridge and Ronald Turnbull (eds): *The Eclipse of Scottish Culture.*
[4] Labour MSP Jenny Marra, *Scottish Parliament Official Report*, 29 September 2011.

that, are claims to unique inferiority. Ultimately, I suppose, whether you are taken in by the latter idea all comes down to whether you think you are entering a *real* country at the Carter Bar, or just crossing into another part of what James VI wanted to called the 'Middle Shires'. UK Prime Minister Boris Johnston evidently takes the James VI view:

> I point out to my honourable friend what he knows very well: there is no such thing as a border between England and Scotland.[1]

Yet, curiously, many of these very people who avert their eye from the Scottish Border seem now to take a stance on borders elsewhere that is a hundred times more inflexible than mine. Today, at the Carter Bar there stands one forlorn little monument to that fact.

In 1993, a beacon was erected here on the Border to celebrate the (then fairly uncontentious) creation of the European Single Market. At that time, nobody seriously envisaged a situation where the UK might withdraw, not only from the European Union, but from all the most obvious trading relationships with its European neighbours.[2]

Someone has ripped the plaque off the Carter Bar's European beacon now. It looks rusty. I don't think it has been lit of late. It may – if the reader will momentarily forgive the extreme hyperbole – never be lit again in our lifetimes.[3]

***

The description of today's journey may give a clearer idea of where the Border lies than of where there might be any sensible place to walk. This is because, for virtually the whole of today, there is no path – or anything resembling one. I have tried to map out a reasonably sensible route but it would be fair to judge, from all the information I have, that today is going to be tough going. The area we are walking today is described on a map of 1754 as:

---

[1] Boris Johnson, House of Commons. *Hansard,* 1 July 2020.
[2] In fact, by the time of our walk, speculation was already beginning as to whether the Scottish Border might eventually come to represent a border of the European Union, if an independent Scotland were to return to the EU.
[3] We were walking this section of the route in August 2018, at a time when the UK Government was struggling to work out how to bring its own shambolic Brexit negotiations to any conclusion. At the European referendum in 2016, it is worth recording, 62% of Scots had voted to remain in the EU. All 32 regions of Scotland (including both the Scottish Borders and Dumfries and Galloway) voted to stay in Europe.

Mountainous and desert parts. Uninhabited. A large waste.

This is not inaccurate.

That said, as we look now into Scotland over the grass-tangled border fence at the Carter Bar, it does not look like a desert. Like an eighteenth-century landscape painting, the view in this morning's sunshine draws the eye out over a balanced composition. Layer upon layer of bright green and purple are laid out carefully for miles till, at last, a horizon shows itself in the unarguable form of the Eildons. Then it is the sky's turn to offer streak upon balanced streak of cloud, till the eye is brought back to the foreground of the panorama, and to the obligatory pair of happy peasants, in this case putting on their rucksacks.

Grant and I set out from the border sign. Immediately, a third figure, a lean, grey-bearded hiker, appears in the frame. His stick is covered in little curved badges that record his various mountain conquests. He asks us where we are going and, without waiting for an answer, starts to offer us advice, based on his many expert attacks on various local hills. He means well, but we are quietly relieved to find that he is going with the prevailing wind, and heading east somewhere.

The weather forecast is sunny and remains good, a fact from which Grant and I are to draw isolated flashes of consolation at some of the lower points of today.

***

The once widely-celebrated (but now widely-forgotten) poet James Thomson, who was born not far away in the village of Ednam, spent much of his childhood here in the parish of Southdean in the early eighteenth century.

Burns was induced by one Thomson-fan, the Earl of Buchan, to write an Augustan and not very interesting poem of praise to Thomson.[1] Burns shortly afterwards mocked Buchan (in a better poem) for the prominent role that the Earl gave himself in the annual Thomson commemoration at Ednam:

> Dost thou not rise, indignant shade
> And smile wi' spurning scorn,
> When they wha wad hae starv'd thy life,
> Thy senseless turf adorn.[2]

---

[1] Robert Burns: 'Ode to the Shade of Thomson'.
[2] Robert Burns: 'Extempore on some Commemorations of Thomson'.

Even allowing for some of my own instinctive prejudices about Thomson (who was the author of the words to 'Rule Britannia'), it is difficult to say even charitably that his body of work much stands the exacting test of time:

> ...The plumy people streak their wings with oil,
> And wait th' approaching sign to strike at once
> Into the general choir. Even mountains, vales,
> And forests seem, expansive, to demand
> The promis'd sweetness. Man superior walks
> Amid the glad creation, musing praise.[1]

The History of Scottish Literature generously says that Thomson and his imitators were, as poets, 'by no means uniformly bad.'[2] It is, however, sorely tempting to ask what powerful dislike Thomson could have had for a simple word like 'birds' that could possibly have driven him to say 'the plumy people' instead.[3]

***

We go south-westwards from the Carter Bar, briefly following the Border as it forms the southern edge of the forest. The line then heads over the top of Catcleugh Shin onto a seemingly unlimited open plateau. Ahead of us lie more expansive skies. The battered little livestock fence runs far off to the horizon, contentedly marking the edge of Scotland.

An American friend, seeing a picture of this fence on my Facebook page, commented that, when set beside some of the more sinister border fences elsewhere,[4] this one is pleasantly understated and unthreatening. It is also a very convenient guide for us, in the absence of any path. The fence, we conclude, is our friend, and we start our walk along its Scottish side. It has been a dry summer, and small pools have become strange, isolated mudflats under our feet. There is little sign of sheep or cattle, and already the heather is knee-high in places. Among it, Grant and I soon find ourselves picking our way across a few incongruous and long-forgotten remnants of little coal workings.

---

[1] James Thomson: *The Seasons.*
[2] Mary Jane Scott, in *The History of Scottish Literature.*
[3] Having said all that, Thomson's *The Seasons* was probably an influence on Alasdair Mac Mhaighstir Alasdair's 'Òran an t-Samhraidh' and 'Òran a' Gheamhraidh', which are far more interesting poetic takes on the same subject.
[4] In November 2018, President Donald J. Trump shocked a world by then already desensitised to his tweets, when he told a cheering crowd that 'barbed wire, if used properly, can be a beautiful sight'.

Though the day is bright, this is a lonely and slightly uneasy landscape in places. We look south towards the English Redesdale Valley, and imagine the sound of gunfire from the Otterburn Ranges.

This is in fact a place with a particularly sinister literary association. Where we are trudging now is where Robert Wringhim, the central and terrifying character of James Hogg's masterly novel *Confessions of a Justified Sinner*, is described fleeing manically at the very end of his life. He is being pursued by the Devil, or his own subconscious, or both.[1]

Hogg (the 'Ettrick Shepherd') had a very humble background, a fact that allowed him to write much more irreverently than Scott. He left school aged six, to work as a herd, when his father's farm failed. Hogg's initial education therefore came directly from the oral tradition of the Borders, through his mother Margaret Laidlaw, famed for her repertoire of songs, and from his grandfather Will Laidlaw.[2]

In the *Justified Sinner*, Wringhim wanders from house to house on the Border here, crossing our own path and provoking noisy apparitions in the byres he sleeps in, as he shambles northwards towards his death. Wringhim records in his diary:

> August 3, 1712 – This morning the hind has brought me word from Redesdale, whither he had been for coals, that a stranger gentleman had been traversing that country, making the most earnest inquiries after me, or one of the same appearance; and, from the description that he brought of this stranger, I could easily perceive who it was. Rejoicing that my tormentor has lost traces of me for once, I am making haste to leave my asylum, on pretence of following this stranger, but in reality to conceal myself still more completely from his search. Perhaps this may be the last sentence ever I am destined to write.[3]

Hogg produces for us here a very specific type of Calvinist, one whose excess is not, as might idly be assumed, in some pharisaic idolatry for the Law, but in its polar opposite – antinomianism. This latter idea requires some explanation to a modern audience, but is essentially the premise that, once the Elect have been predestined to be saved, it is largely a matter of irrelevance whether they then lead good or wicked lives.[4] Emboldened by this particular

---

[1] Hogg never quite reassures the reader completely as to which of these two it is.
[2] We will encounter Laidlaw shortly on our walk, in the context of the fairies.
[3] Hogg, James: *The Private Memoirs and Confessions of a Justified Sinner*.

doctrinal outlook, Hogg's character is a genuine serial killer, created a century before the reading public was quite ready for one:

> [It was] more congenial to my nature to be cutting sinners off with the sword than to be haranguing them from the pulpit, striving to produce an effect which God, by His absolute predestination, had for ever rendered impracticable.

Yet the Ettrick Shepherd, as always, leaves the door open to both rational and supernatural explanations of events. If it is the latter here, then this is not the jokey Auld Nick of Burns, or the unnervingly human Satan of Milton that Hogg has set loose across our path today. This is – forgive me – the real Deil.

***

We trudge on to Duntae Edge. This will be hard going. I bear in mind that J.L. Mack described Duntae Edge as:

> ... the most evil piece of ground which I encountered on the Border Line from sea to sea.

It doesn't seem all that bad. But then Grant and I haven't quite realised yet that we are lost.

Here at Duntae Edge, the Border briefly becomes the Black Needle Burn as it heads south. Mack describes this stretch as difficult and wet walking, and the map suggests it looks safer to follow the burn than to go near the 'area of shakeholes' which are marked between here and the forest to our west. Where this burn meets the Green Needle Burn, a path of sorts leads up to a good viewpoint at Wylie's Craig. Here, on a clear day, is said to be a fine view west and east. It perhaps rivals the Carlin's Tooth, which claims to be a very rare place in Scotland where the Solway Firth and the North Sea can both just about be seen at once.

Unfortunately, today we see none of this. We err together away from the Border by loyally following the fence (which Grant and I are soon no longer to regard as our friend). It misleads us into a dense, deer-leaping conifer wood which engulfs us and then spits us out well inside Northumberland. We can see a lonely

---

[4] Something pretty close to this theology had been espoused by Rev Thomas Boston, in Hogg's native Ettrick, in the period during which the novel is set. I was startled to hear a visiting preacher quote Boston favourably during a Gaelic service in the Isle of Lewis within the last ten years.

farmhouse now, something we did not expect. We are at Kielderhead.

I make a mental note not to walk into a forest again without taking a compass bearing first. Possibly because Grant was a Territorial, I am suddenly reminded, for some reason, of a story which a Swiss friend tells about her father. All the men in her village were doing their required annual military training one year. They got lost, and accidentally invaded Lichtenstein. I decide not to tell Grant the story, in case it comes across as pointed in any way. We are both equally culpable.

In fact, we have only wandered a mile-and-a-half or so from the Border, but we have lost height, and the climb up the Scaup Burn and Kielderstone Cleugh back to the ridge again is a slow and gruelling one. We clamber first upwards through an assault course of felled trees. A carpet of rotting grey branches gives way like a series of little elephant-traps under our every step, and we trip continuously over large tree stumps for around an hour.

I don't mind variable weather, and I enjoy a walk even when it has its tribulations. The reader should not trust those hillwalkers though who try to claim they enjoy every minute of every walk. I have more respect for the honest assessments of J.L. Mack who, a century ago on a wet day here, described the terrain he found under him by saying:

> There is no pleasure to be derived from it.

Suddenly, I have a horror of what might happen if the expert and talkative hiker whom we met at the Carter Bar were suddenly and unaccountably to reappear, and offer us cheery advice about why we should not have come this way. Not being of Robert Wringhim's murderous disposition, I am alarmed that the thought does flash, briefly and unbidden, across my mind that *it would take a long time for him to be found out here.*

For another hour after the tree stumps, we clamber up through dense heather and ferns and moss, and every other substance on which man was never intended to walk, up the side of the Kielderstone Cleugh. It is the kind of walking where I cannot comment much on the scenery, as I have to concentrate on what I see underfoot, trying to guess where my next footfall will land. The guidebook had promised of the Black Needle Burn:

> ...thyme, catspaw, rock roses and the yellow mountain pansy.[1]

---

[1] Alan Hall: *The Border Country: A Walker's Guide.*

I see bog-cotton, blaeberries, downie thistles, hairy oobits.

***

At last though, we see the Kielder Stane. We are back on our route, and back in Scotland. The Kielder Stane is a huge and impressive 1,500-ton natural lump of sandstone. The Border makes a point of going in a tiny horseshoe here, just so it can say it has gone through the middle of the stone.[1] Some accounts suggest that the cracks in the stone's side were used in centuries past as a very remote post office box address, where reivers and others left each other cryptic messages. It seems a long way to come.

In fact, the role of the Kielder Stane in reiving legend is possibly owed, in the main, to comparatively recent poets. John Leyden's 'The Coutt of Keeldar' is for instance included in Scott's *Minstrelsy*, but this gothic effort is clearly not an old ballad:

> Green vervain round its base did creep,
> A powerful seed that bore;
> And oft, of yore its channels deep
> Were stain'd with human gore.
>
> And still, when blood-drops clotted thin,
> Hang the grey moss upon,
> The spirit murmers from within,
> And shakes the rocking stone.[2]

It is said to be unlucky to go around the stone three times widdershins (i.e. anticlockwise). As the background reading for today has been quite supernatural in theme, and as our good luck has not been unalloyed, we err on the side of caution. Un-angered, the stone does not shake today.[3]

---

[1] This little kink in the line seems to date from 1778, when agreements were reached about disputed land ownership here. Up until the first half of the nineteenth century, however, there seems to have been continuing disagreement about the status of some land here around the Carlin's Tooth and Hartshorn Pike. Both of these hills eventually ended up in Scotland, while a section of Peel Fell ended up in England. These are probably questions of detail not completely resolved until the Ordnance Survey maps came out in the 1860s. A number of boundary stones in this area seek, however, to mark a line between the domains of the Percies and the Douglases and, in so doing, to mark the Border.

[2] John Leyden: 'The Coutt of Keelder', from Scott's *Minstrelsy of the Scottish Border*.

[3] In a similar (not entirely serious) spirit of honouring local superstitions, many years ago Malc and I tried to propitiate the Cheese Well on Minchmoor near Traquair. One

The Border heads south-west, in the form of the Kielderstone Cleugh, up to its source on Peel Fell near Jenny Storie's Stone, which looks south over Deadwater Fell.[1]

On Peel Fell, the panoramic view alone would make the last couple of hours worthwhile. In the late afternoon's light, the world is cobalt blue for untold miles around. A blazing red tongue on the horizon is, I think, the Solway Firth, providing for the first time some visible idea of where our walk is ultimately taking us. In Scotland, we can see across to the Cheviot, Yarrow and Ettrick, as well as – just – to Skiddaw and Blencathra in the English lakes.

Somewhere just to our north-west here, lost in the forest, are two ancient roads into Upper Liddesdale. These are the Whele Causay and another track strangely called 'Note o the Gait'. The latter is thought to have been travelled in November 1745 by Bonnie Prince Charlie, after a disappointing recruitment drive in Jedburgh and Kelso. The Prince is supposed to have muttered, as he made his way into England, 'Tak note o the gait'.[2] The last part of this sounds more than unlikely,[3] but is worth it as a story, if only to imagine today, from this high vantage, the distant sight of Charles Edward and his long train of Highlanders, trailing their tartan way over this landscape, as they head for Derby.

***

In the mid nineteenth century, an awe-struck visitor to the poet John Leyden's birthplace at Cavers near Denholm[4] remarked:

> It is not every day we stand under the thatch-clad roof
> …where was born one whose name time will bear written
> in undying characters on its wings until those wings droop
> in the darkness of eternity.[5]

---

is supposed to keep the fairies here happy by making them offerings of cheese, dropped into the spring. Having walked for some days by that point, Malc and I unfortunately had no cheese left, so we offered the fairies 'Smash', a then-popular brand of instant mashed potato. The well erupted angrily in a spray of foaming, other-worldly tatties.

[1] Deadwater Fell lies a couple of miles within England but was chosen as the title for a 2020 Channel 4 Scottish murder mystery starring David Tennant. Filmed in Dunlop, Ayrshire, the name of the hill was presumably chosen simply for its eeriness.

[2] i.e. 'remember the road', a remark which was perhaps held to be the Prince making a mental note of the way back to Scotland, should he need to retreat north (as of course he did).

[3] Walter Elliot points out that the road's name is much more likely to refer to a 'notch' (i.e. narrow stretch) of the road, where it passes between hills.

[4] Not far from Hawick.

[5] *Wilson's Tales of the Borders,* Vol. VIII.

In 1902, W.S. Crockett describes how Leyden's birthplace was open to tourists every day, and says, 'Leyden's name is not likely to be forgotten'. [1] In fact, it very largely has been. It is not readily possible to find anything even half-recently in print under Leyden's name.

Perhaps, however, a few words of Leyden's poetry do live on in the public imagination. 'The Ballad of Sir Patrick Spens' is a genuinely old ballad to which Leyden is likely to have made a few (worthy) additions before he contributed it to Scott's *Minstrelsy*. [2] Some of the best-loved lines in the Scottish ballad tradition are therefore likely to be partly Leyden's own work:

> To Noroway, to Noroway,
> To Noroway o'er the faem;
> The King's daughter of Noroway,
> 'Tis thou maun bring her hame. [3]

While Leyden's own poetic output may be mixed, this son of a Teviotdale shepherd exceeded even the expectations of a 'lad o pairts'. He is described as having delighted high society ('notwithstanding the repulsive sharpness of his native accent'[4]) with his endless knowledge. Leyden studied for the ministry but was a 'stickit meinister' (i.e. one to whom no congregation ever actually offered a job). Still, he kept picking up languages – Latin, French, German, Italian, Old Icelandic, Persian, Hindi. He collected a medical degree with ease, becoming a surgeon in the East India Company.

After a while as a hospital superintendent in Madras (where he mastered another few languages), Leyden died in Java in 1811 aged 35. He is said to have spoken some 36 languages by the time of his death. It is doubtful whether any individual in Scotland can beat that record, and for that distinguished fact alone, Leyden's short life deserves some recognition. [5]

***

Lost somewhere, a couple of miles into the modern forest on our west now,

---

[1] W.S. Crockett: *The Scott Country*.

[2] See Thomas Crawford: *Walter Scott*.

[3] *Minstrelsy of the Scottish Border*.

[4] Rev James Morton, in his introduction to *The Poetical Remains of the Late Dr John Leyden*.

[5] By a strange coincidence, the village of Denholm also produced another linguistic genius, Professor James Murray, who single-handedly compiled what was eventually to become the *Oxford English Dictionary*.

are the remains of the Wheel[1] Kirk. Edward I of England spent the night here in 1296, on his way back from his atrocities at Berwick, and on his way to do cursory penance (for these or other unspecified crimes) at the shrine of St Ninian in Galloway. In 1347, his grandson Edward III made clerical appointments to the Wheel Kirk, to emphasise what he viewed as his right at that time to southern Scotland.

From here, Grant and I head downhill for a while, along a three-inch-wide gap in the heather. This sheep-track, after today's pathless expedition, feels like a veritable escalator by comparison. Then we go briefly through another forest, Myredykes Plantation, and follow the tree-line, which yet again is the Border, past Rushyknowe. Finally, we see ahead of us, over a watery country of mosses and felled trees, the neighbouring farms of Deadwater (England) and Myredykes (Scotland). Between the two farms, parked beside the 'Scotland' sign, is the car.

The two farmhouses do not, in likelihood, mean to look quite as accusingly as they do, either at us or at each other. Yet they watch as pointedly over the landscape as do the birds of prey which land on the lone trees, left here and there for their use in these felled forests. We tread around rushes and into long, wet grass, while unseen crows lecture us in sarcastic terms. The sobering grey landscape is strangely appropriate for the Covenanters' conventicle which was described being held here three centuries ago.[2] Perhaps thinking of these events, one writer has bravely offered the assessment that:

Deadwater was not always so dull and depressed as it is now.[3]

This place stands in great contrast to our starting point today at the Carter Bar. Deadwater is perhaps the least-celebrated of all road-crossings of the Border, the least likely of all to inspire any piper to stand waiting for tourists. Deadwater is impressive on its own lonely terms though. Here is not the Border of Sir Walter Scott's pageantry, but the Border which Alexander Gray was perhaps thinking of:

Through fields where the ghosts

---

[1] Often also spelled 'Whele'.
[2] See 'The Shoes Reversed' by Thomas Gillespie, from *Wilson's Tales of the Borders*, Vol. XX. A number of lonely places like this along the Border line recall these events, including Peden's Cleugh at Southdean and Peden's Stone at Castleton, both of which refer to outdoor sermons given there by the Ayrshire preacher Alexander Peden. Incidentally, Peden (if the reader wishes to make the acquaintance) makes a cameo appearance on the Bass Rock in the Firth of Forth in Robert Louis Stevenson's *Catriona*.
[3] John Byers: *Liddesdale*.

Of the marsh and the moorland
Still ride the old marches,
Despising the plough.

This is my country,
The land that begat me.
These windy spaces
Are surely my own.
And those who here toil
In the sweat of their faces
Are flesh of my flesh,
And bone of my bone.[1]

---

[1] Alexander Gray: 'Scotland', from *Selected Poems*.

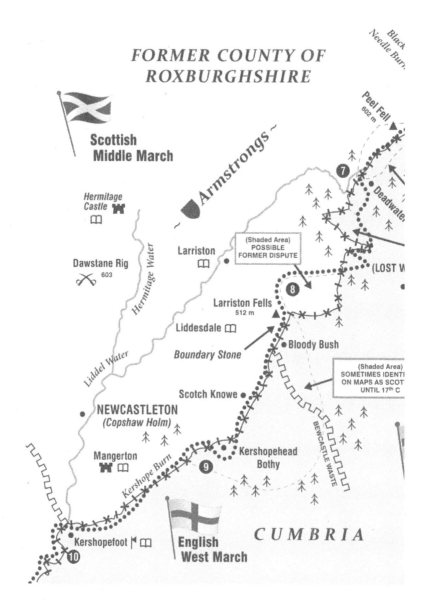

FORMER COUNTY OF
ROXBURGHSHIRE

*Black
Needle Burn*

Scottish
Middle March

Armstrongs

Peel Fell
602 m

Hermitage
Castle

7

Deadwater

Dawstane Rig
603

Larriston

(Shaded Area)
POSSIBLE
FORMER DISPUTE

8

(LOST W

Hermitage Water

Larriston Fells
512 m

Liddesdale

Boundary Stone

Bloody Bush

(Shaded Area)
SOMETIMES IDENTI
ON MAPS AS SCOT
UNTIL 17th C

Liddel Water

Scotch Knowe

NEWCASTLETON
(Copshaw Holm)

Mangerton

Kershope Burn

Kershopehead
Bothy

9

BEWCASTLE WASTE

Kershopefoot

10

English
West March

CUMBRIA

Map 5: The southern ends of the Middle Marches, from Carter Fell to the
Kershope Burn.

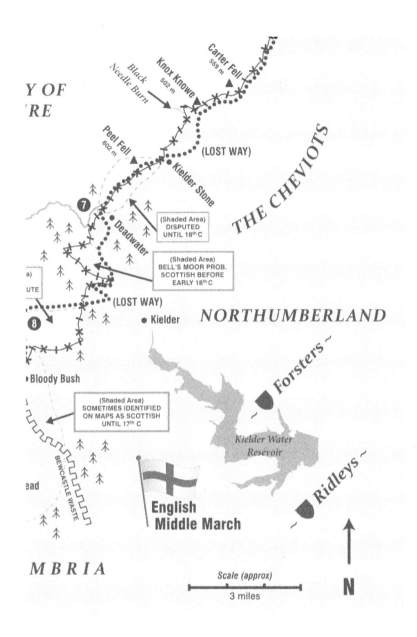

Y OF
'RE

Black
Needle Burn

Knox Knowe
502 m

Carter Fell
559 m

Peel Fell
602 m

Kielder Stone

(LOST WAY)

THE CHEVIOTS

7

Deadwater

(Shaded Area)
DISPUTED
UNTIL 18th C

(Shaded Area)
BELL'S MOOR PROB.
SCOTTISH BEFORE
EARLY 18th C

a)

UTE

(LOST WAY)

8

• Kielder

NORTHUMBERLAND

Forsters ~

►Bloody Bush

(Shaded Area)
SOMETIMES IDENTIFIED
ON MAPS AS SCOTTISH
UNTIL 17th C

Kielder Water
Resevoir

BEWCASTLE WASTE

ead

Ridleys ~

**English
Middle March**

M B R I A

Scale (approx)

3 miles

N

Day 7: From Deadwater to Larriston Fells

Circa 4 miles of actual Border. (Very considerably longer, as a walk, when the errors described below are included)

The Catrail and Y Gododdin; Ghost trains; Wild men of Liddesdale; Hermitage Castle; Newcastleton; The Bells Burn; Lost among the Sitka spruce; Is Scotland real?; Larriston Fells; Kielder; Last train to Deadwater.

I drive southwards from Hawick towards the Ideal Line,[1] stopping to take in the view at Robert's Linn on the Slitrig Water.

Here, with the aid of a tourist information notice board, I can see, beyond an ocean of ferns, the Catrail. This is perhaps another ancient border, but one which ran, not east-to-west, but north-to-south. It is in fact a system of earthworks and ditches, extending from here perhaps[2] as far north as Roberton or Galashiels. Barely discernible in most places, it has sometimes been argued that the Catrail marked an old boundary, at some point, between the Britons and the Saxons. The notice board explains this, in dubiously epic terms, as a struggle between St Kentigern and the wizard Merlin.

In an even older time, before the Saxons, the people on each side of this boundary (or one somewhere near it) were *both* speaking something resembling Welsh. These were the Selgovae (or Rheged) on the west and the Gododdin (or Votadini) on the east. The kingdom of the Gododdin stretched southwards from their capital in Din Eidynn (Edinburgh) into what is now northern England, until the Angles defeated the Gododdin at the battle of Catraeth.[3]

Y Gododdin, is almost certainly the oldest known substantial literary work written in Scotland. It was probably composed somewhere between our own Border and Edinburgh, and praises heroes of the Battle of Cartraeth,[4] perhaps around the end of the sixth century:

> *O winveith a medweith yd aethant*
> *E genhyn llurugogyon*
> *Nys gwn lleith lletkynt*
> *Cyn llwyded eu lleas dydaruu*
> *Rac catraeth oed fraeth eu llu*
> *O osgord vynydawc wawr dru*
> *O drychant namen un gwr ny dyvu*

---

[1] A name which a century or two ago seems to have been regularly used for the Border.
[2] The emphasis here should be on the word 'perhaps'.
[3] Some have linked the name of the *Catrail* here with *Catraeth*. Others (that is to admit, most people) have identified the site of the battle at Catterick in Yorkshire.
[4] The poem possibly synthesises the story of several smaller conflicts in this period.

O winveith a medveith yt gryssyassant
Gwyr en reit moleit eneit dichwant
Gloew dull y am drull yt gytvaethant
Gwin a med amall a amucsant
O osgord vynydawc am dwyf atveillyawc
A rwyf a golleis om gwir garant
O drychan riallu yt gryssyassant
Gatraeth tru namen vn gwr nyt atcorsant

(From the feast of wine and the banquet of mead, they marched
To the strife of mail-clad warriors;
I know no tale of slaughter which records
So complete a destruction.
Before Cattraeth loquacious was the host;
But of the retinue of Mynyddawg, greatly to be deplored,
Out of three hundred men, only one returned.
From the feast of wine and the banquet of mead, with speed they marched,
Men renowned in difficulty, prodigal of their lives;
In fairest order round the viands they together feasted;
Wine and mead and tribute they enjoyed.
From the retinue of Mynyddawg ruin has come to me;
And I have lost my general and my true friends.
Of the regal army of three hundred men that hastened to Cattraeth,
Alas! none have returned, save one alone.[1]

Seeing the Catrail stretch more or less at right-angles away from our own Border provides some cautionary sense of perspective to anyone making the kind of arguments I have been making. It is as well to remember, from time to time, that there were once other tribal groups, before Scotland or England were thought of as countries.

The Catrail does not, however – lest the reader think I am going soft – make the case that Rory Stewart and some others have made for doubting the national existence of Scotland. National identities start in the here and now,

---

[1] Aneirin: *Y Gododdin* (Rev John Williams, ed)

with Irn Bru and *Still Game*, and stretch behind us into a venerable past. They do not start some time arbitrarily in the sixth century and peer forward into succeeding ages, looking for archaeological evidence of nationhood.

I keep driving.

***

There was a railway here once, from Edinburgh to Carlisle, but it closed over half a century ago now, perhaps prompting the unkind remark:

What's the quickest way to get to the Borders?
Invent a time machine and go back fifty years.

There are a number of ways to read the joke.

And yet, lost high up in these hills, as incongruous as the Soviet ships that lie stranded in the dried-up Aral Sea, sit some ghostly railway carriages and a little locomotive. Here, entirely disconnected now from the rest of Britain's rail network, lie a mile or two of functioning railway line in the form of the intriguing but little-publicised Whitrope Heritage Centre. It is only open on Saturdays, so I am not really sure what happens here. A notice explains that you can get a cup of tea, see an exhibition and get a wee hurl along a bit of railway.

I drive on into Liddesdale.

***

The reader – after reading this chapter – is more likely to take a car down Liddesdale to see its historic sites than to traipse on foot (as I inevitably will) along the actual Border a few miles to the south. So I will permit myself to say something about a place or two here in Liddesdale, before I start walking.

I check the weather forecast on my phone. The Met Office curiously predicts entirely opposite weather for the villages of Kielder and Newcastleton, a couple of miles on each side of the Border here. I don't claim that this proves anything (lest the reader still cannot tell when I am joking). In any case, Liddesdale is surely one of the wettest places in Europe. It once had a reputation as being one of the wildest too, a claim based as much on its people as on its landscape.

In Liddesdale, reiving was not merely a form of occasional lawlessness, but was elevated into a system of government. It certainly became a system of literature:

They cross'd the Liddel at curfew hour,
And burn'd my little lonely tower;
The fiend receive their souls therefor!
It had not been burned this year and more.
Barn-yard and dwelling, blazing bright,
Serv'd to guide me on my flight;
But I was chas'd the livelong night.
Black John of Akeshaw, and Fergus Graeme,
Fast upon my traces came.[1]

If the former reputation of Liddesdale is difficult to credit now, then it is as well to consider some reports of the place in the sixteenth century. In 1553, the Lord Treasurer of Scotland recorded the purchase of 'ane byrnyng irne to byrn the thevis of Lyddisdale on the cheik.'[2] In an agreement in the 1520s, the King of Scotland cheerfully admitted the right of the King of England to 'invade, burn rob, slaughter, reive and destroy' in Liddesdale 'at his gracious pleasure',[3] as a means of mutually-beneficial crowd-control. All of this led a shocked apocryphal visitor to Liddesdale in this era to ask 'Are there nae Christians here?', to which he received the reply: 'Na. Oo're aw Elliots an Airmstrangs'.

I drive up to Hermitage Castle, the most famous, complete and palpably sinister of the fortifications that give the parish of Castleton its name. Much of the castle is fourteenth-century, and parts of it older. Early inhabitants included the Lord Soulis who tradition says was in 1320 boiled alive by his tenants in a cauldron in the nearby stone circle on Nine Stane Rig, a story which sadly does not have much reliable basis in fact, but which certainly produces a vivid image:

They rolled him up in a sheet of lead,
A sheet of lead for a funeral pall;
They plunged him in the cauldron red,
And melted him, lead and bones and all.[4]

Another poem tells how the Cout of Kielder and his men once sat anxiously in Hermitage Castle, watching out for any signal that their host's good will

---

[1] Sir Walter Scott: *Lay of the Last Minstrel*.
[2] From the Lord Treasurer of Scotland's Accounts, 1553.
[3] Quoted, among others, by George MacDonald Fraser in *The Steel Bonnets*.
[4] John Leyden: 'Lord Soulis', from *Poems and Ballads*.

was at an end. This sign was normally the serving of a bull's head, but the guests do not realise until too late that even the playing of a tune *mentioning* a bull counts for this purpose:

> ...To wilder measures next they turn:
> 'The Black Black Bull of Noroway'!
> Sudden the tapers cease to burn,
> The minstrels cease to play.[1]

Hermitage was where Mary Queen of Scots rode out to from Jedburgh on 16 October 1566 to meet her lover, the Earl of Bothwell. He had recently been wounded by one of the men of Liddesdale, Little Jock Elliot.[2]

Legend holds that Hermitage is literally sinking under the weight of its own iniquity, but there is little evidence for this. The strikingly brutal appearance of the castle is, however, not softened by today's light rain.

***

I head on for the village of Newcastleton, three miles inside Scotland, and better known to its inhabitants by its old name of Copshaw Holm.[3] The official name of the village reflects the fact that the people of nearby Old Castleton were moved into a new planned village here at the end of the eighteenth century.[4]

It is difficult to think of a very long list of places in Lowland Scotland that are as respectably big as Newcastleton (population 770), but at the same time quite so far from anywhere else. Newcastleton's situation seems, curiously, to have given it simultaneously the wakefulness of a border post, the lively local importance of a market town and all the self-containment of an island. The last comes of being a whole twenty miles (by a winding and often single track road) from the nearest large town, Hawick.[5] The village sits trig and trim around its green. It has three pubs (two of them, surprisingly, right next door to each other), three or four shops, a kirk, a school and a heritage centre.

---

[1] John Leyden: 'The Cout of Keelder'.
[2] Bothwell ended his days insane and kept captive in the Danish Castle of Dragsholm. Tourists in Dragsholm could view what was said to be Bothwell's body, and look for the scar on his forehead inflicted by Little Jock Elliot, until the present Queen of Denmark decided that enough was enough, and his coffin was finally closed.
[3] Pronounced '**Cop**-shae **Home**'.
[4] The ruins of Liddel Castle, at Old Castleton, are where we meet Fergus of Galloway in the *Roman de Fergus* (see Day 3).
[5] The much smaller town of Langholm is a little nearer to hand.

The main road goes through the middle of the village but there is little evidence of through-traffic. Until the 1960s, there were three railway stations in this parish. In fact, the railways largely got to this area before the roads did. A number of tiny communities around here then effectively disappeared along with the trains. The population of Newcastleton itself famously physically blocked the last train on its way to Carlisle, to express their justifiable fears about what the future would hold for them without a railway. One village poet commented in 1969:

> When Beeching's pen, and no his brain,
> Left us aa without a train,
> He cut oor railway wi impunity
> And left the Holm a puir community.[1]

Today however there is much bunting in evidence in Newcastleton, and I ask a passing lady why this is. 'Dae ye no ken it's for VE Day?' she replies, her brow furrowed in wonder at my stupidity. I almost press her as to why the 73rd anniversary of VE Day should be marked with so much more ceremony in Newcastleton than in the rest of the country, and – more to the point – why four months later. But I think it wise to ask no more.

In 1795, around the time of the new village's construction, the minister of this parish was James Arkle,[2] who clearly wondered quite how he ended up here. He describes Liddesdale as 'bleak and wild to a high degree', and notes that until a few years earlier, 'not a yard of road has attempted to be formed' in his parish:

> There is much intercourse with Hawick and Langholm
> …but the difficulty of travelling to those places is
> inconceivable. Through these deep and broken bogs and
> mosses we must crawl, to the great fatigue of ourselves, but
> the even greater injury of our horses.[3]

---

[1] Marius Ferguson Carruthers: 'The Waverley Line', from Walter Elliot: *The New Minstrelsy of the Scottish Border*. The reference is to Richard Beeching, whose recommendations as chairman of British Railways in 1963 resulted in 4,000 miles of railway being abandoned.

[2] While on the subject of Liddesdale ministers, perhaps the most unlikely son of the Liddesdale manse worth mentioning here would be Dr John Armstrong, who published a sex-manual in blank verse (*The Oeconomy of Love*, London, T. Cooper, 1736).

[3] *Statistical Account of Scotland.*

Arkle adds grimly that local tradition asserts that earth taken from Liddesdale is considered so accursed that a handful of it will have the effect of banishing rats in nearby Teviotdale.

The landlord of the Grapes Hotel looks at me doubtfully when I say where exactly my friend Alan Masterton and I plan to walk tomorrow. I have a lingering fear that Alan, brought up as he was between the roundabouts[1] of Cumbernauld, is going to concur, when he arrives here tomorrow, with the bleak assessments of Rev James Arkle.

***

The next morning, I meet up with Alan in Newcastleton's Douglas Square.

Alan emerged, after seven years as my employee, as my good friend. He will not, however, escape unscarred from the next section of the walk. I hope and trust he will still be my friend.[2]

Describing Alan with isolated pieces of information does not quite do him justice. I could mention his degree in Celtic languages, or the tattooed political messages up his arms (along with what seem to be unrelated images of goblins and lighthouses). I could mention his fondness for zombie films or for biscuits. Each of these things gives a possibly incomplete and misleading picture. Alan is in fact is a very efficient local councillor in North Lanarkshire.

We have hopes of walking all the way from Deadwater to the Kershopehead bothy today, going deep into the heart of the Newcastleton and Kershope forests, but this is not to be. St Paul warns that 'The letter kills, but the Spirit gives life'.[3] Regrettably, my interpretation of the Narrow Way along the Border today is to prove, like so many types of fundamentalism, to be actively dangerous. This will turn out to be far and away the most unpleasant day's walking either of us has had in our lives.

Still, taken in the round, I think it will be worth doing; even if the four miles' progress along the Border which we will notch up today is not, of itself, impressive. I will realise our predicament only some time after we start walking today – and long after Alan has realised it.

If the reader is tempted to follow our route today, please do not.

***

---

[1] The curious reader will have to wait a little farther still for any explanation of the wider significance of roundabouts in this story.
[2] He is.
[3] *2 Corinthians*, Ch 3: v 4-6.

Deadwater Farm is inside England by a field. Alan and I begin our walk from here. Unbelievably, there was once a railway station here. The Border Counties Railway branched improbably off the Waverley line at Riccarton Junction and headed along the banks of the North Tyne, over the Border and on towards the village of Bellingham. Deadwater was a station so isolated that it did not even have a proper road all the way up to it.

From the old station, Alan and I look hopefully down the line of the former railway track. Just beyond the station somewhere lies Hawkhope Hole. This was once the site, according to an interesting local tradition, of a village created by families fleeing from the clearances in other parts of Scotland. Two hundred years ago, it consisted of about eighteen smallholdings.[1]

By walking the railway southwards for a couple of miles, we are in fact missing out one odd little angle of the Border. Instead of following that corner, we briefly take a straighter shortcut over the most solid ground I can see in this boggy little corner of England. It is the safest and most pragmatic decision I am to take today.

The Bells Moor, this triangle of unwalkable land, whose hypotenuse is around two-and-a-half miles long, was almost certainly once in Scotland. So, by coincidence, the railway probably takes us more or less along an older version of the Border. We are not making any irredentist statement by taking this particular route. We are just taking a shortcut. A dispute between landowners over Bells Moor, probably around three centuries ago, seems the most likely reason for the long, strange and otherwise unexplained dog-leg in the Border that exists here now.[2] Whatever the reason, one little part of England here now lies to Scotland's north.

The old railway meets the road at an isolated house at Bellsburnfoot. Walking any further south on the road here would take us into the village of Kielder but, instead of (sensibly) so doing, we leave the road and head right. We follow the northern edge of the Kielder Forest until we come to Scotland at Bells Linn. Here are the remnants of the medieval Bell Kirk. Eric Robson says that a large block with what may have been a baptismal font in it survives inside the ruined farm buildings that stand now on the site.[3] When the Border followed its old course, before Bell's Moor changed hands, the Bell Kirk

---

[1] I have been unable to find out any more about this intriguing story, or indeed any explanation as to why evicted families from elsewhere chose such an isolated spot, exactly on the Border line, to make new lives. If the reader can tell me, I would be very interested to hear.

[2] An alternative (and entirely possible) explanation for the Bells Moor anomaly is given by Nigel Tranter in his novel *Sword of State*. In this fictionalised account of the thirteenth-century boundary commissioners, Tranter has them reaching a view that if Kershope Castle was in England, then so too should be the lands around this area.

[3] Eric Robson: *The Border Line.*

(which served as a meeting place for the Wardens) would have been a few yards inside Scotland.[1] Today, it is a few yards inside England.

We want to follow the Bell's Burn, which is the Border here, but to do that we need to cross one of its tributaries. This is a task more easily said than done. We clamber through dense orange bracken and ferns, up to our shoulders.

We climb two fences and conclude that the only way across the burn is to wade, which we do. I manage, momentarily, to drop one of Alan's boots, not (as he is later to complain on Facebook) into the burn, but into a pool beside it. It is no less wet for the distinction, I concede.

At the little waterfall at Bells Linn, we head west through more ferns and bracken to follow the English edge of the Border to Anthon's Linn. From there, we plan to cross the burn northwards, back into Scotland. It is heavy going underfoot. The Border here, heading southwards, is still the Bells Burn, which we jump a couple of times at this, one of the more obscure of Border crossings.

We look for Anthon's Linn, another little waterfall on the Border, possibly named after a lawless Englishman by the name of Anton Armstrong, who led a revolt in Liddesdale in 1541, burned Bewcastle, and enraged Henry VIII. Sadly, we do not quite find Anthon's Linn. The burn takes us into the depth of the forest. Initially, this is quite interesting. On the outskirts of the forest, there are wildlife, carpets of red fungi, daylight, room to walk. We follow, it is probable, the wrong sike,[2] and with too much confidence.

The forest we are walking now had extended by the 1970s to cover an area bigger than London. This is not the old Jed Forest of huge oaks or Scots pines though. We struggle now against another species altogether – Sitka spruce – first merely brushing the branches away from our faces, then actively tearing at them with a genuine hatred. We soon both wish we had come armed with machetes. I visualise us hacking our way through the jungle, to tell the people of Newcastleton that the war is over.

***

In the depths of a forestry plantation, even the most dedicated national romantic has to start talking about borders in very slightly ironic terms. This is probably healthy, occasionally. After seventy or so miles of meditating on the Border, I feel it is acceptable to be a little postmodern about it now, at least fleetingly. Alan demands, nonetheless, to know which country we are in. For once, I genuinely don't know. His look is an accusing one. Should I

---

[1] Mack reports that the kirk was certainly considered to be in Scotland in 1604. It has however been marked on maps as English since the late eighteenth century.
[2] A sike is a watercourse one size smaller than a burn.

make something up? I sense he will know.

Trying to think what someone of actual substance might do in this situation, I recall a scene in the film *Max Manus*, where the Norwegian wartime resistance hero of that name is walking with his friend from Norway into neutral Sweden, to re-group there with other Norwegian patriots. As they trudge through the endless dark impenetrable forests, Manus stops and announces, tongue in cheek:

> «*Vi må da være i Sverige nå. Merker du ikke det hvordan naturen sakte forvandles, blir mer svensk?*»[1]

I feel I got the joke anyway. It may be the wrong moment to explain it to Alan though.

I dwell on the strange fact that, for the first time for me on this whole expedition, the Border really is invisible. I no longer see a disembodied line stretching out ahead of me.

The experience reminds me, oddly, that as a Scot you regularly meet people who seem to believe that you come from a country that does not quite *exist*. It is doubtful whether this experience can be good for a person. In the U.S., I have been asked whether Scotland is 'mythical or real'. In London, I have been asked whether Glasgow is 'on the mainland of England', and even in Scotland I have listened to professors airily explain to me that the country I come from was 'extinguished'[2] in 1707.

I quote extreme examples in all these categories (as the reader will have seen, by now, is my tendency). However, if Scots were to take these types of claims to non-existence at all seriously (as sadly some do) they would certainly find that it impacted on them psychologically.[3] So too, it begins to cross my mind, might I be stuck in this forest for very much longer.

I look at the map for encouragement. The place names along this stretch of the Border do not provide any: Sour Shank, Foul Mire, Drowning Sike.

---

[1] 'We must be in Sweden now. Haven't you noticed how the natural scenery is slowly changing, how it is getting more Swedish?' *Max Manus*: Norskfilminstitutt, 2008. Author's translation.

[2] Professors James Crawford and Alan Boyle were quoted in *The Herald* on 12 February 2013 as saying '[After] the union, Scotland certainly was extinguished as a matter of international law, by merger into either an enlarged and renamed England or into an entirely new state.'

[3] Feeding enthusiastically into this neurosis, Professor Hugh Trevor-Roper once devoted a whole book, *The Invention of Scotland*, essentially to demonstrating that Scotland was not there. Professor Roper's declarations about the 'fake' nature of Scotland regrettably invite awkward comparisons with his own views on the so-called '*Hitler Diaries*', which he enthusiastically declared to be genuine in 1983.

In any case, the Border does at this point at least confound all those who argue that it is not visible from space. The online O.S. map on my phone now demonstrates that much to me conclusively via satellite. We have not, it turns out, wandered very far into England. I inwardly give up on getting to the bothy tonight though, and realise that the only safe option is to head west, out of the tree factory and into the countryside.

***

I realise the need for commercial woodland. I understand the benefits of trees. Yet these particular trees, it might well be argued, are not part of any local ecosystem. In any case, in our present battered situation, Alan and I find them to be increasingly without merit. One local man made this sad observation when this area was first planted, as a response to the emergencies of war:

> It can scarcely be denied that these far-stretching dark forests
> are out of harmony with the natural features of the Borders;
> but, sad to say, the bitter struggle for national existence leaves
> little room for sentimental objections.[1]

Alan and I take turns to fall down holes and drag each other out. I give up the pretence of being cheerful. The trees become ever closer and closer-set. Moving even a yard in any direction now involves physically prising apart the branches with our chests while covering our faces with our hands, as best we can. The needle-covered branches slap us without respite, seemingly for their sport. We go on like this for perhaps another two hours.

I now see that we have not gone very far. I inwardly curse the Forestry Commission for making a desert and calling it a forest. With Archbishop Gavin Dunbar's words in my mind, I curse the hairs of the Commissioners' heids; likewise their hens, if they have any.

At this point, Alan howls. This time, he has fallen down a hole of exceptional size and wetness. He has also not enjoyed my own benefit – wearing glasses – and has been bashed in the eye with a branch. My capacity for guilt is well-developed enough as it is, without me speculating now whether the branch that hit Alan was sprung back on him by his own efforts or by mine. I conclude hopefully that we will never know. I pull him out of the hole and have a look at him. He has had a poke in the eye – a sore one, but hopefully

---

[1] John Byers: *Liddesdale.*

not injurious.

I have just followed the Border a bit too literally this time. We need to keep heading west. I no longer care where we go now, as long as we leave the clutches of the Sitka spruce behind. I am steering our poor vessel by compass alone. There is nothing to see, and only the relentless swearing of Alan to be heard behind me, in time with the constant movement of the branches. We stagger westwards, like creatures from Tolkien, for perhaps yet a further two hours.

***

We listen for any sounds of wildlife that might tell us when we are near the edge of the forest. Eventually, the hills of Scotland start to edge above the tree-line, and our hope returns. My classics teacher[1] once told us how exiled Greeks miserably crossed continents and then rejoiced when they saw the sea, shouting the primordial sea god's name: 'Thalassa! Thalassa!' They knew they could navigate their way home now. That is how I feel now about seeing a ridge of hills. It seems we got lost briefly somewhere around the Kielder Observatory,[2] but we have made our way back west, and are not far now from Larriston Fell.

And lo – a proper path has been provided to us too. In fact, it is the path we would have been wiser to have taken via the village of Kielder in the first place. It would have been simpler than trying to follow a political boundary quite this zealously. We walk back to Kielder. Here, the forest takes on a wholly different character: Scots pines and clearings, fresh air, people, marked ways and hope.

The tiny English village was largely created for the forestry industry. Not far south beyond it are the Kielder Water reservoir and dam, opened in 1982. These created the largest man-made lake in northern Europe and caused a whole valley, including a number of houses and a school, to be flooded. Kielder has one B and B, a campsite, and a pub.[3] The area is now home to around half of England's red squirrels. Longer ago, it was a habitat for wildcats.

Sir Walter Scott claimed that the Duke of Northumberland had told him that, within his father's memory, the people of Kielder had been 'all quite wild'. He had said that the men 'were savage and could hardly be brought to rise from the heath, either from sullenness or fear', and that the women here

---

[1] From Xenophon: *Anabasis*. If the way to assess former teachers is by how much you remember of what they said, then Mr Shanks wins by a wide margin.

[2] A couple of miles from the Border, this observatory boasts among the darkest skies in England.

[3] The Angler's Arms, which sells food.

'had no other dress than a bedgown and petticoat'.[1] Unsure what to make of these observations, I keep them to myself for present. We leave Kielder behind. Looking over my shoulder, the village appears now as just a few well-tended gardens fighting a constant war against the overwhelming odds around them of rushes and bracken.

The old railway line takes us back eventually to Deadwater. A more unlikely claim for Deadwater even than its old station is that, just beside it and a few yards inside Scotland, are the remains of a *bathhouse*. A bathhouse would probably have been useful and welcome by this point today. Scarcely believably, there was in fact a health spa here from the late eighteenth century, long before the railway came. It is a very strange image. While refugees from the clearances sought a place of safety on the Border here, wealthy people, (some, no doubt, with cleared estates or recently-enclosed commons to their names) somehow came here to bathe and take the waters. The bathhouse lasted for a hundred years or so, and the spring-water from the 'magnesia wells' here seems to have been particularly popular among those who suffered from scrofula. I file this last fact away for any potential future use.

We drive back to the Grapes Hotel in Newcastleton for some food. The bar is full of people with Roxburghshire accents dressed up as American G.I. soldiers. They are taking part in a pub quiz. In this round, the questions all seem to have one of two multiple-choice answers: 'Benny Hill' or 'Frank Sinatra'. I am concerned that Alan may think he is hallucinating now. I explain to him that this is in fact not a V.E. Day commemoration at all, but a World-War-Two-themed charity event. This also explains the bunting. Alan's eye is still sore though.

There had to be one day like this on my walk, I suppose. I apologise to Alan that he was present for it. I am now cheerfully four miles further on with my project, but poor Alan has been subjected to an afternoon with very little to recommend it.

---

[1] Quoted by Mack from Sir Walter Scott's *Journal*, 1827.

Day 8: From Larriston Fells to Kershopehead

(Circa 7 miles)

Lock the Door Larriston; An unexpected straight line; Political protest on the Border in 1707; The Bloody Bush and the Boundary Stone; Hobb's Flow and the Lamisk Ford; A Liddesdale drow; The Kershope Burn; Jock o the Side; Remembering the Little People; The Kershopehead Bothy.

Lock the door, Lariston, lion of Liddisdale!

Lock the door, Lariston, Lowther comes on!

The Armstrongs are flying,

The widows are crying,

The Castletown's burning, and Oliver's gone!

Lock the door, Lariston! High on the weather-gleam

See how the Saxon plumes bob on the sky!

Yeoman and carbineer,

Billman and halberdier -

Fierce is the foray, and far is the cry!

So runs James Hogg's praise of Elliot of Larriston, and all other reivers, in full-blooded, alliterative terms. The song makes no apologies and takes few prisoners (unless the latter should, perhaps, have some commercial value as hostages).

It is to Larriston in Liddesdale that I have come again this May morning. I have persuaded Malc to pick up on the trail again with me. Today, we will take up roughly where Alan and I turned back in our curtailed adventure in September. Once more, I am setting off in the hope of reaching what is (for me) the, by now, slightly fabled Kershopehead Bothy. After my last experience of these forests, I have studied the map over the winter till the shape of the Kershope Burn is branded onto my brain.

Our starting point today is a couple of miles down the Liddel Water from Dawstane Rigg. This is the (possible) site of the Battle of Degsastan, fought around 603 AD between Áedán mac Gabráin, King of the Dalriadan Scots, and Æthelfrith, King of the Northumbrian Angles. The battle, wherever exactly it really was, assisted the Kingdom of Northumbria in first claiming the eastern part of what we now think of as the Scottish Borders.

We get as near to the Border as we can by vehicle, driving up the uncertain track beyond Larriston farm steading to the lonely house at Larriston Rigg. Here, as we start walking, a man cutting his grass takes a cheerful interest in where we might be going. He recommends a barely-discernable parting in the undergrowth on the distant hillside. This perforated grey-green line, he says, will lead us up to the ridge above. At the next house we come to, Upper Larriston, the road finally peters out near the site of some old lime kilns.[1] From here, we stride off into the bog cotton and on towards the horizon.

It is forecast to start raining at 3pm, so we lose no time in setting off over Larriston Fells. After two miles, the view opens out before us and we stand at a vantage point not far from the rickle of stones known as the Grey Lads.[2] After green Liddesdale, the view is a contrasting one. We suddenly look out now over miles and miles of bog and felled forests.

***

The Border does not follow any obvious natural features for a while now, but the edges of the forests here visibly mark out a sudden right-angle in Scotland's edge. In fact, the differing patterns of planting and felling mean that the two countries are stained different colours on satellite photos here as distinctly as they are on political maps. Malc and I aim for the line that none else today are here to see.

Admittedly, like many politicians, I am good at seeing invisible lines, not least those that mark out parliamentary constituencies.[3] For example, if the reader has the patience to hear about this, in the last independent Scottish Parliament, this particular constituency was Roxburghshire. One of the men who jointly represented Roxburghshire then was Sir Gilbert Elliot of Minto, who had, I am sure, many faults. However, Elliot did distinguish himself (like several other representatives of Border constituencies) by voting against the Union of 1707. I provocatively commend his example to all who represent the Borders in Parliament today, in that one respect at least.

Significantly, Elliot is *not* listed among those members who accepted sudden and largely unexplained payments from the Government in the run up to the crucial parliamentary vote on the Union. Historians take differing positions as to how much these payments aided the London Government in getting the outcome it sought, but it is difficult to believe that the money was exactly a hindrance.[4]

---

[1] This is in fact somewhere near the presumed site of the Larriston Tower, whose door we have to hope was locked.

[2] The name is from Anglo-Saxon *hlaed* or Old Norse *hlad*, both simply meaning 'heap'.

[3] If the reader wearies of hearing about invisible lines by now, it is surprising how many people find them as interesting as I do. I have, for example, more than once climbed a hill in Norway to find that someone has lovingly built a monument there to a long-abolished county boundary.

[4] At one end of the scale of payments was the eye-watering £12,325 Sterling which

Meanwhile, however, some 96 local petitions were at this very time being raised *against* the Union by the general public throughout Scotland. These incuded several here along the Border line. Some of the current elected members for this part of the world (who rarely tire of explaining how enthusiastic Borderers have ever been for the Union) might want to consider the uncompromising petition presented to the Scottish Government by over 1,300 people in Berwickshire on 16 December 1706:

> Wee, the barons, freeholders and others within the same shire undersubscriving, Having seen the Articles of Union agreed upon by the Commissioners, ...in which they agree that Scotland and England shall be united in one kingdom, shall be represented in One Parliament ...And seeing it does evidently appear to us that [this] is contrair to the Honour, fundamental Laws and Constitutione of this Kingdome, ...and that the samine is destructive to the natione ...wee do confidently expect ...that yee will support and preserve the soveraignty and independency of this Croun and Kingdom...which have been so valiently maintained by our heroick ancesters by the space of near tuo thousand yeirs.[1]

All this said, there is (the reader may decide) a disconnect here between the political tone of much of what I have been saying and the actual politics of the Border today. The reader may feel I require a long-overdue reality-check. So, it is now time for me to acknowledge something, even if through the written equivalent of gritted teeth: at no point on my expedition will I have walked through any Scottish constituency which is *not* presently represented by a Conservative MSP or MP. The southern edge of Scotland today represents a fringe of blue on Scotland's political map.

While both the Borders and Dumfries and Galloway voted for devolution in 1997, in the 2014 referendum, it would be fair to surmise that all the parishes I am walking through voted 'No' to independence – probably by two to one.

There is no doubt that the Border, as an issue, was used to full effect here by the 'No' campaign in 2014. Although the Scottish Government set out its

---

ended up in the hands of the Duke of Queensberry, probably representing a multi-million pound sum today. At the other was the pitiable £11 and 2 shillings which the impoverished Lord Banff gratefully accepted as (to use his own word) 'encouragement'.
[1] Karin Bowie (ed): *Addresses against Incorporating Union, 1706-1707.* I am delighted to see that some (very possibly related) people who share my surname have signed the Berwickshire petition. Roxburghshire presented a similar address.

intention to have an open border upon independence,[1] Labour joined with the Conservatives in threatening to build customs-posts along the *English* side of the Border, if Scots voted 'Yes'. Clearly this threat was made by people who had never actually *seen* what long stretches of the Border (such as today's) actually look like.

Without trying to claim that such Border scare-stories were the only factors explaining the concerns of those 'No' voters in Duns who did their weekly shopping in Berwick, they were certainly among them.

***

Looking back over our shoulders for a few miles, the fine detail of the Border line here was probably always a little hazy in places until the last 150 years.

It has been suggested, for instance, that a small stretch of the Border, running roughly north-eastwards from here back as far as the Bell Kirk (which we passed yesterday), was once considered disputed ground. The Border perhaps once favoured England with marginally more wild land than it does now, and possibly followed a straighter line between here and the Thorlieshope Pike. One map of 1837 by J. Duncan certainly still shows a string of small patches of land along that line marked as 'Disputed'. This uninhabited landscape is in fact wide open enough to have made the task of drawing any exact Border line here no easy one for mapmakers down the centuries.

I mention all this for the sake of completeness. Any short gap between where *exactly* Alan and I left the Border last time and where Malc and I join it today can perhaps be explained away by praying in aid such ancient little border-uncertainties. If it cannot, then I am not walking all the way back out here again, just to fill in the missing two miles.

The Border always surprises. For the next two miles, however, it does something new and truly extraordinary: it goes in a straight line.

The line here (J.L. Mack advises) is the one established on a map of 1770 by Matthew Stobie. The likely reason for such a strangely arbitrary[2] straight line lies in previous land-ownership disputes. That said, some later maps than Stobie's do seem to express ongoing uncertainties.[3] In any case, the dispute has long since been settled. So, straight line it is, for a while now, and the longest of these I have encouered since I first started walking.[4]

---

[1] Scottish Government: *Scotland's Future*.

[2] If the reader still does not accept my central premise about the non-arbitrariness of Scotland's Border, then they may find smug amusement in my choice of words here.

[3] Duncan's 1837 map continues to regard a long, thin strip of land on either side of this straight line as 'Disputed'.

[4] Until this point, no truly straight section of the Border has been more than a couple

To a Scot, straight borders (and there are quite a number in the world[1]) look as strange on the map as might rectangular contour lines. So intricate are Scotland's edges on all sides, that nations, states and provinces with straight borders look, to a Scot, like trees which nature has decided to give a few massive and perfectly square leaves. In many countries, I venture to guess, such lines (drawn, as it were, by rulers using rulers) do not carry as many layers of ancient meaning as a wavering burn or ridge does here. So, in Scotland, two whole miles of straight border feel very odd indeed.[2]

We join this part of the Border at the Bloody Bush, named after an incident when some of the men of Liddesdale killed English raiders who were camped here. Here the Border is marked by a huge, incongruous stone obelisk with a series of price lists engraved on its sides. The 'Boundary Stone', as it is called, was set up here to mark a fairly short-lived toll-road over the Border, and still lists all the tolls payable. These begin at the halfpenny a day required of anyone moving calves and increase in an upward scale. Ponies once carried coal in creels this way into Scotland until railways arrived elsewhere. The stone announces, to anyone listening, that the landowners on each side of the Border require twopence from anyone so carrying coal, on pain of prosecution.

A lone mountain-biker pechs up the toll road past us through the old turnpike gates, heedless of the obelisk's demands. The stone predates bicycles, in any case, so these do not feature on its otherwise very comprehensive list. The sound of disembodied bike wheels persists faintly across the hills, long after any cyclist can be seen.

It is silent again. The rain is on now, not in great sheets or dauds, but in a slow sound-suppressing smirr that promises to settle, as in an old chair, for days. We follow the ancient, rickety remnants of a long, straight border fence, until the Border starts to wander reassuringly away again from the straight and narrow.

***

This is Hobbs Flow. Malc and I tread around the place suspiciously, wary

---

of hundred yards long. The exception to this comes in the form of three stretches of straight line lying just to the east of Kirk Yetholm (the longest of these being just under a mile in length). We did not really see much of these ourselves, however, as we wandered away from the line here briefly on Day 3, in order to go into Kirk Yetholm for the night.

[1] The Canadian province of Saskatchewan, as well as the U.S. states of Wyoming and Colorado, are in fact perfectly rectangular. New Mexico and Utah are pretty close to it.

[2] That said, we will encounter another interesting (and quite old) three-mile-long straight line on Day 11.

of a warning from J.L. Mack of the danger of being 'engulfed in morass' here. It is certainly hard walking. Hobb's Flow makes more than one attempt to seperate us from our our boots. For an hour or two, the pair of us jump over rivulets, constantly testing the rushes and heather under our feet for their safety. We alternately soak our socks and trip over tree stumps, anticipating, as usual, each other's every next cautious footstep and every next grimly-sceptical remark. Soon, however, we find the next of our Border burns, the tiny Clark's Sike, as it prises its way between an English and a Scottish forest, under a huge, uniform, whitewashed-ceiling sky.

I am relieved now to see a landscape that looks more navigable than I had feared; many sections of the forests on either side of the burn have recently been felled. Taking some care that we are following the right watercourse, we walk alongside Clark's Sike into a forest clearing and keep to its Scottish bank, making tactical incursions whenever the English bank seems slightly more walkable. My fear that we would be drawn siren-like by the sound of the burn into another black Sitka-oblivion proves groundless. Our legs ache though at our appallingly slow progress.

We chance upon a rotting little wooden signpost, sinking with us into the bog. Scraping off pale lichen, we find that it points behind us 'To Bloody Bush'. We wonder why on earth a signpost was put up here to link two such obscure and inaccessible places in such a formal way. A feeling dawns on us both that we may be part of some tiny minority who approach the Kershope Bothy from the east.

The rain today is not an event. It is a silent, steady-state reality, just as much as land or sky are. We take the elements' hint, and put on our waterproof trousers. I am suddenly and soddenly driven to recall at this point how James IV wore a chain about his waist as a penance for what he felt was the ambiguous role which he had played in the death of his father. One story tells of how this chain nearly had the effect of drowning James in the pool at Ladykirk.[1] Another says that he ominously took the chain off as he approached Flodden. I remember all this at present for no particular reason other than because, today, a seam in my rain-soaked trousers has somehow managed to saw a penitential red line horizontally across the top of one leg.

Seeking out the shelter of the lonely bothy among the trees now takes on the same importance in our minds that catching sight of the International Space Station presumably occupies in the thoughts of free-floating astronauts. I check my compass. We both silently realise that we have had enough of following the Border quite this literally for one day. We reckon we can be permitted to wander a hundred yards into Scotland for a while, in search of a

[1] See Day 2.

slightly easier life. So we follow the Queen's Sike briefly, as it leads up from Clark's Sike, and find a forest track that follows close to the Scottish bank of the border burn. Walking today's final three miles on solid ground will now take us a fraction of the time that it took us to complete the first four along the Border itself.

This is the first path I can recall walking on in what feels like a very long time. Apart from a couple of miles of old railway at Deadwater, this is the first time any significant stretch of my expedition has taken me along any proper path since I left the Pennine Way, some three days' walking behind me. For a good while ahead of us now, paths and roads will lie under our grateful feet.

We are at Scotch Knowe, at or near the site known of old as the 'Lamisk Ford'. Here an old Roman road perhaps once crossed our Border, and in so doing eventually formed the boundary between England's Middle and West Marches. The line now marks the boundary between the English counties of Cumbria and Northumberland. We follow the path over the amusingly-titled Havering Bog,[1] whose name, Malc and I conclude, may reflect the state of our recent conversation. The next bog we pass is Yearning Flow, whose name, we in turn decide, honours our eagerness to stop walking now.

The rain persists quietly as we pass Scotch Craig. By the time the Yearning Sike trickles into Clark's Sike, the latter has gained the more dignified-sounding name of Kershope Burn. In any case, it is still the Border, and we walk on its Scottish bank for some time till we find a good place to jump into England, in which country we have heard the bothy to be.

***

Though the road is good now, the weather could probably be better. A *Liddesdale drow* is defined in an 1841 dictionary as 'a shower which soaks an Englishman to the skin.'[2] Other Scots dictionaries make no reference to the nationality of the afflicted, but add the phrase to the countless others which Scotland has for precipitation.[3] As we make our way down the Kershope Burn, the drow becomes as real a presence on our minds as it is on the rest of us. Perhaps it is best summed up in the words of one local bard:

---

[1] To *haiver*, in Scots, is of course to speak nonsense.
[2] Quoted, among others, by Graham Robb: *The Debatable Land.*
[3] *The Scots Thesaurus* (Iseabail MacLeod ed, Aberdeen University Press, 1990) lists something like 400 Scots words under the headings of 'wind, storm, rain, mist, snow, frost, thunder, lightning.' In 2015, Susan Rennie at the University of Glasgow went further, and suggested that Scots had 421 words for snow alone (far outdoing, on that basis, the fifty generally accredited to the Inuit). Scottish Gaelic has countless more words for precipitation.

The rain for days cam soakin doon,

An dark the heavens lookit.

The sky it wore an angry froon

An a' the worl was drookit.[1]

The poet, John Byers, goes on to describe how a summer rainstorm persisted, (worse, he observes, than the great Common Riding flood of 1847), until a man named Noah from near Copshaw Holm built a boat. Today, the drow sets about its determined mission of needling its way through Gortex.

Incredibly, Sir Walter Scott seems to have been the first person to attempt to take a wheeled vehicle into Liddesdale, when he came here to seek out the region's ballads two centuries ago. Our way down the Kershope Burn today takes us through a landscape now largely unrecognisable from that time. The country is covered in rows of trees. The Border line here has been pacified. There are no people here today, wild or otherwise. There are just seas of conifers, and in Old Testament numbers.

***

Liddesdale once had its own 'Keeper' under the Warden of the Scottish Middle March. This appointment recognised this area to be an ungovernable world of its own, even by Border standards, and one requiring its own specific officer. This concern was reciprocated by the English authorities. In 1552 the English warden ordered that the Border along the Esk and Liddel, all the way up here to the Kershope Burn, should be watched every night by a force of sixty men.

One of those being watched for here was doubtless Jock o the Side, the reiver famed in the ballad of that name.[2] He is less romantically accounted for by the poet and (significantly) judge, Sir Richard Maitland:

He is weil kend, John of the Syide,

A gretar theif did never ryide:

He never tyris

For to brek byris,

...Yit, or I die,

Sum sall thame sie

---

[1] John 'Bluebell' Byers: *The Liddesdale Drow.*
[2] 'Jock o' the Side' (*Child Ballads*, 187A).

Hing on a trie,
Quhill thay be deid.[1]

Crossing the burn, we see at last, high up in the trees on the English bank, the Kershopehead Bothy. We plot a path up past the crumbling dry-stone fanks that prove that a shepherd lived here once. We certainly did not expect it to take six hours to walk seven miles today; we are glad now to establish that the bothy is not a mirage. The little stone house sits comfortably in the thicket of nettles that seem always to surround an old human habitation.

A mile or two from here was the scene in 1849 of the grisly murder of Thomas Davidson, a gamekeeper from Bewcastle. Two people called Hogg and one called Turnbull – all suspected poachers – were tried in Carlisle for the killing. Turnbull hanged himself in his cell and left grafitti saying, 'The two Hoggs are guilty. I am innocent.' The Hoggs were nonetheless found *not* guilty and quietly left the country. The monument to the victim, which once stood on a desolate hillside, is now doubtless almost lost in trees.

I feel there is fertile ghost-story material in all this. Malc has heard all my anecdotes, so I hope, as I open the wheezing door into the bothy's darkened kitchen, that there is someone new in here to unsettle with all this information tonight around the fireseide. There is not, but any disappointment I might feel about that is lost in the sudden and magnificent sensation of being dry.

***

Kershopehead deserves to be highly rated among bothies. We light the stove with the sticks that our unknown predecessors have kindly sawn for us, and the fire roars into instant life. Grateful, we hang our soaking possessions around the mantlepiece like offerings at a clootie well. Socks laid across the stovepipe hiss, boil and then very quickly start to combust. We have others. After cooking our food on the stove and opening our flask of whisky, we feel all the smugness that comes of being inside on a wet evening.

I cannot but recall here now how, many years ago, Malc and I hiked to another bothy like this, at the top of a very misty Yarrow Valley – James Hogg country at its most mysterious. We looked in at the old house there at Nether Phawhope. When the door of that other bothy creaked open that day, three or four very startled-looking student backpackers who were sitting around the fire jumped out of their skins, as Malc and I emerged, half-bearded and fully-bedraggled, out of the dark and swirling elements. They did not seem

[1] Sir Richard Maitland: 'Aganis the Thievis of Liddisdail', from *Ancient Scottish Poems*. *Byris:* byres, *sie :* see, *quhill:* till, *or:* before.

keen to speak to us so, after an awkward pause, I tried helpfully to break the ice. I am much better now at this particular task than I was in my youth.

At this point, as Malc now recounts widely, I memorably attempted to open up a conversation with my young peers by saying:

> 'A relative of mine saw the fairies here in the eighteenth century.'[1]

There was, as I recall, a very uncomfortable silence. We hurriedly ate our pieces while the students looked into the embers studiously, as if they might fear the evil eye itself. At Malc's exasperated but kindly prompting, we disappeared into the storm again, leaving the others to make what they could of the previous few minutes of their up-to-then sheltered lives.

Tonight, though, it is my turn to jump. The dark and stooping figures of two men suddenly appear from nowhere and flicker past the kitchen window. The sneck on the door rattles open.

Two mountain bikers join us – a junior doctor and a PhD student from the north of England. We all gladly share our provisions. I sense inwardly that Malc would prefer if the conversation were kept relatively mainstream this evening, so this time I offer our bothy-mates no tales of the supernatural. I explain we are walking the Border, something which seems suddenly to solve a mystery for them. 'Ah!' they exclaim together. 'So that explains that dotted line on the map.'

All of us are asleep long before night falls fully on Kershopehead. Silver wraiths of mist encompass the little house about. The bothy wrings them all out though, like cloots, into one single drip of water that falls steady into a barrel outside. The stove burns slowly out. Malc snores.

---

[1] This claim to a family connection is not strictly true. He was in fact only an in-law of one of my relatives. Will Laidlaw, better known as Will o Phaup, is claimed to have been the last man in the Borders to have seen the fairies. His grandson, the writer James Hogg, recorded that, one All Hallows Eve around 1740, Will saw a large group of female fairies baking bread. On another occasion, the creatures came to Will asking him for a mysterious silver key, but disappeared when he asked them where 'in the name of God' they came from. Will also stumbled one night near Moffat upon a bearded giant who was busy writing labels on enormous barrels. It seems.

Day 9: From Kershopehead to Kershopefoot
(Circa 6 miles)

A forest with ghosts of shepherds; The Bewcastle Waste; Out of the trees; The Kershope Burn and the Liddel Water; Kershopefoot and days of truce; Hobbie Noble and Kinmont Willie; Armstrong country; Into Scotland's West March.

We are away before our cyclist friends, who (being grateful to have come in to a fire last night), are sawing sticks now for those who come after us. We gather our possessions and sweep the floor. Hillwalkers staying in bothies should have the manners to remember that these places were not, on the whole, originally intended for birdwatchers escaping human company. They were in fact generally once someone else's house. So, in that polite spirit, I offer one more story about the Kershopehead bothy before we go.

J.L. Mack writes that, sometime around 1900, a Scottish shepherd who was living here brought a Scottish minister all the way out here to conduct his daughter's wedding. The minister suddenly remembered that, here in England, by law clergy could only perform marriages in church buildings. This was in direct contrast with the situation in Scotland, where it was at that time still very unusual for ministers to use churches for weddings. The minister decided in the end to walk the couple and their guests down to the burn, and scramble a few paces into Scotland for the ceremony, to keep it legal.

Today, like the wedding guests of old, we step out from Kershopehead and cross the burn. The rain is heavier today, and not going to stop; we might as well resolve to enjoy it.

Writing in 1926, Mack warns this about today's route:

> Woe betide the unfortunate person who endeavours to walk alongside the Border line along the banks of the Kershope Burn.

This was probably fair advice then but, since the forest was planted, there is in fact now a forestry road (marked as an official footpath, and also much-used by mountain-bikers) which follows the Scottish side of the burn. Kershopehead to Kershopefoot is therefore not a long or difficult walk by anyone's definition – not even by ours. We will be there by lunch-time.

In the past, pinning down an exact Border line in these remoter areas may have been no simple business. One theory is that the Border here was once actually three or four miles further in Scotland's favour. Some (no doubt highly contentious) claims of this kind seem at least to have been made by

Scotland in the sixteenth century for the wild area from Kershopehead as far south as Christianbury Crags.[1] Today, however, we will follow the long-accepted legal Border along the Kershope Burn.

The first house we pass is at Scotch Kershope (its sister house, English Kershope,[2] being on the other side of the burn). Indeed, this represents the first inhabited house that the Border has passed directly by since lonely Deadwater. The path crosses over the burn and into England.

***

Bewcastle, referred to in Hogg's song about Larriston, is a little village lying some eight miles to our due south now in England on the other side of the impressively-named Bewcastle Waste. Among several other claims to fame,[3] Bewcastle was the scene in 1559 of perhaps the first recorded international football match between Scotland and England. George MacDonald Fraser memorably describes how the game was not without incident:

> Six Armstrongs came to Bewcastle to play a match against six of the local English boys, and after the game there was 'drinking hard at Bewcastle House'. However, it happened that a Mr William Ridley, an Englishman, 'knowing the continual haunt and receipt the great thieves and arch murderers had with the captain of Bewcastle' determined to capture the Armstrong footballers while they were on English ground …The Armstrongs had been tipped off, and Mr Ridley's ambush party found themselves suddenly set on by more than 200 riders. Ridley and two of his friends were killed, thirty taken prisoner, 'and many sore hurt, expecially John Whytfield, whose bowels came out but are sowed up againe.' The result of the game is not recorded.[4]

---

[1] Eric Robson in *The Border Line* says that a book by John Johnson and John Goodwyn with the comprehensive title *A Book of the Survaie of the Debateable and Border Lands belonginge to the Crowne of England, lying betwixt the west and east seas and aboundinge upon the Realme of Scotland Taken in the Year of Our Lord God 1604* shows for the first time a final abandoning of any Scottish claim to a line via Christianbury Crags. The Border may once have lain there near a ditch named (rather grandly) 'the Fosse of the Galwegians'.

[2] mountainbothies.org records how some of the last inhabitants of Kershopehead in the 1930s, a forester and his family, used to walk as far as English Kershope once a week to pick up the groceries left there by a van.

[3] The village of Bewcastle is home to an amazing seventh-century carved stone cross, and also the remnants of a Roman fort.

[4] George MacDonald Fraser: *The Steel Bonnets*.

The Bewcastle Waste also makes an appearance in Scott's short story 'The Two Drovers', the tale of a Highlander and an Englishman on their way south together while droving cattle to markets in England:

> The pair of friends had traversed with their usual cordiality the grassy wilds of Liddesdale, and crossed the opposite part of Cumberland, emphatically called The Waste. In these solitary regions, the cattle under the charge of our drovers derived their subsistence chiefly by picking their food as they went along the drove-road, or sometimes by the tempting opportunity of a start and 'owerloup', or invasion of the neighbouring pasture, where an occasion presented itself. But now the scene changed before them; they were descending towards a fertile and enclosed country, where no such liberties could be taken with impunity, or without a previous arrangement.[1]

In Scott's novel *Guy Mannering*, the Bewcastle Waste also features as the scene of the obligatory 'arduous journey' required of any self-respecting literary hero of the Romantic era.[2] The novel's central character, Bertram, meets the good-natured farmer Dandie Dinmont, (who has his farm, 'Charlieshope', somewhere on the Liddel Water[3]) just as he is crossing back into Scotland over the Bewcastle Waste. Here – it being the eighteenth century now – he is assaulted, not by reivers, but by landlowping highwaymen.

We probably cross these characters' paths somewhere on our walk today, though where exactly is difficult to pinpoint. Nearby Conscouthart Moss has been suggested as the setting for these scenes, and there is certainly a 'Dinmont Lair' and a 'Dinmont Lair Knowe' marked near the Havering Bog. Whether the character gets his name from the place or whether, like Meg Merilees' Cave[4] near Wigtown, the place is more likely named in honour of Scott's character, I do not know. In any case, even after he is attacked, Dinmont himself definitely knows he is on the Border line, saying dismissively of his injuries:

---

[1] Sir Walter Scott: 'The Two Drovers', from *The Chronicles of the Canongate*.
[2] As far as my own arduous journey is concerned, I have of course already faced that, somewhere between Deadwater and Larriston Fells. I can now relax, as much as the hero of any account of this kind ever can.
[3] Here there is actually a farm with the suspiciously similar name of Thorlieshope, not far from Dawstone (with which latter farm, in fact, Dinmont himself says his own farm borders).
[4] Otherwise known as Dirk Hatteraik's Cave, after another of Scott's characters.

'Hout tout, man – I would never be making a hum-dudgeon about a scart on the pow …but we'll be in Scotland in five minutes now.'[1]

***

We pass over the fields of Day Holm, which get their name because the place was once set aside for days of truce,[2] following the Kershope Burn's English bank. Here the trees on our (Scottish) right hand finally clear, before we pass a road-end into Scotland at Kershope Bridge. Eventually we reach Kershopefoot, an English hamlet of a few houses, some of whose gardens almost line up against the Border itself.

At a spot on our right called Flatt, a field called Tourneyhome lies just between our path and the river. J.L. Mack and others identify this as a former venue for trials by combat for both Scottish and English disputants. Mack also advises that Kershopefoot has the only station where it is (or was) perhaps possible to see a train standing with the engine in Scotland and the guard's van in England.

Near Kershopefoot, half a mile inside England, is seventeenth-century Stonegarthside Hall, probably built around a much older house. It can now be rented out for the week, presumably complete with its pair of courting sixteenth-century ghosts.

Kershopefoot, soporifically quiet as it seems today in the rain, makes more than one violent appearance in the ballads. One of these is in 'Hobbie Noble', which tells the story of a man banished here from just over the Border, and then tricked and set upon by the men of Liddesdale:

> Now Hobbie was an English man,
> And born into Bewcastle dale;
> But his misdeeds they were so great,
> They banish'd him to Liddesdale.
>
> At Kershope foot the tryste was set,
> Kershope of the lilye lee;
> And there was traitor Sim o the Mains,
> With him a private companie.[3]

---

[1] Sir Walter Scott: *Guy Mannering*
[2] Day Home is where, it seems, the warden meeting was held that led to Kinmont Willie's capture (as mentioned a page or two hence).

It was also here at Kershopefoot that the infamous reiver Kinmont Willie was captured by English rivals, despite it being the traditional time and place for a day of truce:

> Had Willie had but twenty men,
> But twenty men as stout as he,
> Fause Sakelde had never the Kinmont ta'en,
> Wi' eight score in his companie.
>
> They led him thro' the Liddel-rack,
> And also thro' the Carlisle sands,
> They brought him to Carlisle castell,
> To be at my Lord Scroope's commands.[1]

As the ballad goes on to recount, Kinmont Willie was eventually re-captured from Carlisle by his friends in 1596. In reality this was more of a jailbreak operation than the heroic national enterprise that Scott's version of the ballad suggests, and it almost certainly involved the cooperation of elements on the English side.

One of the main participants in the raid on Carlisle, Dickie Armstrong of Dryhope, is known to have had other less celebrated episodes to his name. In one of these, he visited a certain Hecky Noble with a hundred of his friends, stole two hundred cattle, destroyed nine houses, and burned Hecky's son and pregnant daughter-in-law alive.[2] Learning all this about Dickie does have a sobering effect. Perhaps thinking of all that too, Pippa Little has written about what a day of truce in Kershopefoot might perhaps have looked like to a woman:

> Hard-bitten aye: by loss
> And sorrow, those scavengers .
> There's only sleep keeps a truce.
> In men's dreams, spilled blood dries,
> It's drink that runs over.
> …it's Sandy's Tom to hang.[3]

---

[3] 'Hobie Noble', *Child Ballads* 189A.
[1] 'Kinmont Willie', from Scott's *Minstrelsy of the Scottish Border*.
[2] Recounted in George MacDonald Fraser: *The Steel Bonnets*.
[3] Pippa Little: 'Truce Day', from *Foray: Border reiving women*.

In 2013, somewhat strained comparisons with these wild times were drawn by *The Guardian*, when the Royal Mail moved the local post box over the Border from Kershopefoot, and, after a local outcry, eventually had to return it.

***

Somewhere around this point, we are leaving Scotland's Middle March and entering the West. Some would argue that we actually crossed that slightly indistinct line a little earlier this morning.

At Kershopefoot, the Kershope Burn runs at last into the winding Liddel Water, which now carries the Border with it southwards. In a much earlier era (perhaps the fifteenth century), it is possible that the Border here may in fact have followed the Liddel Water for a few miles further upstream beyond Kershopefoot. For five hundred years at least, however, Kershopefoot has marked the confluence of two border-rivers. So, we cross the bridge here back into Scotland.

We have left a car here, and now drive towards Newcastleton, heading into Scotland and deepest Armstrong country. We pass the slender remains of Mangerton Tower. One ballad describes how one Mangerton laird famously shoed his horse back-to-front, in order to confuse his pursuers:

> Lord Mangerton them orders gave,
> 'Your horses the wrong way maun be shod;
> Like gentlemen ye mauna seim,
> But look like corn–caugers ga'en the road.'[1]

We pass Millholm, with its stone cross. Legend has it that another Armstrong laird of Mangerton, slain at Hermitage Castle[2] in the fourteenth century, was borne along this way. His funeral party rested here at the cross on its way to nearby Ettleton kirkyard.

Later, in 1601, Robert Carey sought to harry the Armstrongs of Liddesdale here on behalf of the English Crown. Carey's forces met here at the confluence of the Kershope Burn and Liddel Water, on a grassy mound from where they sought to drive the local population away to their traditional hiding places on

---

[1] 'Jock o' the Side', from Scott's *Minstrelsy of the Scottish Border* (corn-caugers are corn carriers). This is a story I remember clearly my father telling me when I was very small (it is nice now to confirm I did not imagine it). Reversing horseshoes is a method of avoiding detection which more than one Gaelic folk tale also ascribes to Robert the Bruce.

[2] He was killed either by one of the de Soulis family or by the Earl of Angus.

the lonely Tarras Moss.[1] Graham Robb notes laconically in his account of the fray that the grassy mound in question is:

> …just downstream from the Riverview caravan park for the
> over fifties at Mangertoun.[2]

We are tired, wet, but duly pleased with ourselves. Before we head to Jethart for sustenance, I pause here near the Border, not merely (as Malc idly claims) to mark my territory, but to reflect. We have done better than the English knights who surveyed the Border in the thirteenth century ever managed;[3] two Marches have been inspected now in full, and only the controversial West remains.

---

[1] The Tarras Moss was described (somewhat strangely) in MacDiarmid's poem 'Tarras' as 'This Bolshevik bog! Suits me doon to the grun'!'.

[2] Graham Robb: *The Debatable Land*. I should add that I have been unable to find anything to suggest that the Riverview Holiday Park discriminates in any way against people under the age of fifty.

[3] And they had an advantage over Malc and me, in that they had horses.

CHAPTER 7
The West March

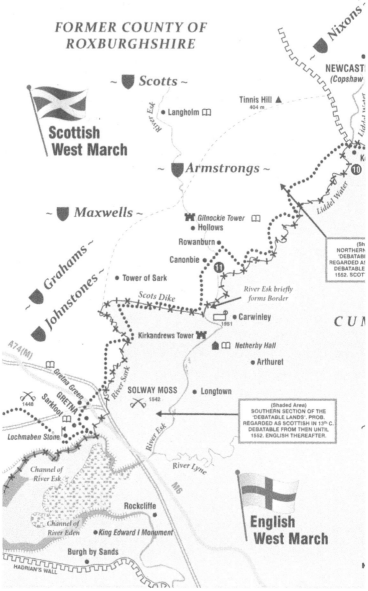

FORMER COUNTY OF ROXBURGHSHIRE

Nixons

NEWCAST (Copshaw)

~ 🛡 *Scotts* ~

Scottish West March

Tinnis Hill ▲
404 m

River Esk
● Langholm 🏛

~ 🛡*Armstrongs* ~

Liddel Water

K

10

~ 🛡 *Maxwells* ~

🏰 *Gilnockie Tower* 🏛
● Hollows
Rowanburn ●
Canonbie ●
11

Liddel Water

(5h
NORTHERN
'DEBATABl
REGARDED AS
DEBATABLE
1552. SCOT

~ *Grahams* ~
~ *Johnstones* ~

● Tower of Sark

Scots Dike

*River Esk briefly
forms Border*

A74(M)

🏛 Gretna Green

● Carwinley
1951

C U M

Kirkandrews Tower 🏰

🏛 *Netherby Hall*

● Arthuret

River Sark

🏛 GRETNA
Sarkfool
1448

SOLWAY MOSS
⚔ 1542
● Longtown

(Shaded Area)
SOUTHERN SECTION OF THE
'DEBATABLE LANDS'. PROB.
REGARDED AS SCOTTISH IN 13th C.
DEBATABLE FROM THEN UNTIL
1552. ENGLISH THEREAFTER.

Lochmaben Stone

River Esk

River Lyne

*Channel of
River Esk*

M6

Rockcliffe ●

*Channel of
River Eden* ● *King Edward I Monument*

English West March

Burgh by Sands ●

HADRIAN'S WALL

Map 6: The Scottish and English West Marches, including the former 'Debatable Lands'.

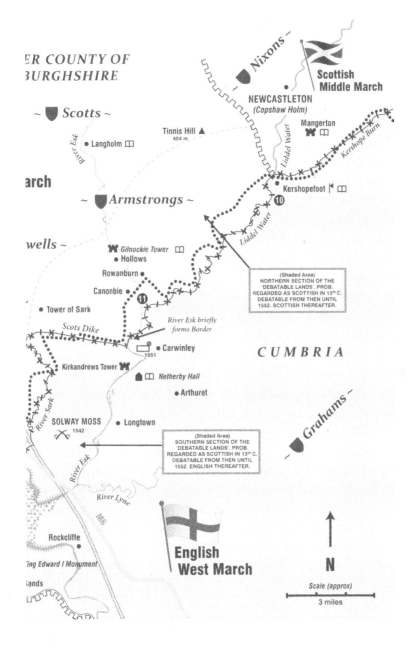

ER COUNTY OF
BURGHSHIRE

~ Scotts ~

Nixons ~

Scottish
Middle March

NEWCASTLETON
(Copshaw Holm)

Tinnis Hill ▲
404 m

River Esk

● Langholm

Mangerton

Liddel Water

Kershope Burn

arch

~ Armstrongs ~

Kershopefoot

⑩

wells ~

🏰 Gilnockie Tower
● Hollows

Rowanburn ●

Canonbie ●

⑪

Liddel Water

(Shaded Area)
NORTHERN SECTION OF THE
'DEBATABLE LANDS'. PROB.
REGARDED AS SCOTTISH IN 13th C.
DEBATABLE FROM THEN UNTIL
1552. SCOTTISH THEREAFTER.

● Tower of Sark

Scots Dike

River Esk briefly
forms Border

Kirkandrews Tower 🏰

● Carwinley
1951

CUMBRIA

🏰 Netherby Hall

● Arthuret

River Sark

SOLWAY MOSS
✕ 1542

● Longtown

~ Grahams ~

(Shaded Area)
SOUTHERN SECTION OF THE
'DEBATABLE LANDS'. PROB.
REGARDED AS SCOTTISH IN 13th C.
DEBATABLE FROM THEN UNTIL
1552. ENGLISH THEREAFTER.

River Esk

River Lyne

M6

Rockcliffe ●

'ing Edward I Monument

English
West March

N

Scale (approx)

3 miles

iands

189

Day 10: From Kershopefoot to Canonbie
(Circa 8 miles)

The Muckle Toun o the Langholm; Neil Armstrong – from Langholm to the moon; The tale of Burns's sock and MacDiarmid's H.P. Sauce; The Liddel Water; The Debatable Lands; Dumfriesshire – the borders of the Borders?; Rowanburn and Lang Sandie; Gilnockie Tower and Johnnie Armstrong; Canonbie – the debated capital.

> This is tae gie notice that there's a muckle fair tae be hadden in the Muckle Toun o the Langholm on the 15th day o July auld style[1]…and a land lowpers and dub scoupers…that come here tae breed hurdums or durdums, huliments or buliments, hagglements or bragglements…they shall be taen, …and their lugs shall be nailed tae the Tron wi a twal-penny nail.

So is announced the 'Cryin o the Fair' every year in 'the Muckle Toun o the Langholm'. Langholm lies seven miles inside Scotland, and so more than qualifies for a visit. I call in on my circuitous way back to Kershopefoot, where I will soon join Malc on the Border trail again.

The Muckle Toun's much-repeated claim to bigness[2] (its population is 2,300) may seem somewhat overstated, but these things are relative. Langholm was in fact once a major centre for the textile industry. Today, in the Narrows of Langholm's old town centre, lorries hurtle on to Carlisle, shaking venerable shopfronts.

Langholm was an early-adopter of rugby in Scotland, and sepia ranks of players adorn the walls of the town's pubs. Outside Langholm's stately little town house, meanwhile, is a sort of Langholm Pantheon, where varied monuments remember some of the town's other famous sons. The engineer Thomas Telford is to the fore, as is no less a figure than Neil Armstrong, the first man on the moon. Armstrong came here in 1972 to be made a freeman of the burgh, after the Langholmites worked out that his ancestors had gone to America, via Ulster, from this part of the Border some generations earlier. In fact, this was a gesture which seemed genuinely to move Armstrong:

> My pleasure is in knowing that this is my home town, and in the genuine feeling that I have among these hills, among these people.[3]

---

[1] i.e. according to the old Julian calendar, and so (in modern terms) 28 July.

[2] The claim of 'The Muckle Toun' is incidentally not quite so overstated as that of Malc's native Biggar in Clydesdale (the two towns are very much the same size). Biggar's unofficial Latin town motto is '*Londinium magnum est, sed Biggar Biggar est*' ('London's big, but Biggar's Biggar').

Among other memorials, one plaque commemorates the poet and translator William Julius Mickle (1734-1788), who is the probable author of the well-known song 'There's nae luck aboot the hoose', the only lines for which he is really remembered:

> For there's nae luck aboot the hoose,
> There's nae luck ava;
> There's little pleasure in the hoose,
> When our gudeman's awa.[1]

***

Hugh MacDiarmid's plaque, when seen beside Mickle's, seems pointedly smaller, considering the two poets' relative importance. MacDiarmid (or C.M. Grieve, to use his real name) was born here in 1892, and allegedly asked for his own epitaph to read 'a disgrace to the community'. While he has perhaps not *quite* achieved this status, it is difficult not to detect a certain cautiousness in the way Langholm views him.

MacDiarmid was the most significant of a group of figures who put a literary bomb under many cultural assumptions about Scotland. A self-prop-agandist (unhelpfully for the home-rule movement at the time, he listed his chief recreation in *Who's Who* as 'anglophobia'), MacDiarmid was kicked out of the SNP for communism and expelled from the Communist Party for nationalism.[2]

Not surprisingly, given MacDiarmid's modernist (and often aggressively elitist) outlook, he did say some things which were almost calculated to perplex and irritate his native town. With characteristic modesty, MacDiarmid regularly compared himself (more than favourably) with Robert Burns. So it is perhaps worth comparing Langholm, just for a moment, with Ayr, a town which has built its tourist industry around Burns. The patient reader will no doubt also humour me, therefore, by allowing me to compare for a moment the respective fates of Burns's sock and MacDiarmid's bottle of H.P. Sauce.

To explain, I have an early childhood recollection of visiting the Burns museum in Alloway, which in those days had much of the atmosphere of a

---

[3] Neil Armstrong: Address to the assembled people of Langholm, 1972.
[1] See Frank Millar: *The Poets of Dumfriesshire.* Jean Adam in Greenock also claims authorship.
[2] One of the founders of the SNP, John MacCormick, described MacDiarmid (not unfairly) as: '…having done invaluable work in the whole field of Scottish literature [but]… politically one of the greatest handicaps with which any national movement could have been burdened.' John MacCormick: *The Flag in the Wind.*

reliquary. One of the revered exhibits I remember seeing was labelled, 'A sock, believed to have belonged to Robert Burns'.

By way of contrast, when MacDiarmid's widow died near Biggar, Malc tells me that he somehow got the task of helping to catalogue away in the local museum everything that was left in the poet's house. One item he recalls carefully labelling as: 'Hugh MacDiarmid's H.P. Sauce Bottle'.

I am fairly certain that there are Burns fans who would still (literally) kill for Burns's sock. They might, in some cases, even credit the object with miracles. It is to take nothing away from MacDiarmid's achievements to say that I can be sure that his own bottle of H.P. Sauce, by contrast, is now forgotten in storage somewhere. Perhaps it has long since gone the way of most of Scotland's medieval relics.

I wander up to the MacDiarmid Memorial on Whita Hill, just outside the town. The wind is snell and fierce and uncompromising. Appropriately. Jake Harvey's red oxidized-steel monument to MacDiarmid takes the form of a huge open book depicting images from his poems, including some taken from Langholm's common riding:

> Drums in the Walligate, pipes in the air,
> Come and hear the cryin' o' the fair.
> A' as it used to be, when I was a loon
> On Common-Ridin' day in the Muckle Toon.
> The bearer twirls the Bannock-and-Saut-Herrin'
> The Croon o' Roses through the lift is farin',
> The aucht-fit thistle[1] wallops on hie;
> In heather besoms a' the hills gang by.[2]

Standing in long, rough grass, the monument looks out over Langholm. Beyond the town, in spots where the sun breaks through, lie little oases of bright hillside; then, the black outline of wind-blasted frontier hills. Someone has left lying on the base of the monument a little piece of slate, on which they have scratched the words of a MacDiarmid verse:

> The rose of all the world is not for me.
> I desire for my part

---

[1] As an interesting aside, Langholm must be one of very few places to have an 'official thistle grower'. He claims that the thistles which he grows, for ritual use in the Langholm Common Riding, rival any others in Scotland for size.
[2] Hugh MacDiarmid: 'A Drunk Man Looks at the Thistle'.

Only the little white rose of Scotland
That smells sharp and sweet – and breaks the heart.[1]

Someone else has put a bit of paper under the slate, briefing MacDiarmid with their vews about Brexit. I read it, have to agree, and put it back carefully under the stone for the poet's continuing attention.

Langholm may caw deeply cannie about Hugh MacDiarmid. However, the town will, I hope, in time see through his multiple layers of double-bluff and bombast, and overlook his improbable attempts to mention Langholm in the same breath as Lenin.[2]

I was, in any case, wrong on at least one thing about MacDiarmid. Though he may never inspire the love that Burns does, it seems that the best of MacDiarmid's lyrics do have the power to inspire votive offerings.

***

In my car, I follow Malc's thirty-five year-old campervan as it struggles up a brae. A long stream of other (and, I have no doubt, similarly patient) traffic follows us. We leave the van beside the Cross Keys, the whitewashed seventeenth-century coaching inn at the little village of Canonbie, before making our way by car, yet again, to Kershopefoot.

Today there is a modest breeze and a clear sky. I am, as ever, looking forward to a day's walk with Malc. We walk into Scotland at Under Burnmouth Farm,[3] heading southwards along the B6357. Today's walk can be summed up simply; we will walk along the Scottish bank of the Liddel Water for the whole length of that river that forms the Border. Malc asks me why we are not doing all this by kayak. It does sound quicker. I had not considered this possibility, and I do not advocate it to the reader, unless they have considered it thoroughly themselves.

I began this expedition in parts of the Merse I knew well. But here is unknown territory for me now. To borrow the words of one explorer from a couple of centuries ago, I feel that I am five miles west of the 'U' in 'Uncharted'. Walking westwards from here takes us not only through Scotland's West March, but also into the infamous 'Debatable Lands'.

The Debatable Lands have not actually been in any debate since the middle

---

[1] Hugh MacDiarmid: 'The Little White Rose'.
[2] Hugh MacDiarmid: 'The Seamless Garment'.
[3] Here at Upper Burnmouth, John Byers records in his book *Liddesdale* that Lord Balmerino, one of Prince Charles Edward Stuart's lieutenants, slept a night. Byers adds that, 'The bed in which he slept was kept as a memento until it fell to pieces.'

of the sixteenth century. They have a history, however, which is fairly Balkan in character. By that, I mean not just that this was once a *genuinely* disputed section of the Border, but that the area has been characterised in the past by long-running blood feuds. As instance of the latter, we hear in the ballad 'Lord Maxwell's Last Goodnight' about the Maxwell who has killed the Johnstone who has killed his (i.e. the Maxwell's) father, and who must flee Scotland as a result:

> Adue, Lochmaben gaits so faire,
> And the Langholm shank, where birks bobs bony!
> Adue, my leady and only joy!
> Trust me, I may not stay with the.
> Adue, fair Eskdale, up and doun,
> Wher my poor frends do duell!
> The bangisters will beat them doun,
> And will them sore compell.
> I'll reveinge the cause mysell,
> Again when I come over the sea;
> Adue, my leady and only joy!
> Fore, trust me, I may not stay with the.[1]

The name 'Debatable Lands' is occasionally (and infuriatingly) misused to describe the Borders region in general. In fact, it defines a relatively small and very specific parcel of once-disputed land. This area was described in detail by Sir Robert Bowes in 1550[2] and is (as ever) most succinctly deliniated by J.L.Mack:

> This tract of country was bounded on the west by the River Sark, on the east by the Esk and Liddell, on the north by the Bruntshiell Moor and Tarras Moss, and on the south by the estuary of the Esk. It measured about ten miles from north to south, and three and a half from east to west…and com-prised almost half the parish of Morton, a considerable part of the parish of Canonbie and the whole of the parish of Kirkandrews …As to its previous ownership, in the thirteenth century it was not debatable at all, but admittedly Scottish soil.

---

[1] 'Lord Maxwell's Last Goodnight' (*Child Ballads*, 195). Maxwell fled to France and came home in 1613, only to be beheaded. *Bangisters*: lawless persons.
[2] *A Book of the State of the Frontiers and Marches betwixt England and Scotland, 1550*, as quoted by J.L. Mack.

Graham Robb, by contrast, advances a case that the Debatable Lands were always:

> ...not so much under dispute, as recognised by both countries as neutral ground.[1]

This view seems to suggest that the Debatable Lands were some sort of equivalent to Moresnet, the little triangle of land which Belgium and Germany[2] both agreed to regard as No Man's Land between 1816 and 1920 (something which Moresnet's 3,000 officially-stateless inhabitants marked by adopting a national anthem in Esperanto).

I find it difficult to see how the Debatable Lands got their reputation if they were ever truly looked upon in this way. Both governments probably realised that the sheer effort required to pacify and meaningfully adminster the Debatable Lands was not worth the while. It was simpler to claim the lands nominally, treat them as a buffer zone, and periodically lay them waste whenever their lawless inhabitants got completely out of hand. A yet more matter-of-fact take is offered by one local writer in 1844:

> This Debatable Land was, however, hardly worth debating about, seeing that it is a bog, a marsh, a quagmire, a swamp, across which a man cannot pass at hazard lest he sink.[3]

This was threap land. 'Threap' is a Scots word for a very Scottish thing, and means to subject something to (probably endless) highly-opinionated controversy.

As we will see tomorrow, a diplomatic settlement of this dispute did eventually come about. Today we are walking in the northern part of the Debatable Lands, the section which was in 1552 recognised by both parties as Scottish, and which continues to be recognised as such today.

***

We walk along the dandelioned verge in the sun, passing the farms of Lawston and Longrow on our left, congratulating each other about how pleasantly easy all this presently is. After a couple of miles, we turn left down

---

[1] Graham Robb: *The Debatable Land.*
[2] Initially, the two parties were Prussia and the United Kingdom of the Netherlands.
[3] Peter Orlando Hutchinson: *The Chronicles of Gretna Green.*

the road into Liddelbank Farm, keen to make sure we do not stray too far from the Border itself.

A path from here takes us back down to the riverbank, through an Amazon of high summer nettles. I fairly but unhelpfully point out to Malc that, unlike me, he has chosen to wear shorts today.

We poke our way with dead branches past dead farm steadings, beating back a path for ourselves, with all the satisfaction of childish explorers. Here, among the ever-darkening trees, we must ford a decent-sized burn as it runs into the Liddel Water. In so doing, we cross the boundary of two modern local authorities, passing from the Scottish Borders into Dumfries and Galloway. More anciently put, we cross between Roxburghshire and Dumfriesshire.

I have studied all this on the map, but it has not crossed my mind till now that the word 'ford' here might well mean a crossing last used a hundred years ago, on a day when the burn was not – as it is today – in spate. Malc scores a re-taliatory point, after my remark about nettles and shorts; we have to wade well over our knees and so, for a while now, it is I who must do without trousers at all.

This burn is (or has been) variously called the Mere Burn or March (i.e. Boundary) Burn, though it is marked on O.S. maps as the Muir Burn (i.e. the Moor Burn). Whether this name reflects the fact that it runs from a moor[1] or that it runs into the national Border, marks a county boundary or indeed stands at the eastern edge of the Debatable Lands, I do not claim to know. Encountering so many boundaries in the space of a couple of sentences, however, invites speculation about where 'The Borders' actually are as a region. That is, (not to put things overly metaphysically) I wonder briefly what the borders of the Borders might be.

George MacDonald Fraser takes one particular historical view of all that, and holds that the Borders comprise:

> ...Northumberland, Berwickshire, Roxburghshire, Cumberland and Dumfriesshire. Add Selkirk and Westmoreland to taste.[2]

In Scotland however, when the phrase 'The Borders' is used today, it is definitely only the Scottish areas that are usually intended. Scottish Borderers often talk about 'on the English side' or simply 'Northumberland' when they

---

[1] The burn flows out of what is now a large plantation, at the other side of which are the standing stones at Windy Edge. These are the 'Bounder Stane' which once marked the northern corner of the Debatable Lands.

[2] George MacDonald Fraser: *The Steel Bonnets*.

are talking about what people in England tend to call England's 'Border Country'.

In fact, to most Scottish Borderers, 'The Borders' means specifically the old counties of Selkirkshire, Peeblesshire, Berwickshire and Roxburghshire. It means, in other words, more or less the area covered today by Scottish Borders Council, plus, (a strong argument can be made) this very easternmost little corner of Dumfriesshire.[1]

Malc and I are glad to have that matter sorted out. We are still more grateful that we have so far managed to keep our rucksacks (containing in my case, I am very conscious, my trousers) dry during our crossing into Dumfriesshire. We clamber up the steep and slippy banks of the Liddel through the trees towards Harelaw Mill, grabbing on to ever more slender branches as we go. We have to repeat the whole sorry wading procedure at another burn. It is not too deep, but it is uncertain going. I remember, half-way across and too late, a previously received wisdom (from a war film) about it being best to keep a pair of socks on for grip in this situation. Malc's advice about kayaks crosses his own mind again, but he has too much tact to mention it.

I advise the reader to ignore my route and stick to the main road, which, just beyond Harelawslack Farm, we eventually consent to join again.

***

The rolling farmland on this stretch of Border could not be more different to the wilds and forests of the Middle March. Yet the farms we pass today are smaller and more independently-minded-looking than those we can remember, further back still, in the Merse. The Border along the West March here is definite enough, but it is not marked by the stark distinctions we saw drawn by history in the East March, or by nature in the Middle one. Not since Berwick have I had to concede any real (if only historical) sense of debatability[2] along any significant stretch of Border. H.V. Morton described the West March this way:

> Wild centuries have left their mark along the Border, giving
> to each comfortable farmstead a rather startled look, and to
> each fat hayrick an air of vague uncertainty.[3]

---

[1] On one thing there is universal agreement; people in Galloway, as well as those in northern and western parts of Dumfriesshire, live nowhere near the Border. They laugh when they are occasionally mis-described as 'Borderers', merely because they live in the southernmost outcrop of the country.

[2] This, however, is a debate that really has been settled now for four and a half centuries, beyond even any of the sort of lingering ambiguities that still exist in Berwick.

Coming to the main road again, we turn left for a couple of miles, passing Harelawhagg Farm, and a river-bend with the appealing name of 'Hog Wash'. Then we walk on through the sparse Scottish settlement of Harelaw and the long, thin ferm toun at Linn's View. Here, a row of houses looks intently at England, as if it were the front row of a cinema.

It seems there is a scarecrow competition taking place locally, judging by the variety of these to be seen today in people's gardens around here. Some care has been given to creating one scarecrow which – it would seem – moons cheerfully at the Border, which is not far over the road from him.

We reach the road-end for Crookholm Farm. We take this road back to the river, as I am concerned we should be following the Border here even more diligently than we already are. Malc is less concerned about that, but humours me, not for the first time. His doubts are well-founded; we wade through a third burn. We walk along the Scottish bank of the Liddel for a wee bit here. After the farm steading, there is no obvious path for a few hundred yards, so we pick an improbable way through the scrub until, climbing up the side of the valley, we find ourselves looking down into the farm of Rowanburnfoot. A young dog in the distant steading hears or smells us; his manic barking ricochets for a mile either way along the Liddel Water.

It was here in November 1745 that Prince Charles Edward Stuart (for we meet him again) crossed into England, staying the night at Riddings Farm, on the English side. Here he dreamed, we can have little doubt, of a more comfortable bed in St James's Palace.

Today, this is where perhaps the most impressive border bridge of all sweeps over the river: the disused Liddel railway viaduct. We make an effort at getting onto the bridge, keen to see the view it would afford us far along the valley. The viaduct, however, is comprehensively shut off with high fences. Notices warn of the penalties for incursions. So, we walk northwards instead, along the old overgrown railway line, on which stand now quite aged trees. The dog has given up shouting at us from Rowanburnfoot. We clamber along the long-forgotten railway, through cuttings and along embankments, into the little village of Rowanburn.

Here by the roadside are two monuments to different eras. One, a pit-wheel, recalls Rowanburn's mining heritage. The other is a statue to the memory of the reiver Sandie Armstrong, known *inter alia* as Lang Sandie of Rowanburn, who had a fastness here. Sandie was hanged in 1606 along, it seems, with several (possibly eleven) of his sons. He had been on the run for almost six years, hav-

---

3 H.V. Morton: *In Scotland Again.*

ing been a member of the ambush crew who had murdered the Scottish Warden Sir John Carmichael (a feat of agility against the forces of law which earned Sandie his continuing status here as local hero). One of Sandie's sons is claimed to have penned these words before he was executed:

> This night is my departing night,
> For here nae langer must I stay;
> There's neither friend nor foe o' mine,
> But wishes me away.
>
> What I have done thro' lack of wit,
> I never, never can recall;
> I hope ye're a' my friends as yet;
> Goodnight, and joy be with you all! [1]

Today, Sandie's larger-than-life effigy peers into the road, seemingly menacing the driver of the Newcastleton bus into letting him on without a fare.

The main road takes us towards Canonbie. For a stretch here, the Liddel Water (which is still the Border) runs parallel with the Esk. This means we have to cut away from the Border for a short while now. There are no bridges over either river here and, after spending too much of today with my feet sliding over riverbeds and my boots hanging around my neck, I have no enthusiasm for any more. Unlike Young Lochinvar,[2] Malc and I have little inclination to make a dramatic swim across the Esk, and have brought neither broadswords nor towels with us in any case.

***

Scott said – unconvincingly – of the Border reivers that 'they abhorred and avoided the crime of unnecessary homicide'.[3] As we have seen, the reivers' society was in fact indisputably vicious, but it did create a poetry. The *Godfather* trilogy does not justify the actions of the New York Mafia, but neither does the behaviour of the New York Mafia undermine the merits of *The Godfather*.[4]

A little laughably, at the end of the film *Braveheart*, the Scots are described

---

[1] 'Armstrong's Goodnight' from Scott's *Minstrelsy of the Scottish Border*. Quite why Scott associates these words with this man is not clear.
[2] On whom, more tomorrow.
[3] Quoted by George MacDonald Fraser: *The Steel Bonnets,* among others.
[4] Mario Puzo: *The Godfather*. London, Arrow Books, 2009.

as 'warrior-poets'. G.M. Trevelyan sums up the legacy of the reivers rather more effectively, but makes a not dissimilar claim:

> Like the Homeric Greeks, they were cruel, coarse savages, slaying each other as beasts of the forest; and yet they were also poets who could express in the grand style the individual fate of the individual man and woman …The whole cut-throat population felt this magnanimous sorrow.[1]

The Border ballads are not short of material that expresses exactly these feelings:

> Gae dig a grave, baith wide and deep,
> And a grave to hald baith him an me;
> But lay Christie Graeme on the sunny side,
> For I'm sure he won the victorie.[2]

High above a sharp bend of the Esk, two miles north of tonight's destination[3] of Canonbie, these and other reiving sentiments are embodied in the shape of Gilnockie (or Hollows) Tower. Now restored as a centre for the Clan Armstrong worldwide, this is one of the finest remaining peel towers. Its unflinching grey silhouette is broken only by a couple of small windows here and there, like narrowed eyes. Together with one heavily-barred little door, these scant openings are all intended to minimise the chances of Gilnockie's residents being 'scomfished' (i.e. smoked out) by aggrieved neighbours. It strikes me as the kind of place where the wife of the house was, from time to time, in the habit of slamming a dish of spurs on the table.[4]

Within Gilnockie's thick walls, tickets are being sold by a friendly Terie,[5] who makes me a cup of tea and strikes up conversation:

---

[1] G.M. Trevelyan *The Middle Marches*. Newcastle, Northumberland and Newcastle Society, 1976.
[2] 'Graeme and Bewick' from Scott's *Minstrelsy of the Scottish Border*.
[3] In the interests of painful honesty, I should say that this account of a detour to Gilnockie is in fact from another day's visit and did not form part of the route for Malc and me.
[4] This story is told about both Charleton of Hesleyside and Scott of Harden. The hint behind the dish of spurs was of course intended to encourage the men of the house to go out looking for some of their neighbours' cattle.
[5] i.e. a native of Hawick, so named from the words of the town's mysterious anthem *'Teribus ye Teri Odin'*. This claims to have been a war-cry used at Flodden. Numerous inconclusive theories have been advanced as to what the words might mean, and in what, if any, language.

'Whaur aboots are ye frae?'
     'Frae Ashkirk, originally.'
'Ye mean ye're frae Hawick?'
     (with unintended but pronounced defensive-ness):
     'Ashkirk is a mile nearer tae Selkirk as it is tae Hawick.'
'Hmm. Ah weil. At least oo'll can aw agree aboot thon ither
place, ayont Selkirk.'
     'Galae?'[1]
'Oo'll hae nae sweirin here.'

This somehow puts me at ease. In this monument to the Borders' venerable traditions of inter-territorial suspicions, there is something deeply reassuring and courteous about the efforts this man has gone to, just to seek out some shared local foe, on whose depravity we can all, presumably, agree.

He tells me about the tower and its history, as well as its exhibitions. These include one on the reiver Johnnie Armstrong and another about the astronaut Neil Armstrong, who visited the tower in 1972. Today, a portrait of the latter stares blankly through the golden reflective visor of his space helmet and into the blazing log fire of a reiver's kitchen. Intriguingly, I also learn from my host about a cow which wandered into the tower one day, climbed up the spiral staircase to the roof and, whether simply tiring of this world or as a gesture of resignation towards all reivers, threw herself off the top. It is a strange and slightly troubling image, but I am assured there is a photo from 1943 to prove it.

Johnnie Armstrong built his tower around 1520. In 1528, that tower was burned by Sir Christopher Dacre, the Warden of the English West March. It seems to be a matter of real and admitted confusion whether the tower we are in now, or another one nearby, was Johnnie Armstrong's tower.[2] In any case, the one that has survived is a very worthy claimant.

Johnnie came to an infamous end in 1530, when he and many of his Armstrong retainers were hanged at Carlenrig in Teviotdale, after James V ensnared them into thinking they were being invited to join him on a hunt. James did himself few favours by rejecting Armstrong's offer to cut a deal:

     'Away with thee, thou false traitor!

---

[1] Galashiels.
[2] The earthworks marked nearby as 'Gilnockie Castle' may in fact be the remnants of the Gilnockie Tower burned in 1528. I fear I may already have angered the shade of James Logan Mack by even referring to what he considered to be Hollows Tower as 'Gilnockie'.

No pardon I will grant to thee,
But, to-morrow before eight of the clock,
I will hang thy eightscore men and thee.'

O how John looked over his left shoulder!
And to his merry men thus said he:
'I have asked grace of a graceless face,
No pardon here is for you nor me.'

In another version of the ballad, Armstrong makes an even more direct
remark to the king:

To seek het water beneath cauld ice,
Surely it is a great folie.[1]

Within three days of this encounter, the Armstrong estates were in the hands
of the Maxwells, which raises some interesting questions about the Maxwells'
potential role in this entrapment. Ultimately, however, the most disquieting
account of James's expedition to this part of the Border is found in 'The lament
of the Border widow', which claims to be the words of the wife of Cockburn
of Henderland, hanged by James V in Cockburn's own front doorway.[2]

I tuk his body on my back,
And whiles I gaed and whiles I sat;
I digg'd a grave and lay him in;
And happ'd him with the sod sae green.

But think na ye that my heart was sair;
When I laid the moul' on his yellow hair?
O think na ye my heart was wae,
When I turned about away to gae?[3]

***

Malc and I arrive finally in Canonbie, the tiny 'capital' of the Debatable Lands.

---

[1] Both of these are versions of 'Johnnie Armstrong' (*Child Ballads*, 196).
[2] It is reasonably well established that Cockburn was actually hanged in Edinbugh.
[3] 'The Lament of the Border Widow', from Scott's *Minstrelsy of the Scottish Border*.

The village name reflects the fact that there was an Augustinian priory here from 1165. The original village was in fact on the other side of the Esk, beside the priory which Henry VIII of England's forces destroyed at the time of the Battle of Solway Moss[1] in 1542. The village was described then as sharing a border with England on one side and as having debated territory on the other three. Canonbie has unambiguously been in Scotland since 1552.

The village was the scene, as late on as 1602, of a trial by combat between two Englishmen: Thomas Musgrave and the chivalrously-named Lancelot Carleton. Carleton had accused Musgrave of offering to hand over the castle of Bewcastle to the Scots. This may well have been the very last such formally-organised trial anywhere along the Border. The details of the agreed weapons are recorded meticulously but the outcome is unknown.

More recently, in 2001, Canonbie became the sad scene of Scotland's first outbreak of foot and mouth disease. This epidemic resulted in the slaughter and burning of animals on a massive scale here and across many parts of the UK. The outbreak also resulted in a UK general election being postponed and – more unthinkably than that – caused Selkirk Common Riding to be cancelled.[2]

By this time, hungry, we fully appreciate why Canonbie (population 390) was the subject of centuries of protracted, pitiless warfare; it boasts a pub and at least two shops.

The campervan finds a home for the night near the hamlet of Penton,[3] just over the Border. There, we find ourselves – more than a little oddly – the only residents of an otherwise empty caravan park. We celebrate today's walk, and the prospect of tomorrow's final triumphal lap. As the calor gas flame hisses under long-anticipated steaks and tattie scones, Malc and I feel that the words of at least one local ballad are now particularly apt:

> They gave him a wheat loaf to eat,
> And after that a can o beer;
> And they a' cried with ae consent,
> Eat brave Noble, and make good cheer.[4]

---

[1] On which, more tomorrow.
[2] A makeshift common riding, without horses, did in fact take place that year on a much-reduced scale. The Covid-19 pandemic meant a traditional common riding was also impossible in 2020.
[3] The emphasis of the place name is on the second syllable.
[4] 'Hobie Noble', (*Child Ballads*, 189A.)

Day 11: From Canonbie to Gretna
(Circa 9 miles)

*The Liddel Strength; Destiny arrives; Netherby and Young Lochinvar; The Esk;
Fish wars on the Border; The Scots Dike ends the debate; Armstrongs and
Grahams; The River Sark and the Battle of Solway Moss; Three writers cross the
Border by train; The Quintinshill disaster; A roundabout argument resolved;
Gretna Green and runaway marriages; The Devil's Porridge;
Where Sark rins over Solway sands; Wi' a hundred pipers an a' an a'.*

Today is the final day of our walk.[1]

If the reader climbs Everest or wrestles crocodiles – indeed, even if they are
an accomplished climber of Scotland's Munros – then the feat I have described
in this account may seem a pedestrian one, in both senses. However, it is no
less real for all that, and it is not quite over yet. The walk ahead of us today
illustrates, perhaps more than any other single day before it, just how varied a
country Scotland really is. The final nine miles of Border have a history as
rammed full of sturdy ingredients as a Hogmanay black bun.

Today, Malc and I will slice a significantly straight line through the middle
of the Debatable Lands, before we emerge blinking into the little tourist-Vegas
that is Gretna Green, and walk out towards the vastness of the Solway Firth.

In Canonbie, it is raining steadily, but the weatherman's pessimism is ill-
founded; after an hour or two, the rain relents, and the day is dry. We walk
three miles southwards along the B7201, through Woodslee Farm, to join the
main Edinburgh to Carlisle road, the A7. This morning, on our left, we again
see two rivers running in parallel: the Liddel Water and the Esk. It is still the
further away of these, the Liddel, that is the Border just now, until it runs into
the Esk not far away.

Near the place where the two rivers meet is the site of a castle called the
'Liddel Strength',[2] which lies just inside England.

The Liddel Strength is mentioned in an 1165 charter of William the Lion,
King of Scots. The motte and bailey here were captured by Longshanks, but
eventually destroyed by the Scots in 1346. It has all the usual gruesome castle-
tales to its name. For instance, it was here in 1346 that King David II of
Scotland is said to have responded to a plea for mercy from the English
commander Sir Walter Selby by making Selby watch his own two sons being
strangled in the minutes before his own summary execution.

One curiosity about the Border line itself at this point lies near the old railway

---

[1] For the moment.
[2] The Liddel Strength is not to be confused with Liddel Castle, near Newcastleton,
where Fergus of Galloway made some of his (fictional) appearances.

which runs beside the Liddel Strength. Building the line meant diverting a small section of the river here, but *not* moving the Border. The latter, by that point, was considered more or less immovable. So the railway company isolated a little sliver of Scotland on the newly-formed 'English' bank of the Liddel Water. It is a kind of industrially-made Scotch Haugh, if the reader can remember as far back as that near-equivalent little international oddity on the Tweed.

The fields beyond the castle lie in the English parish of Arthuret.[1] The hamlet of Carwinlay here is often identified as the site of the battle of Arfyderydd, fought between two Welsh-speaking princes in AD 573. Here, King Riderch Hael of Strathclyde was slain. Afterwards, according to some versions of events, St Kentigern ran into a 'hairy, naked madman' who was fleeing from the battle. This was said to be the king's bard, Myrddin Wyllt, who in turn then gets identified with the Arthurian wizard Merlin.

Going southwards, the Esk is the Border now – even if only for half a mile – and so we walk very briefly along its Scottish bank. Soon, on our right, a two-foot-wide border-burn trickles into a pipe under the road and then out into the Esk on our left. The burn marks the edge of Scotland, and also the edge of someone's front garden. I have to wonder if the owner built the house here to make a point. A life-size wooden figure in the front garden certainly makes his own feelings clear. This green-kilted sculpture of tree-branches holds its arms skywards in a Braveheart 'freedom' gesture, clutching a large saltire.

On our left, in the Esk, a tiny (and probably nationally-bisected) island lies midstream in front of the Marchbank Hotel. The hotel itself is – just – inside England. We pause near here at the 'Scotland' sign on the A7, and for a very specific reason.

***

I gave warning as far back as Coldstream that I would probably describe another episode involving the Stone of Destiny. It took place here, at this border roadsign by the Esk, on Auld Year's Day 1950.

It was here that the Stone came home, not by military force or political lobbying, but in the borrowed car of four penniless, idealistic young students from the University of Glasgow. There is something touching about this episode that fully justifies the place it has since earned in Scotland's folklore. The story is a rebuke to all cynicism.[2] An account of it was later written by

---

[1] The place name here is encouraging for those looking for Arthurian references, though almost certainly misleadingly so.

[2] It even renders in some ways irrelevant the doubts of some historians as to whether Edward I actually got the right stone in the first place.

one of the students, Ian Hamilton, who had somehow managed to hide inside Westminster Abbey on Christmas Eve[1] and remove the Stone from the Coronation Chair.

This has inspired several songs, including a famous one by Donald MacIntyre from South Uist (who spent most of his life in Hamilton's native Paisley):

> 'S gur coma leam i 'n Cearrara
> An Calasraid no 'n Calbhaigh
> Cho fad' 's a tha i 'n Albainn
> Nan garbhlaichean cas.[2]

This escapade, as well as representing the righting of an old wrong, sought to remind the world that Scotland was still there and still mattered, at a time when the country was slipping entirely off the political and cultural agenda of the UK. This was a time when hundreds of thousands of people had signed a petition calling for a Scottish Parliament,[3] and had been utterly ignored. In its own gentle, daring, eccentric way, the Stone helped to challenge many assumptions about Scotland.

Hamilton's account is not just an eloquent claim for Scotland's existence; it is also a song in praise of youth and adventure. The reader will not be too surprised to hear that reading it made a big impression on my young mind:

> We had not seen a police car for the last hundred miles. The next town was the Border town of Longtown. ...Here on the bridge was the ideal place for a roadblock. We grew tense and tenser... My mouth was dry, and my stomach fluttered like a white flag in a storm.
>
> Two miles further on, at half past two in the afternoon, we came to a sign that said 'SCOTLAND'. We passed the

---

[1] There is something coincidentally appropriate about the Stone being liberated at Christmas and coming home just in time for the Bells at Hogmanay. In 1950, these were still widely viewed as 'English' and 'Scottish' festivals respectively.

[2] 'I don't care whether it's in Kerrera, Callander or Calvay. As long as it's in Scotland, rugged and precipitous.' Calvay, incidentally, is the uninhabited island near Eriskay on which had been wrecked S.S. *Politician* in 1941, famously laden with whisky. Donald MacIntyre: 'Òran na Cloiche', from *Sporan Dhòmhnaill*.

[3] The Scottish Covenant movement, led by John MacCormick and others, reached its peak in 1949 and claimed to have gathered two million signatures. Its petition read: 'We pledge ourselves, in all loyalty to the Crown and within the framework of the United Kingdom, to do everything in our power to secure for Scotland a Parliament with adequate legislative authority in Scottish affairs.' It was dismissed out of hand by the Labour Government of the time, and by the Conservative one that came after it.

sign and gave a little ragged cheer, and shook hands. We were most moved. Success is a strange thing, and much nearer to tears than to laughter. A handful of miles into Scotland, we stopped. The symbol of her liberty had come back to Scotland.

We stopped and drew the coat back and exposed the Stone to the air of Scotland for the first time in six hundred years.[1]

***

From the border sign on the A7, we look into England. A mile away is Kirkandrews Tower, built by the Grahams around the year 1540, in a period when the loyalties of Kirkandrews parish, and indeed of the Grahams themselves, were genuinely unclear. The place name does seem to suggest that Scotland's patron saint is somehow staking a claim.[2] In any event, after a long-disputed history, the district has been in England since 1552.

Just beyond the tower is the palladian Netherby Hall (also in England). In Scott's *Marmion*, Young Lochinvar swims the River Esk here and arrives at a wedding in Netherby just in time to rescue his love from marriage to another, before bringing her back safely over the Border:

> O young Lochinvar is come out of the west,
> Through all the wide Border his steed was the best;
> And save his good broadsword he weapons had none,
> He rode all unarm'd, and he rode all alone.
> So faithful in love, and so dauntless in war,
> There never was knight like the young Lochinvar.
> He staid not for brake, and he stopp'd not for stone,
> He swam the Eske river where ford there was none;
> But ere he alighted at Netherby gate,
> The bride had consented, the gallant came late:
> For a laggard in love, and a dastard in war,
> Was to wed the fair Ellen of brave Lochinvar.

---

[1] Ian Hamilton: *The Taking of the Stone of Destiny*.
[2] J.L. Mack points out that Edward I's *Ragman Roll* of 1296 refers to Kirkandrews as being in Dumfriesshire (i.e. in Scotland). As to the name of the church, Nigel Tranter's novel *Kenneth*, provides a fictionalised explanation, saying that the relics of St Andrew paused there on their way to Fife.

While the incident is legend, both Lochinvar's family (the Gordons of Kenmure) and the setting for the drama, Netherby, are real enough. The story achieved an even wider fame in 1923 when its account of moustachioed villains and timeously-rescued heroines was found to be virtually perfect material for a silent film.

In reality, Netherby was the scene of less romantic (but no less powerfully-felt) cross-border tensions. The fish garth which was constructed by those on the English bank of the Esk to trap salmon here in the middle of the fifteenth century was a source of international difficulties for decades. Once people upstream in Scotland worked out why salmon were no longer ascending the Esk towards them, Scots destroyed the fish garth several times, leading to full-scale diplomatic attempts to resolve the matter by both Scottish and English monarchs. These included a number of inspections, as well as conferences held at the Lochmaben Stone near Gretna, but the debate smouldered on until at least 1543.[1]

In Scott's *Guy Mannering* we find a description of salmon fishing of a later and very different kind around here:

> …[It is] peculiar to Scotland, [and] may be called a sort of salmon-hunting. This chase, in which the fish is pursued and struck with barbed spears, or a sort of long-shafted trident, called a waster, is much practised at the mouth of the Esk …The sport is followed by day and night, but most commonly in the latter, when the fish are discovered by means of torches, or fire-grates.[2]

The present (mainly eighteenth-century) house at Netherby was probably built around a sixteenth-century Graham peel tower. Long before that though, there was a Roman settlement here known as Castra Exploratum. It was so-called because (and this is not easy to visualise now, so far inland) there was once a port here. Here were based *scafae exploratoriae*, Roman reconaissance vessels which sailed out from Netherby to keep watch for Rome over the Solway Firth. Essentially, their job was to prevent people from simply going round the end of Hadrian's Wall. It is likely that much of a Roman town ended up underneath the house's ever-expanding floors.

---

[1] Scott observes in his original footnotes to *Redgauntlet* that, much later on than all this, Sir James Grahame of Netherby constructed a new fish garth here, provoking renewed local violence. Scott goes so far as to say of this episode that: 'A renewal of the Border wars had nearly taken place in the eighteenth century'.

[2] This sport – otherwise known as leistering – was also once practised on the Tweed.

At this point on our walk – thanks to the civil servants of two child-monarchs[1] – the Border veers suddenly and sharply away from the Esk. It cuts over the main road in front of us, up the little burn, past the Braveheart scarecrow, and continues far over to our west in a conspicuously straight line.

***

A long, straight line of trees marches now into the far distance through fields of cattle. We are at the eastern end of the Scots Dike or, as it is often also known in Scotland, the March Dyke.[2] This is the three-mile-long earthwork, dug in 1552, to mark this stretch of the Border and end discussion about the Debatable Lands. The dyke runs from the Esk to the Sark, and still forms the Border here today.

Two commissioners were chosen by each government, with the French Ambassador as arbiter. Meeting on this spot, they drew a three-mile straight line over the Debatable Lands. The section to the north of the line (representing slightly more than half of the disputed territory) is in Scotland as a result, and that to the south is in England.

The French Ambassador decided that the line should begin where we stand now, at the Esk, 'opposite the house of Fergus Graham'. His advice about exactly where it should end was, however, slightly disregarded when the ditch, and its little wall of spoil, was eventually dug. In the end, for both governments, a priority was to make sure that the line at least theoretically separated Armstrongs from Grahams as much as possible. The dyke left the parishes of Kirkandrews and Canonbie (for the most parts) in England and Scotland respectively, with the parish of Morton split in two. It would be nice to think that this last fact gives us the present bizarrely-logical name of the Scottish parish of Half Morton.[3]

The dyke is now planted over entirely with a very long, narrow stretch of woodland. Many sections of the dyke (particularly those around its middle) have been ploughed up in the process of planting and felling, much to the protest of J.L.Mack, who a century ago managed to publish photographs of some of what was subsequently lost. The dyke is said once to have had stones

---

[1] Mary Queen of Scots and King Edward VI of England.

[2] 'Dike' is the spelling used in the (England-originating) place name, but 'dyke' is the more common Scots spelling used for a field-wall, and so this inconsistency will be observed throughout.

[3] The strange name is in fact possibly a reflection of a later ecclesiastical (as opposed to international) boundary dispute. In the seventeenth century, the (Scottish) parish of Canonbie annexed part of the (Scottish) parish of Morton. This did not actually leave very much of the old pre-Scots-Dike parish left. Calling it Half Morton today is probably being quite generous.

at each end bearing the arms of Scotland and England, though these are no-where to be seen.[1]

Malc and I wander into the flickering shadows of the groaning woods, to see if anything of the dyke remains. I had expected there to be nothing to see at all, yet there the Scots Dike clearly and amazingly still is. The trench that the two governments ordered the best part of five centuries ago is still a good few feet deep in some places. Someone has even gone to the length of coming away out here to place a small cardboard notice on a stick:

Caution: Imaginary Border Line. Please cross and enjoy.

I am not sure in exactly what spirit the notice was written. It strongly reminds me of the cardboard labels bearing instructions which are found in the early chapters of *Alice's Adventures in Wonderland*. There is, in fact, nothing imaginary, and the Border here is particularly visible. In any case, we take the notice's advice to heart, and thoroughly enjoy the Scots Dike.

Interesting as all this undoubtedly is, I must confess that I had not expected that walking the Scots Dike would take quite so long. We search out the best route we can: sometimes in Scotland; sometimes in England; sometimes along the ridge of the dyke itself, in those places where that can still be seen. We walk through the woods among land-lowping rabbits and along the edges of rain-blasted arable fields, which today look determined to defy harvesting. In a brief, eerie clearing, the silence and the trees are both suddenly broken by huge *War of the Worlds* electricity pylons that hum loud over the Border before the sound of wind in leaves is resumed.

The Scots Dike looks on the map like a straightforward walk. I think I may even have sold it as this to Malc. In fact, we climb again and again and again over the countless fences of adjoining fields in each country, passing between Glenzierfoot Farm (in Scotland) and Coultard Scar (in England). The line of trees still stretches far away, over what passes for a horizon in this flat and farmed landscape. Inevitably, Malc and I end up wading again, this time for what we are both now determined is to be the final time of our expedition. J.L.Mack said there were only two rivers worth speaking of that the Border crosses (rather than forms): the Whiteadder and the Bowmont. He obviously did not walk the Scots Dike on a day when the Glinger Burn (which cuts straight through the dyke itself) was in spate.

Further along the dyke, we see two more farms, Greenknowe and Cubbyhill, on our Scottish and English sides respectively. We follow the more-or-less

---

[1] We did see what looked like a more recent marker stone, half way along.

straight, bureaucratic line westwards for its whole three miles, until the dyke finally ends, and we come to the road at Crawsknowe. We are keen now to get a solid road under our feet. Malc is, in fact, sufficiently desperate to do this that he shows signs of trying to fight his way through an unpromising, massive hedgerow, just to find tarmac. We find a gate onto the road, in the end. To our right, a few hundred yards into Scotland, lies the farm of Tower of Sark, once the fastness of the legendary reiver Kinmont Willie. Instead of heading that way though, we follow the little road southwards down the English bank of the River Sark.

***

We walk past a farm with a strangely obvious name – Englishtown – which found itself officially in England in 1552. The farms of Cadgillfoot and Greenwrae, meanwhile, can be seen just over the river in Scotland. The little Sark, as it runs now from the Scots Dike to Gretna, has changed its course in detail many times across this flat country. In 1740, the rector of Kirkandrews commented on how the Border here had not in fact changed to correspond with the river, but that locals knew exactly where the line was.

It might be assumed that all such subtleties have long-since been lost and that the Border now simply follows the river wherever it currently flows. In fact, the O.S. Map shows that the line does wander a good few yards away from the banks of the Sark in several places, in old horse-shoe shapes which probably reflect the course of the river as it ran when first mapped by the Ordnance Survey a century and a half a go. If there are further changes to the Sark's course in future (as seems probable), I would guess it unlikely now that the Border will move with the river.

We are now firmly in Graham territory. Of all the reiving families, perhaps the Grahams had the most flexible nationality of all.[1] It is difficult not to feel sorry for their fate. James VI sought to destroy Grahams – whenever he was not busy seeking out Gypsies, witches, MacGregors, Catholic plotters, or Armstrongs – meaning that some 150 Graham families were eventually rooted out and transported to the Low Countries. When that did not work, they were transported to Dublin. When they started coming back from there too, it was suggested that they be planted in Ulster. The Lord Deputy of Ireland objected that the Grahams were 'a fractious and naughty people', and too much to contemplate adding into the already complicated picture in the north

---

[1] As Scott puts it of the Grahams, in *The Lay of the Last Minstrel*: 'They sought the beeves that made their broth/In Scotland and in England both.' The English Warden Scrope, meanwhile, referred to the Grahams on both sides of the Border as 'caterpillers', because of their tendency to destroy crops.

of Ireland, but people with the name Maharg can be found in Ulster to this day. It is widely understood that these are in fact Border Grahams who decided to reverse their names in an effort to achieve respectability in their new home.

None of these attempts to remove the Grahams from this part of the Border seem to have been ultimately successful. Even in these days, when declining numbers of people have land-lines and even fewer feel any sociable urge to list them in the phone book, a quick search of a ten-mile radius of Gretna produces eighty Graham households, distributed equally on each side of the Border.

At the little humphy-backit Corries Mill Bridge (not far from the well-named Drowned Cow Moss), we cross into Scotland. This is the final time we will make a border-crossing and, a little disappointingly, one of the few such moments not to have been marked for us by a 'Scotland' sign. We follow the Sark's Scottish bank through Campingholm and Westgillsyke farms. Over in England now lie the old peat workings[1] of the Solway Moss while, to our west, the Scottish countryside rolls away into Annandale.

The Battle of Solway Moss took place here in 1542. It belongs firmly in the long and cherished tradition of 'disasters for Scotland'. Henry VIII of England had asked his nephew James V of Scotland to follow him in breaking with Rome, something James was reluctant to do. Relations were not helped when James stood his uncle up in York after a meeting had been arranged there. In the end, at Solway Moss, the English commander Wharton's troops routed perhaps as many as 19,000 Scots who had been raised by Lord Maxwell, the Warden of Scotland's West March.

This was the final humiliation for the young James, and was followed quickly for him by a fever. As he lay dying at Falkand Palace, he fortold sadly (and inaccurately) that his only child, his baby daughter Mary, would be the end of the Stuart dynasty:

It cam wi a lass, an it will gang wi a lass.[2]

***

Our way takes us over the railway line that runs northwards to Glasgow. Looking a mile to our left from the bridge lies the unprepossessing Gretna

---

[1] The Solway Moss has not always been a stable landscape. On 16 November 1771, some 1600 acres of bog burst and flooded 28 farms under 30 feet of peat.

[2] This remark referred to the fact that the Stewart family had obtained the Scottish crown by marrying Marjory, daughter of King Robert the Bruce. James assumed that another family – perhaps that of his Tudor uncle – would now take the Scottish crown away from the Stewarts by marrying his own daughter. He had not considered the possibility that she (Mary Queen of Scots) might, in fact, marry a man called Stuart (Henry Stuart, Lord Darnley).

Junction, where trains cross the Border. As we have seen now, many border crossings have provoked a literary response. Perhaps few have done so as convincingly or with such variety as Gretna Junction.

Probably the most widely-known of these is in 'Night Mail', by the English poet W.H. Auden. The whole structure of that poem famously evokes a lonely mail train hurtling through the darkened Border countryside, carrying its cargo of postal orders over Beattock and on towards Glasgow.

A very different poem is Norman MacCaig's 'Crossing the Border', which certainly reads as if the poet is thinking of this same train journey. With typically precise imagery, MacCaig draws on flashes of scenes from the reiving times, and speculates about some of the forces that drag him on.[1]

This same spot also produced perhaps the best of all the short stories by R.B. Cunninghame Graham. Cunninghame Graham was many and varied things: an aristocrat, a socialist, a celebrated gaucho cattle-rancher in South America, a Liberal MP and a founder of both the Labour Party and the SNP. Today though, what matters for us is one compelling story, 'Beattock for Moffat', which he wrote about a train crossing the Border exactly here.

After an exile in London, an old shepherd is travelling one-way with his wife and brother, as they try to get him back home to Moffat in Dumfriesshire. He does not last quite that far, but he lives just long enough to cross the Border. The story is not as sentimental as it sounds; in fact it neatly inverts many sentimental expectations of the time. The dying man and his brother speak on the train in matter-of-fact terms that shock the old man's well-meaning but ultimately tactless Cockney wife:

> [They] began to talk, after the Scottish fashion, of the funeral before the anticipated corpse.
>
> 'Ye ken, we've got a braw new hearse ootby, sort of epescopalian-lookin, wi' gless a' roon', so's ye can see the kist. Very conceity too, they mak the hearses noo-adays. I min' when they were jist auld sort o' ruckly boxes, awfu' licht upon the springs, an' jist went dodderin alang, the body swayin to an' fro as if it would flee richt oot.'

The old man crosses the Border, in both senses:

> Gretna, so close to England, and yet a thousand miles away

_____

[1] MacCaig returns to this same journey (almost certainly when he is talking at least as much about mortality as about borders) in 'London to Edinburgh'.

from it in speech and feeling, found the sands flying through the glass. All through the mosses, which once were the 'Debatable Land' on which moss-troopers of the clan Graeme were used to hide the cattle ...the repatriated Scotchman murmered feebly that it was 'bonny scenery', although a drearier prospect of 'moss hags' and stunted birch trees is not to be found.[1]

***

Standing on the same bridge over the railway, here at Quintinshill, we turn to look the other way. Immediately to our right now is a sorrier spot than most. This was where the UK's worst ever railway disaster took place. It is a tragedy that calls out to be remembered, more than it generally is, for its sheer scale and for the official incompetence which surrounded it.

Here, a few hundred yards inside Scotland on 22 May 1915, two goods trains lay in passing loops while a northbound passenger train was waiting on the southbound line between them. The passenger train was struck by a troop-train heading for Liverpool. This was filled with new recruits to the 7th Battalion of the Royal Scots. Intended for a different kind of carnage – Gallipoli – these were, in the main, very young men from the Musselburgh and Leith areas around Edinburgh.

Roughly a minute later, a northbound express sleeper train collided with the wreckage of both these trains, at which point the gas lighting on the rickety wooden carriages of the troop-train caught fire, consuming all five trains in the area in flames.

Two signalmen were jailed in Scotland, essentially for completely forgetting how many trains were in one place at the same time. The railway companies were less willing to take any corporate responsibility.[2] A newspaper editorial from that week draws parallels with older tragedies near this same spot:

> It may be questioned whether, in the long and bloodstained story of the Debatable Lands, where the tragedy took place, there is set down anything more startlingly and poignantly tragic than the fate which, in the course of a few minutes of shock and flame, practically wiped out of existence a half battalion of the 7th or Leith Royal Scots ...an incident as

[1] R.B. Cunninghame Graham: 'Beattock for Moffat', from *Rodeo*.
[2] The compensation eventually paid out varied wildly between the payments offered to the families of railway workers and those of first-class passengers.

214

heart-rendingly mournful as any recorded in Border history.[1]

One writer records that the firm of Julius Pintsch supplied the highly-flammable oil gas for the troop train's lighting. They had also, it is alleged, recently been very involved in the development of the poison gas which had just been deployed by German forces on British and Allied trenches.[2]

News of the accident only reached the police in Carlisle after a sailor hitch-hiked there and told them. When the police then telephoned the railway company, they were told that the company believed the fire was 'out', but that possibly an ambulance might be a sound precaution. Emergency services eventually arrived on the scene three hours after the accident.

It is thought that 227 people were killed, and 246 injured.

***

We walk out of the under-stated, under-rated lowland countryside and into the full, pitiless blast of Scottish tourism at Gretna Green.

Between us and the Border now, we can see the visitors arriving thick and fast. We watch them peeling off the English M6, just beyond where it subtly becomes Scotland's M74.[3] Roundabouts bounce cars and coaches, as if in a pinball machine, towards the big tourist prizes: Gretna Green's Old Blacksmith's Shop, Gretna's[4] Old Toll Bar Cafe and, beyond those, the Kentucky Fried Chicken of Gretna Green Services.

Malc sees me watching the distant roundabouts, and smiles. I am not quite clear how the story of the 'roundabout incident' ever gained such circulation before the advent of social media, but it did. It is now so widespread that it might as well be embraced. There is little point now in me further gainsaying the story's main features, which the reader will doubtless already have pieced together in any case. If I have met the reader, I have probably already been introduced to them anyway as 'that guy who once camped by mistake on a roundabout in the middle of the night'.

It was moonless and snowing when Stuart Rivans[5] and I accidentally pitched our tent on a traffic island beside a roadworks, in the belief that it was

---

[1] *The Scotsman*, May *1915*.
[2] See John Thomas: *Gretna: Britain's worst railway disaster (1915)*.
[3] The southernmost section of the M74 is in fact the A74(M), if that distinction by any chance matters to the reader more than it does to me.
[4] Gretna and Gretna Green are two different villages, but so close to each other that it is difficult not to talk about them both in the same breath. Gretna is the name of the parish containing both settlements.
[5] See Day 5.

somewhere else completely. That was sometime around 1991, but I recall as if yesterday the jeers from road workers and passing motorists when we emerged the next morning from our frozen tent.

It was not a roundabout. It was just a sort of traffic island. In Tobermory. But roundabout it is now, in folklore at least, and who am I to argue with folklore?[1]

***

The Old Toll Bar Cafe has large signs, announcing it to be the first house in Scotland, and the last. Bonnie Prince Charlie, needless to say, stayed at Gretna on his retreat northwards. It would have been quite surprising, really, if he had not. Presumably he stopped to eat a scone.

An unpublished Latin diary shows that Rev. James Gatt, minister of Gretna at that time, made a sharp exit to Bowness in Cumbria when Charles Edward and his Highland troops approached, leaving his wife to cook for a number of the latter when they took up uninvited residence in his manse. Gatt describes the Hanoverian victory thereafter in verse, praising the arrival of the Duke of Cumberland's government forces in Carlisle, in poems with heroic themes like 'Impius heu saevit toto Mars orbe Britanno.'[2] At other times, Gatt writes mainly on rather dry subjects (and insists on doing so in Latin), but he does produce one poem in relevant praise of 'The delights of Gretna':

> *Pars Orientalis munitur flumine Sarcae*
> *cuius aquae tenues Anglicae prata rigant.*

> (The eastern side is guarded by the slender Sark,
> Whose gentle stream waters English meadows.)[3]

This pastoral scene – still there, if you leave Gretna's retail centre and look for it – is not what the tourists seem interested in. Today, as Scotland's official wedding capital, and also the country's most self-publicised gateway, Gretna Green seems to be thriving in equal measure on bus parties and wedding receptions. As one official brochure unironically advertises the place:

---

[1] The idea that we had gone so far as to camp mistakenly on an actual *roundabout* is almost certainly a conflation with a strikingly but coincidentally similar incident in the 1961 *Broons* Book.
[2] 'Impious war rages in the whole British world'.
[3] Quoted in Frank Miller: *The Poets of Dumfriesshire.*

Gretna Green: the power of love meets with a passion for
shopping

I have doubts whether two such radically different conditions could long
cohabit.

As we walk through the village, two coachloads of international tourists
are being unloaded beside the Old Blacksmith's Shop. A hundred excited
people soon begin to video every inch of the surrounding pavement and street
furniture. I am not completely clear what they have come to Gretna Green
to see, but they seem to be enjoying themselves. Fair play to them.

Probably one of the harsher assessments that has been made of this place
comes from Alistair Scott:

> Gretna Green stands alone as a sordid example of frontier
> Scotland.[1]

That does seem a little judgemental. It must be said though that Gretna
Green is like nowhere else we have walked through on our whole expedition
for sheer commercialisation. It does come as a bit of a shock to the system,
after a hundred miles of visiting fairly out-of-the-way places. Recent additions
include the 'Gretna Outlet Village' shopping centre and a 'courtship maze',
shaped like two wedding rings. For many years there was a 'Lovers' Leap
Motel', which certainly does seem to hold at least some echoes of the Little
Church of Elvis.

Reading my way along the Border has, happily, meant discovering a lot
more of Sir Walter Scott. It is therefore only fair, perhaps, that we now at last
see Scott's other great invention – tourism – in tooth and claw.

***

Gretna Green is, of course, famed most as a place for runaway marriages.[2]
These began when the Marriage Act of 1754 came into force in England.
Thereafter (in England), parents could legally veto the marriage of anyone
under 21. In Scotland, meanwhile, it was still possible for boys and girls as
young as 14 and 12 respectively to marry with or without parental consent.
Scots Law also still allowed for 'irregular' marriages, meaning that, if a

---

[1] Alistair Scott: *Native Strangers.*
[2] In Peter Orlando Hutchinson's *The Chronicles of Gretna Green*, the claim is made
(three-quarters in jest) that Gretna Green was where Sir Gawain of King Arthur's
Round Table got married.

declaration were made before two witnesses, then almost anybody (in Gretna's case, an enterprising blacksmith) had the authority to conduct a marriage ceremony. One such blacksmith 'minister' in Gretna claimed to have married some 3,000 couples.

By the 1790s, the *actual* minister of Gretna, Rev John Morgan, was railing against these weddings, complaining that people were beginning to get the impression that they were something to do with him. He called for action against what he called Gretna's self-appointed 'priests', describing one such as:

> ...a fellow without literature, without principles without morals and without manners. His life is a continual scene of drunkenness.[1]

Morgan adds that this celebrant is doubly deceptive; he is in fact a tobacconist, and not even the blacksmith he makes himself out to be to the tourists. In 1834, Morgan's successor, Rev James Roddick, describes the village's lucrative wedding venues as 'altars to Baal',[2] and calls for them to be outlawed. He goes so far as to hint that Gretna Green is in fact a very convenient place for bigamists.

Possibly not unrelated to this last suspicion, a comic opera called *Gretna Green* was an unaccountable success in 1783. Between arias and double-entendres, its hero, Rory the blacksmith-registrar, declares:

> Come ye young, and come ye auld,
> Come ye rich and come ye needy.
> I'll chain ye for a purse of gold,
> And sure ye cannot think me greedy!
> Rory, Rory, the god of marriage,
> To me ye drive in four-wheeled carriage!
> My temple's here on Gretna Green,
> Rory, the blacksmith god of marriage![3]

Today there do remain some differences in marriage law which might still prompt the very occasional genuine runaways. For example, unlike in England, in Scotland sixteen and seventeen-year-olds still need no parental consent to marry. In 1856, irregular marriages were legally reined in for the most part,

---

[1] *Statistical Account of Scotland.*
[2] *New Statistical Account of Scotland.*
[3] Charles Stuart: *Gretna Green: A Comic Opera.*

though this has not diminished the appeal of Gretna.

***

We walk under the main road, over the railway, and into the adjoining village of Gretna,[1] where a fully-fledged international customs post operated on the drove road from 1612 until 1707.[2] Gretna (in contrast to its more picturesque neighbour) is largely a modern planned village, set out mainly during the First World War. It boasts a greyhound racetrack and a football club, the latter of which stands in a sort of strange symmetry with the anomalous football club in Berwick, where we started.

Gretna F.C. long competed in junior English football, leading Clyde fans on one occasion to deride Gretna as 'an English pub team'. Perhaps stung by this, Gretna joined the Scottish Football League in 2002, aided a couple of years later by a steroid-like injection of cash from a wealthy benefactor. Gretna briefly and spectacularly made it to Scotland's Premier Division and the Scottish Cup Final of 2006. They lost there to Hearts in a penalty shoot out, before immediately crashing and burning. A successor club, Gretna 2008, now plays in the much more modest East of Scotland Football League.

One part of Gretna's history, which until very recently was certainly not advertised to the tourists, is its munitions factory. Yet the map shows that HM Factory Gretna (as it was originally called) is truly vast. The former factory and its associated military bases take up most of the English countryside that lies between Longtown and Gretna, and dwarf both villages. It used to be even larger, straggling for nine miles west into Scotland and taking in a large satellite site at Eastriggs.[3] Gretna Green's tourist trap in fact sits right in the middle of a very industrial area. Graham Robb observes that the sight of the munitions factory from the M6 is:

> ...a scene to test the resolve and the high spirits of the English couples who come to be romantically married at Gretna Green.[4]

As an aside, the munitions factory was the reason why (possibly uniquely

---

[1] Gretna possibly means 'gravelly haugh' (from the Old English *groeten halth*). Another option is that the last syllable comes from the Norse for 'island', reflecting the fact that the village was once surrounded at high tide.

[2] At what is now the Old Toll Bar Café.

[3] See Chapter 8. A number of the sites here have now been wound down, but there are still some in use by the Armed Forces.

[4] Graham Robb: *The Debatable Land.*

in Scotland) pubs in Gretna were operated until the 1970s by civil servants, who were under government instructions not to allow people to get drunk.

***

In making this journey, I have built up an unexpected respect for the scholarship (if not, generally, the conclusions) of the former MP for Penrith and the Border, a respect which until this point has kept me from referring to him as Rory 'the Tory' Stewart.[1] Sometimes, however, rhyme drives sense and, until this point, I have not been confronted by an actual concrete expression of Mr Stewart's unionism. I am today.

The large 'Hands across the Border'[2] cairn, or 'Auld Acquaintance Cairn' (built in much the same shape, strangely enough, as the alien spacecraft in the film *Independence Day*) was constructed at Mr. Stewart's instigation. It squats, just on the Scottish side of the border bridge, on Gretna's Sarkfoot Road. The cairn bears an explanatory notice which Mr Stewart himself has clearly penned. Curiously, the monument has been built *on* the Border to emphasise the argument that the Border is *not* there. The notice refers back to a supposed:

> ...period when this region was a 'middle land', part of neither Scotland nor England and independent of both.

If this structure were, as it is often presented, merely a monument to friendship between Scotland and England, I could readily add my own stone to it. It is not. As the cairn's own politically-charged website makes very clear, it is instead built 'as a testament to the Union', and as an expression of something called 'Union Love'. It was constructed in 2014,[3] needless to say.[4]

I realise that such Union Worship (as distinct from straightforward political

---

[1] Mr Stewart in fact left the Tory Party in 2019.

[2] As far as I can see, this initial proposed name for the cairn was abandoned, along with an ill-considered attempt during the referendum campaign to find enough anti-independence campaigners who might be willing to stand in a protesting human chain along the entire hundred miles of Border.

[3] The year of Scotland's independence referendum. In fact, I could see that more than one painted stone had already sneaked its unauthorised way into the cairn, bearing on it a blunt assessment of the Union, of which I am certain that the cairn's instigators would not approve.

[4] This cairn is in fact likely to be dramatically upstaged soon by another structure a couple of fields away. At time of writing, plans are at an advanced stage to build a 50-foot high 'Gretna Landmark' or 'Star of Caledonia' sculpture with the twin aims of announcing Scotland to motorists on the M74 and celebrating Scotland's scientific heritage (particularly the physicist James Clerk Maxwell). While it remains to be seen what this looks like, early indications suggest a sculpture with all the potential to rival the iconic significance of the Angel of the North in Gateshead.

support for the Union) is a reality for some people in Scotland, but I am no nearer getting my head around that now than I was when I first set off from Berwick. Former UK Prime Minister Theresa May certainly embraced such a cult, and regularly referred in reverentially-hushed tones to our 'precious' union, remarks which invited many unkind online comparisons with the character Gollum in Tolkien's *The Lord of the Rings*.[1] One of the most incongruous (and most derided) of such offerings was when Mrs May suggested in 2018 that the great legacy to humanity of Robert Burns was that his birthday provided the opportunity to hold a Burns Supper in Downing Street – so proving again beyond doubt the importance of 'our enduring union'.

Nobody else has come to see Gretna's union cairn today. It is probably best that I say nothing much further about it, and instead leave any comment on this very final stretch of the Sark here to Robert Burns's own much more capable assessment:

> Fareweel to a' our Scottish fame,
> Fareweel our ancient glory;
> Fareweel ev'n to the Scottish name,
> Sae fam'd in martial story.
> Now Sark rins over Solway sands,
> An' Tweed rins to the ocean,
> To mark where England's province stands-
> Such a parcel of rogues in a nation![2]

***

Our route takes us away now from Gretna's tourist megastores, through their prairies of car parks, and into a quiet road of bungalows. Then, leaving the road, we make our way down an avenue of thistles towards the shore at Sarkfoot. Here we cut across the fields to follow the last few yards of the Sark, before it runs onto the sands of the Solway Firth. It is the highest of

[1] To be fair to Mrs May, her language now sounds hamfistedly respectful towards Scotland, when set beside the scarcely-concealed contempt on display from her successor, Boris Johnson. In January 2019, Mr Johnson said it mattered 'not one jot' to him what the Scottish Parliament thought about Brexit, independence or (by more than implication) anything else. Such pronouncements are no doubt meat and drink to the authors of popular Scotland-sceptic hashtags such as *#rebuildthewall* (which, of course, show amusingly little awareness of what rebuilding Hadrian's Wall would actually imply for the good people of much of Northumberland).

[2] Robert Burns: 'Such a Parcel of Rogues in a Nation'. The rogues were of course Scots. The song decries those members of the Scottish Parliament who allegedly accepted bribes for voting in favour of the 1707 Union.

high tides now; nothing separates sea from agriculture. So, today we will in fact see no sands – just the waters lapping at our weary feet.

The breeze and the incoming tide today seem to be moving as much of the little river upstream as down here. The huge expanse of the Solway is suddenly visible.

Equally suddenly – and a little reluctantly – our journey reaches its long-sought destination.

The expedition that we began in earnest amid my sceptically-observing ancestors in the Merse (indeed, the expedition from which we inwardly pled to be released, in the quagmire of Hobb's Flow) is over. The Border comes to an end in a sound of seabirds, as the Sark empties into the sandy channel of the Esk.[1]

I secretly quite like the rain. I could – some other time – walk further along the Solway coast very happily. All this I would justify to Malc by the fact that, by coming here today at high tide, I now realise we have arguably missed seeing ten whole extra miles of Border. At low water, we would have been able to see the line as it made its way along the channel of the River Esk, and then that of the Eden, far out into the Firth. In fact, it is not until just beyond the town of Annan that the map makers finally put down their pens and the dotted line on the sand stops. To walk there would be to follow the map's Border line well beyond what most people would consider dry land and into the realms of theory. That new challenge is already forming in my mind.

For today, though, the expedition that we began at the North Sea, and then hirpled over hill and through forest for, is at an end. We have to stop somewhere, and the sea is a persuasive place to choose.

Walking the Border demands an imagination, and the exercise pays off if you have access to one – or ideally two. Today, Gretna's tourists ignore our sea-washed and luminously-fertile little field of cows. Clearly, they can't hear the pipers. And yet, only four-and-a half-miles (and two-and-three-quarter centuries) to our left now, beyond the grey munitions factory at Longtown, Charles Edward Stuart is wading the Esk[2] with a Highland host:

---

[1] We saw the Esk very briefly this morning, but it left Scotland for a while to pursue a career in England.

[2] Longtown provided the inspiration behind one of Scotland's best-known tunes. It was here, with the Esk in spate, that Charles Edward Stuart retreated from Carlisle in December 1745. A hundred years later, Lady Carolina Nairne penned the song 'Wi a hundred pipers an a' an a"' to commemorate another incident entirely – Charles's earlier advance *into* England to capture Carlisle (see Chapter 8). On that occasion, he in fact crossed the Eden near Rockliffe. Nairne included, nonetheless, the above verse about the Esk, with its image of Charles's subsequent desperate retreat *northwards*, via Longtown, on his way *out* of Carlisle. This part of the song either confuses or nakedly converts a Jacobite Dunkirk into a Jacobite D-Day.

Wi' a hundred pipers, an' a', an' a'.
The Esk was swollen sae red an' sae deep,
But shouther to shouther the brave lads keep;
Twa thousand swam owre to fell English ground
An' danced themselves dry to the pibroch's sound.[1]

Without the need for much further discussion, Malc and I turn and walk back into the village. We will find that Gretna, because of its continual traffic of eloping couples and outraged fathers, has quite a number of places in which to eat and drink.

---

[1] The song appears in the second edition of *Lays from Strathearn* (1846). Elizabeth Rainford published the musical arrangement five years after Nairne died. In 1958, Lord Rockingham's XI propelled the song to number one in the charts, largely by punctuating it with the frequent assertion that there was *a moose loose aboot this hoose*.

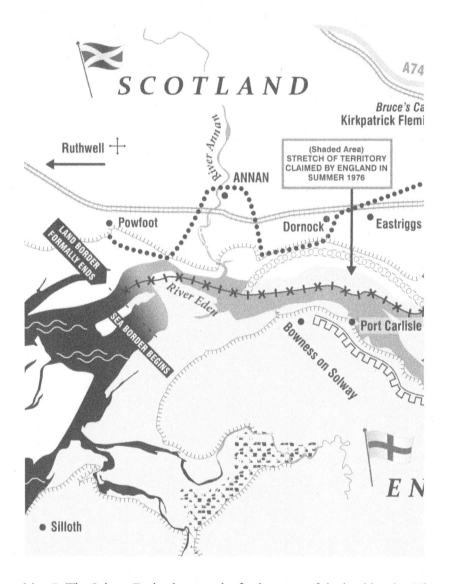

Map 7: The Solway Firth, showing the final section of the land border. This runs over the sands between Gretna and Powfoot, following the mid-channel of the rivers Esk and Eden, before it officially stops, and the sea border finally begins.

The Border legally runs wherever the Eden happens to be visible at low tide. The shaded area shows the six-mile stretch that was disputed, as a result, between Scotland and England for a few months as recently as 1976, when the Eden suddenly altered its course.

A74(M)

e's Cave
Fleming

Gretna Green

☐ 1448

GRETNA

Sarkfoot

River Sark

Longtown

triggs

Lochmaben Stone

River Esk

River Esk

ENGLAND

M6

arlisle

Rockcliffe

River Eden

River Eden

King Edward I Monument

Burgh by Sands

HADRIAN'S WALL

ENGLAND

N

CARLISLE

Scale (approx)

3 miles

CHAPTER 8
Afterthought: Solway Sands

(Circa 15 miles)

The line in the sand; Literary visitors; Robert Burns takes on some smugglers; The Lochmaben Stone; Explosive Eastriggs; A first and last distant glimpse of Hadrian's Wall; Longshanks bites the dust; Wading the Solway with Scott and others; Spiders in Kirkpatrick-Fleming; Annan and Powfoot; Medium filum aquae – the final border dispute of all; Into the Irish Sea.

We idly reckoned that our walk would end at the mouth of the Sark. In fact, the map shows the land-border stretching westwards for another ten miles along the Solway coast. Just about visible at low tide, the line will run now along the channels of the Esk and Eden. This is a book about a line, even if latterly one only in the sand. So, the reader will permit me to follow that line to its salty end.

I have finally[1] persuaded Malc to walk this 'extra' section of Border, as a sort of pedantic encore. We start again near Sarkfoot, in the southernmost streets of Gretna.

***

The writers I have mentioned to the reader so far have, in the main, been Borderers. It would be remiss now though not to mention a few literary visitors to the Border, and particularly to this end of it.

William Wordsworth came, though he wrote mainly of what he anticipated he *might* see a little further north in Yarrow. John Keats visited the Solway to see the setting of *Guy Mannering*. It seems he had not gone so far in his enthusiasm as actually to read Scott's novel, but this did not prevent him from writing a poem 'Meg Merrilies' in honour of its Gypsy character. Coleridge came north too, though he appears to have been keener on Scotland than on the Scots.[2]

A lesser-known visit to the Border was that paid by the English playwright and poet Ben Jonson who (amazingly) walked all the way from London in 1618 to visit the land of his Annandale reiving grandfather.[3] A recently-

---

[1] In fact, before we could walk this final stretch, we had to wait for a brief summer relaxation in some of the country's movement restrictions, following the strange and terrible stillness which had swept over the world in early 2020.

[2] Coleridge was a Cumbrian.

[3] Perhaps because he had heard about how wild the Johnstones still were, Jonson in fact walked via Berwick to Edinburgh instead.

discovered account of his expedition, written by someone who walked with him, now verifies all this.[1]

None of these visits compare though, for sheer rock-star-on-tour qualities, with the 1787 visit to the Borders of Robert Burns. He got to Berwick, Kelso, Duns and Jedburgh, and briefly reached as far south as Carlisle, from which last place he writes to his friend William Nicol. He does so – unusually for his letters – in Scots:

> I hae dander'd owre a' the kintra frae Dumbar to Selcraig[2]
> and hae forgaither'd wi' monie a guid fallow and monie a
> weelfar'd hizzie. I met wi twa dink quines in particular, ane
> o them a sonsie fine fodgel lass, baith braw an bonnie; the
> tither was a clean-shankit straught, tight, weel far'd winch,
> as blyth's a lintwhite on a flowerie-thorn.[3]

Though certainly not a Borderer, Burns lived enough of his life not too far away in Dumfriesshire for us to categorise him here as more than just an amorous literary tourist. In any case, Burns had at least a passing interest – poetic, political and (as we will see) professional – in the Border at the Sark. He was of course also fascinated, if not entirely in earnest, by those other 'border' rivers which form checkpoints between this world and another. [4]

***

Smuggling across the Solway was commonplace until 1707.[5] After the Union, the land border between Scotland and England meant less (from a

---

[1] See James Loxley: *Ben Jonson's Walk to Scotland*.
[2] Selkirk.
[3] From *The Letters of Robert Burns*. Burns's visits are marked by plaques around the countryside. It is considered good luck to touch the one in Selkirk, whenever walking past, a tradition difficult not to see as having origins in a fertility ritual.
[4] I am thinking, of course, of the last scenes of Burns's 'Tam o' Shanter', which must have made some early impression on me. When we were about nine, a friend and I were exploring a lonely and long-abandoned herd's hoose near Ashkirk. Without warning, a ghost walked slowly and determinedly across the creaking floorboards above us. It may in fact have been a rat. If so, it was one of quite exceptional size, and wearing tackety boots. We ran in very genuine terror through the whins, looking back regularly at the black, empty windows of the ruined house, until we reached a nearby burn. We jumped the burn, and then immediately sat down. And there, within sight of the same house, we happily ate our cheese pieces and chocolate Wagon Wheels, in the smug knowledge that no unchancy spirit could cross running water.
[5] This often involved such ingenious covers as 'pregnant' women (carrying animal bladders, filled with whisky, strapped around their waists) who waded across the Solway.

tax-evasion point of view) than did the sea border, just to the west, between Great Britain and the Isle of Man. So, throughout the eighteenth century, much brandy and tobacco found its way into Britain via the low-tax island[1] and then, as often as not, along the discreet little lane here into Gretna that is still known as Whisky Loaning. In Scott's *Guy Mannering*, we meet a Dutch smuggler working on this coast who goes by the name of Dirk Hatteraick. He is based on a real-enough character, once operating around here, called Captain Yawkins. People here believed Yawkins had named his ship the *Black Prince* in honour of the Prince of Darkness.[2]

This black economy was what brought Burns here to Sarkfoot in 1792, when he became involved in one of the more dramatic events of his civil service career: the seizing of the brig *Rosamund*. Burns's celebrity status ensured that this became a news story very quickly.[3] A party of dragoons set out, while the vessel's crew resisted all attempts by them to board. Accounts show that one company was indeed 'led by Mr Burns', and that it approached 'in a martial and determined manner upon her rebellious crew'. The excisemen waded out to the vessel, under fire, until the crew jumped overboard and splashed towards England, leaving Burns and his colleagues to salvage the *Rosamund* and her contents.

A path along the edge of the Esk (which manages today to be simultaneously sea, river, and border) now takes us as far as the farm of Stormont. This was the scene of a battle in 1448 between the Percys and Douglases, known variously to history as the Battle of the Lochmaben Stone or the Battle of the Sark. It was the first major Scottish victory since Otterburn in 1388. It is unclear how many people died, but it is thought possible that almost as many were drowned as were slain.

The battle takes one of its names from the the impressive Lochmaben Stone, remnant of a stone circle,[4] which stands nearby beside the Kirtle Water. There is no loch here, despite the name.[5] The stone, erected around 3,000 BC, was

[1] Until 1765, the Isle of Man was the personal feudal possession of the Duke of Atholl, who then sold it to George III. Although an arms-length possession of the Crown since then, the island is still not part of the United Kingdom. In recent decades, the island's ancient parliament, Tynwald, has gradually assumed many of the powers of an independent state. The Isle of Man is in fact now significantly more autonomous than Scotland.

[2] In *The Smugglers*, by S.R. Crockett, Yawkins gets a mention or two under his own name. This tale of Galloway smugglers and Gypsies owes more than a little to *Guy Mannering* itself, (overlaid with the homespun wisdoms of the Victorian manse). In another Crockett adventure tale, *The Raiders*, Yawkins also appears.

[3] See *Edinburgh Evening Courant*, 8 March 1792.

[4] A second surviving stone can just be seen, hiding in a fence.

[5] The name is in fact from the Old Gaelic *cloch* ('stone') and *Maponus*, who was probably a local god. A Gaelic place name as far south as Gretna is, no doubt, a daily irritant to those people who have a grievance against Gaelic.

for long the south-western corner-post of the Debatable Lands and, up until the Union of the Crowns, was a regular meeting-place for the exchange of hostages. It also marks one end of the Sul Wath, the fording point over the Solway that has almost certainly come to give the whole Firth its name.[1]

***

Walking further west along this stretch of the shoreline sounds attractive, as an idea. From all I can see, however, this would mean squeezing a way between a swift tide and the equally non-negotiable perimeter fence of the huge military sites at Eastriggs. I have prevailed on Malc for us to cut inland for a while instead, via the hamlets of Old Graitney and Rigg, where we join the B721. This does not make for the best of views, for a couple of miles, and there is some tediously-regular waiting in verges and ditches in order to make way for the fast-oncoming traffic.

This takes us into the little village of Eastriggs, billed on signposts as 'The Commonwealth Village'.[2] Sure enough, Eastriggs flies a (seldom-elsewhere-seen) Commonwealth flag, in honour of the community of munitions workers who were hastily assembled and housed here from around the Empire, to work in HM Factory Gretna. This is reflected too in the village's exotically-imperial street names, which include Delhi Road, Brisbane Road, Halifax Road, Ladysmith Road and Dunedin Road.

The munitions factory, once the largest in the world, was born out of the 'shells crisis' of 1915, when Britain realised it had already expended more explosive in France and Belgium than it had initially imagined to be either possible or necessary. Sir Arthur Conan Doyle, visiting the factory at that time, commented on the 800 tons of cordite propellant which the site's mainly female workforce were manufacturing every day, often turning their hair (and, one wonders, their lungs) yellow in the process.[3] Conan Doyle described the substance they were making as 'the Devil's porridge', a comment that now gives a name to the Devil's Porridge Museum at Eastriggs, which tells the factory's story.

The little locomotive 'Sir James' sits guard outside the museum, camouflage-painted and (possibly uniquely among steam engines) built without any place in which to light a fire. Eastriggs was once such an unimaginably

---

[1] A *wath* is a ford. The shape of the coastline here has changed dramatically over the centuries, and it is therefore difficult to say with certainty the exact routes that some of the ancient 'wath' names represent.

[2] The village's chip shop, we find, continues to be called the Commonwealth Takeaway.

[3] Photographs sadly show many of the women mixing these noxious chemicals with their bare hands, which, in many cases, caused both nails and teeth to fall out.

explosive village that locomotives had to be filled with steam elsewhere, before venturing briefly near the place.

***

Looking out from Eastriggs, a mile offshore, the Esk runs imperceptably now into the channel of the Eden, our very last border river of all. Beyond that lie the wilds of the Rockcliffe Marsh and England.

As mentioned earlier, Prince Charles Edward Stuart and his forces waded south across the Eden near Rockcliffe on their way to capture Carlisle. The twentieth-century poet Deòrsa Mac Iain Dheòrsa (George Campbell Hay) seeks to imagine the Highlanders' thoughts then, as they reached England:

> *Nuair a chuir an t-arm an abhainn,*
> *'s a sheas iad air ceud raointean Shasuinn,*
> *thionndaidh iad gun ghlaodh, gun fhacal,*
> *dh'amhairc iad le dùrachd dhainginn*
> *air Albainn, 's rùisg gach fear a chlaidheamh.*
> *Bheachdaich iad 'nan tosd car tacain,*
> *is gheall iad dhi an neart's an gaisge.*
>
> *Sgrìoch na truaillean fo'n stàilinn,*
> *Dh'èigh a' phìob is lean am màrsal.*

(When the army had forded the river, and they stood on the first fields of England, they turned round without either a cry or a word. They looked with steady, purposeful devotion on Scotland, and every man unsheathed his sword. They gazed silently for a while, and vowed to her their strength and courage. The sheaths scraped under the returning steel, the pipe cried out and the march continued.)[1]

Rockcliffe is very near Burgh by Sands where, since 1685, a monument has marked the place where Edward I of England died in 1307. In Scott's *Redgauntlet*, an old Jacobite erupts in an uncharacteristic outburst of feeling when this monument is pointed out to him:

---

[1] George Campbell Hay: *'Feachd a' Phrionnsa'*. Charles and his forces waded south via either the Peat Wath or nearby Rockcliffe Wath, and therefore not *quite* through the 'first fields of England' – but not far off them.

'Yonder monument is erected to the memory of the tyrant Edward I. The just hand of Providence overtook him on that spot. ...Edward's grave is the cradle of our national freedom.'

Edward I has, of necessity, made more appearances in this story than I would have chosen or than he deserves. At least the book ends with him safely dead and buried, or – in his case – perhaps dead and boiled.[1]

Possibly one of the reasons why some prim people in Scotland react badly to our *de facto* national anthem 'Flower of Scotland' is because the tune provides a convenient pause after each of the song's several references to Edward I. Into these metrical gaps, Scotland football fans and others are free to insert any two-syllable assessment of Edward's character which they choose. In general, by any reasonable historical measure of Edward, these assessments are not overly-harsh.

***

Today, the uninviting fenced-off landscape of MOD properties here on the Scottish shore is mirrored on the opposite coastline by an array of enormous masts which conduct a constant, unguessed gossip with nuclear submarines. On the hillside to our right now lies the equally tourist-forsaken former Chapelcross nuclear power station, whose magnox reactor cooling towers loomed over the Scottish coastline here until 2017.[2] Chapelcross's cathedral-like remnants now seem determined to carve out a role for themselves as an unromantic ruin. It occurs to Malc and me, again, that we may have chosen a path less-walked.

The next hamlet, Dornock, by contrast, is a peaceful little place of douce bungalows and ancient orange-sandstone steadings, which peer out with only slight curiosity into the vast silver haar of the firth. The kirk at Dornock is locked. Its graveyard tells stories of sailors and shipowners – the sort of tales we have not heard on this expedition since we left Berwick of distant memory. This meeting with the sea makes me realise we are certainly not in the Borders[3] now. Yet we are – equally certainly – still on the Border, which lies only a few

---

[1] The tradition is that the dying Edward called for the flesh to be boiled off his bones, so that the latter might be carried into future invasions of Scotland. If he really asked this, then the request was not honoured, as Edward's tomb in Westminster Abbey was opened in 1774 and showed little evidence of anything of the kind.

[2] Power generation was only the less disquieting part of Chapelcross's function. It also produced nuclear weapons-grade plutonium.

[3] See Day 10 for some views on where the Borders are as a place.

hundred yards out under the incoming tide. Indeed, this was once viewed as bandit country, just as much as were other, dryer, points along the line. The Solway's various *waths* provided border crossings which were once as identifiable as the Carter Bar or Coldstream Bridge.

The reiver in me is reassured to learn that, as late on as 1626, Scots waded and rowed from here over to Bowness-on-Solway to appropriate the bells of St Michael's Church there. The Scots unfortunately managed to drop the bells, half way home, as they made hurriedly for their boats. A retaliatory English raiding party then set out from Bowness over to Scotland and – more efficiently – removed a bell from Dornock. For four centuries, the Church of Scotland has made regular (though increasingly tongue-in-cheek) demands of the vicar of Bowness to give Dornock their bell back. As for the bells taken from Bowness in the first place, these still presumably lie somewhere out in the mud near a point now called the Bell Pool.

***

Little Dornock, as well as being our final encounter with reivers – all be those reivers with boats rather than horses – has another distinction. Here is the only place on our whole walk where we have come within sight (with a little imagination) of Hadrian's Wall. We encounter the wall, which so many people still imagine marks the Border, for both a first and a last time; over at Bowness-on-Solway is Hadrian's Wall's official western end. Here, for a single fleeting moment, the wall and the Border do in fact come within a few hundred yards of touching.

A long summer evening stretches out. Ignoring, once again, the more conventional tourist hotspots, we walk down to the shore through the grounds of Dornock's meat-processing plant. I am not sure if it was this or some other similar facility on the Solway that provided the inspiration, but it seems relevant now to say that a song with the unlikely name of 'Solway Firth' was released by the U.S. metal band Slipknot in 2019. The song deals with the issue of living a lie, something whose consequences the band compares vividly to the insides of a slaughterhouse.

Neither the lyrics, nor the video (which shows severed arms being thrown around and heads being bashed into sinks), really explain why the song is named after the Solway Firth. It is, strangely enough, quite compelling though, and definitely worth the reader giving a listen.

***

232

Not far from us now, in Kirkpatrick-Fleming, a cave claims to be the one in which Robert the Bruce hid in 1306. Here, according to a (disappointingly-modern) legend, Bruce drew political inspiration from a spider which he saw patiently spinning its web.[1] The cave is now, prosaically (but, for us, very conveniently) in the middle of a caravan and camp site. Following Bruce's example, we seek our refuge for the night there.

The cave doesn't really take much discovering these days. Given away by a nearby large chromium effigy of a knight on horseback, and by the tell-tale smoke of barbecues, it lies roughly between the children's play park and the toilet block. Once we are inside the cave though, we realise that it is (or once was) actually in a very concealed place. High up in a tree-lined ravine above the Kirtle Water, the cave is only accessible now thanks to a modern ramp and steps (earlier tourists were invited to abseil in). A square alcove inside claims to be the niche for an altar, while the National Museum of Scotland holds what are said to be the cave's solid-stone doors.

Whatever the truth of all that, in 1306, Bruce was certainly in hiding somewhere near here, and with good reason. He was being hunted down by Edward of England for having recently dared to be crowned King of Scots. Additionally, some weeks before his coronation, Bruce had been excommunicated by the Pope for the murder of his rival John Comyn. The killing had taken place in a very ill-considered place indeed – before the high altar of Greyfriars Kirk in Dumfries.

It was more than difficult for the medieval mind to grasp the idea that Scotland's hero-king might have done this. Bruce's loyal biographer John Barbour does his best to introduce a note of doubt about what exactly happened, but even he has to concede that this was not Bruce's finest act:

> Nocht-for-thi yheit sum men sayis;
>
> At that debat fell othir-wayis;
>
> But quhat-sa-evyr maid the debate,
>
> Thar throuch he deyt, weill I wat.
>
> He mysdyd thar gretly but wer
>
> That gave na gyrth to the awter.[2]

---

[1] The story is that Bruce resolved here to 'try, try again', after watching a spider refusing to give up. This tale probably first appears in Scott's *Tales of a Grandfather* (First Series), though Scott does not identify a specific cave. Some have suggested that Scott in fact adapted a legend about the Black Douglas.

[2] 'In any case, some men still say, the quarrel happened another way. But whatever was the cause of their debate, I certainly know he [Comyn] died as a result. He [Bruce] definitely acted very wrongly in that, for he showed no respect to the altar.'

Others have likewise done their spider-like best to spin things that Bruce 'merely' stabbed Comyn in the church (without killing him), after being provoked. This version of events invites us to believe that Bruce came out of the church door and sheepishly admitted roughly what had happened, only for his lieutenant Roger de Kirkpatrick then to rush in with a blade, crying 'I'll mak siccar'.[1] Another equally enthusiastic (and possibly rather competitive) friend, Sir Robert Fleming, is then said to have gone one better by decapitating Comyn and announcing, in blood-drenched satisfaction, 'Let the deed shaw'.[2]

It is tempting to think that the village of Kirkpatrick-Fleming gets its name directly from this pair of characters, both of whom sound as if they have been asked by history to take some convenient (and not totally convincing) responsibility for their master's deeds. Sadly, this correspondence of names between the knights and the village is probably not much more than coincidence.[3] It is convincing as folklore though, not least, as Malc tells me (showing a little irritation at my scepticism), to Flemings such as himself.

***

After packing up at Bruce's Cave Campsite, we make our way back to Dornock. This time, we really are on the last brief leg of our walk, and Malc (rightly) lobbies that this time we should walk along the shore. So, we set out into a calm bright morning and along the long expanse of crumbling shingle from Dornock Mains, by the edge of a still-retreating tide. We are about three-quarters of a mile north of the Border.

Out amid the ever-shifting grey distinctions between land and sea can now be seen a few haaf nets, strung out on their wooden frames. Several more stand drying beside our path. These are the traditional means of fishing for salmon and sea trout here, and their use is older perhaps than the Vikings who gave them their name.[4] They are limited now to the Nith, Annan and Eden.

The farm of Seafield now marks the Scottish end of the Bowness Wath (or Annan Wath), walked over by Bruce, Wallace, Longshanks and many others since. People drove their cattle from here to Bowness until, in 1869, a railway viaduct of breath-taking scale was built to carry Cumbrian iron ore to the

---

[1] 'I'll make sure' (i.e. 'I'll finish the job off').
[2] This gleeful remark has been the motto of the Flemings since.
[3] The village name Kirkpatrick predates this incident, and a Fleming landowner added his own name onto the end (to distinguish the place from other Kirkpatricks) only much later. That said, both the Kirkpatrick and Fleming families do have long associations with the area back to the time of Bruce.
[4] 'Haaf' comes from the Norse word for 'sea'.

hungry steel works of Lanarkshire.[1]

Here I realise that the Border line is wearing fast now into both the theoretical and the sea. That said, a faint silver current can still be seen bubbling up from the Eden, marking the Border beneath the waves. The tide – on which I have been keeping a watchful eye – has started to turn, and now comes in at an astonishing rate before our eyes.

In *Redgauntlet*, Scott imagines a last-gasp appearance by Prince Charles Edward Stuart on the Solway coast in the 1760s.[2] The story's hero, young Darsie Latimer, misjudges the tide somewhere near here, as he tries to cross the Solway on foot. He is eventually saved only after a stranger on horseback warns him:

> 'Best make haste then… He that dreams on the bed of the Solway, may wake in the next world. The sky threatens a blast that will bring in the waves three feet a-breast.' So saying, he turned his horse and rode off, while I began to walk back towards the Scottish shore, a little alarmed at what I had heard; for the tide advances with such rapidity, upon these fatal sands …I began a race as fast as I could, feeling, or thinking I felt, each pool of salt water through which I splashed grow deeper and deeper.

We walk up the old railway line from the northern stump of the old viaduct and into Annan town centre. The town is heralded for us by an enormous peal of thunder that shatters the day's heat and splits the sky with black rain. The drains at once overflow, and we run for shelter under a bridge. Looking up from my soaking map, I shout after Malc that the Royal Burgh of Annan (population 9,000) is probably named after Anu, a local goddess of prosperity. Malc does not hear, but a group of fourteen-year-old boys running the other way do, and reckon me the funniest thing they have seen that day. On reflection, I can understand their point.

When there was a bridge to England, Annan must have continued to feel like a town on the Border. Now it feels much more like a town on the Scottish coast. Annan, whose old buildings, including its impressive town hall, are of an almost orange sandstone, has a shipbuilding and engineering heritage. It remains the most industrial place we have walked through since Berwick. The

---

[1] After the railway closed in 1921, the Solway Junction Viaduct formed for a few years a very convenient way for Scots to walk over to England (in which latter country it was possible to get into a pub on a Sunday) until the viaduct was dismantled.

[2] While completely fictional, this episode no doubt draws on an actual, rather pathetic, *incognito* visit made to England by Charles in 1750.

town's distillery, reopened in 2014, provides Scotland once again with one of its most southerly sources of whisky.

I could go on here, and say something about the Battle of Annan (1332) or the origins, in this part of Scotland, of Robert Bruce, and Thomas Carlyle. Perhaps I could even say something of the Solway's modern folklore, including the story of Annan's phantom removal van or the deeply untroubling tale of the Solway Spaceman.[1] But we should probably keep moving while it is still dry.

***

I have mentioned, along my way, the little border disputes and uncertainties which there have been since 1603. The reader will have noted that the very tininess of most of these only serves to emphasise one of my regularly-laboured points. It is appropriate therefore that I have been able to keep the strangest – and by far the most recent – of these disputes till last.

Within the last half-century, a five-mile-long stretch of Border on the Solway Firth has moved twice – not by political or military might, but by the forces of nature. This is because the Border here is traditionally understood to be the *medium filum aquae* (i.e. the mid-point of the stream) of the River Eden at low water. This channel normally runs more or less half-way between the two countries' coastlines.

In July 1976, however, a stretch of the Eden (running between its confluence with the River Esk and the point where the River Annan runs into it) suddenly moved to a new and more northerly channel, running virtually right along the Scottish coastline.[2]

At its most practical, the question immediately arose as to whether the English water authorities could now claim to administer the resulting five-by-one-mile strip of new English territory (if that is what it was). In particular, it was unclear who might now regulate net-fishing there.[3] How could the fishing rights (extending out to a rock called the Altar Stane in the 'old' southern

---

[1] In 1964, local fireman Jim Templeton took a photograph of his young daughter playing at Burgh Marsh on the English side of the Solway Firth. He was surprised when the photo came back from the developers with what appeared to be a space-suited alien standing behind her. It is now fairly well established that this is in fact an over-exposed image of the back of Mr Templeton's wife's head. Mr Templeton's reading of the situation was, it would seem, made in all sincerity. He did not seek the publicity which followed, when the photograph briefly became a worldwide media story. It has subsequently been pored over endlessly online by people who may wish to consider getting out more.

[2] See Map 7.

[3] In some ways, the Border's move northwards actually benefitted Scottish haaf netsmen – such fishing in Scotland required a permit, while in England it did not.

channel), which were granted to the burgers of Annan by James V of Scotland, still be said to belong to them, if the area concerned was now in England? An even more involved question was whether any two parties with a grievance over any such issue could resolve them in court. For an English party to raise a case of this kind in a Scottish court would, of itself, probably involve recognising Scottish jurisdiction in what they considered to be part of England. The same problem arose *vice versa*.

Writing at the time in *The British Yearbook of International Law*, Colin Warbrick reached an interesting constitutional conclusion. He said that the question was in fact one of international law but, because of Scotland's anomalous political position, it was, for the time being, probably unsolvable. He concluded, essentially, that this was an international disagreement between two countries which no longer legally existed. It was therefore a problem that would be difficult to settle because, since 1707:

> ...there are no parties to reach an agreement.[1]

Charting the boundary of a country which does not legally exist is an appropriately odd Scottish thought on which to end this account.[2]

In the end, the Eden went obligingly back to its old southern channel in 1977. When the two parties do legally exist again (from the standpoint of international lawyers), I am sure some amicable and lasting agreement will be reached about the line here – wherever exactly the Eden flows, when the tide retreats, that happy morning.

***

The weather fairs again as suddenly on leaving Annan as it broke when we first saw the town. We walk along the west bank of the River Annan, where a path takes us through a huge garden of sea pinks and yellow wildflowers. On the bank opposite us, fishing boats are being repaired.

At the towering chemical factory in Newbie, we take a short cut down to the shore again at Newbie Mains. Here the Border turns its face seaward, and away from the coastline for the final time.[3]

We walk along the shingle and seaweed, briefly shinning along a pipe to

---

[1] Colin Warbrick: 'The Boundary between England and Scotland in the Solway Firth', *British Yearbook of International Law* (Volume 51, 1980).
[2] The Eden had, in fact, also moved back and fore previously in 1942.
[3] Maps of a century ago actually show the land border petering out here at Newbie Mains, but today's maps will take us another two miles yet.

get across a burn at a place called Bruce's Acre. A long Mexican-wave of oystercatchers[1] rises ahead of us and settles as quickly again behind us, for a whole spectacular mile, until we near the village of Powfoot. There, past the white cottages, and the red Victorian holiday villas which stand around their green, we can see our finishing-post, the Powfoot Hotel. We are determined now to eat there. We wipe our boots and go in.

In a strange miniature echo of Douglas Adams's science fiction novel, *The Restaurant at the End of the Universe*, it strikes me that diners at Powfoot must look forever out at the Border, as it continually comes to its end. Sure enough, between the hotel window now and the distant purple peaks of Blencathra, we can see the very last of the land border as it comes to an abrupt, invisible stop in the face of the Irish Sea. A mile out from here under a thin – it seems suspended – rain shower, somewhere around grid reference 152631, the Ordnance Survey ceases to mark our line.

From that point westwards lies the maritime border – a different type of line completely – marked out into the distance for us today by a faint string of distant wind turbines.[2] After this, Scotland's sea-border will run briefly up against the territorial waters of England, and then those of the Isle of Man, before stretching itself from the Mull of Galloway to the Mull of Kintyre. It will march then with the seas of both parts of Ireland,[3] before it heads west, leaving the Hebrides far to starboard and *Tìr nan Òg* somewhere on the port bow, as it points a course far over the Atlantic horizon, towards Rockall's dark and distant mysteries.

---

[1] I think.

[2] The Robin Rigg Windfarm, while not within Scotland's land borders, is marginally within Scotland's territorial waters.

[3] The sea border between Scotland and the Antrim coast assumed a new political importance in 2021, following the UK's trade deal with the EU. There will be customs checks, for the first time, on many types of goods passing between Scotland and Northern Ireland. Meanwhile, the idea floated by Boris Johnson in 2019 of a bridge from Northern Ireland to Scotland is widely considered to have been either a joke or an overture to Ulster's Democratic Unionist Party. Perhaps it was both. Such a bridge, from Portpatrick to Larne, would cross 21 highly-improbable miles of open sea.

Afterword: Not in Debate

Though I am from the Borders, I have long lived happily at another of Scotland's national extremities – the Outer Hebrides.

Some of my observations about the Borders will be thirty years out of date, but this walk has been an honest attempt to rediscover and to learn. If I had grown up 70 miles north of the Border line, I would have struggled to draw it on a map. If I had lived five miles from it, I might have seen the Border as a matter of fact rather than fascination. But I grew up eighteen miles from it – just the right distance to make it both familiar and exotic. So I have sought here, accurately or otherwise, to verify half-remembered stories about passing peel towers and thief roads, once heard in the back of a childhood car. I hope this walk has allowed me – as well as the much-addressed reader – to accept my own intial challenge to *read,* as well as walk, a way along the Border.

The Border and its Ballads continue to provoke new and significant writing such as Andrew Greig's tale of obsession *When they lay bare*. Historical fiction continues anew in Mark Montgomery's *The Borderer Chronicles*, or Melvyn Bragg's seventh-century Cumbrian epic *Credo*, while Rab Wilson's anthology *Chuckies for the Cairn* shows that poets are still writing in Dumfries and Galloway. Perhaps the most arresting contribution of all comes in the form of Alasdair Gray's science fiction.[1]

Meanwhile Nigel Tranter's[2] historical novels have, for half a century and more now, provided most Scots with one of their very few ways of accessing Scottish history.[3] Among many Tranter novels with a Border theme are *True Thomas, Balefire,* and *The Marchman. The Rough Wooing* and *The Wallace* both also make inevitable and frequent references to the Border, as does Tranter's magisterial trilogy *The Bruce*.

I hope the reader will explore all these recent writers, as well as overcome the last acceptable prejudice of our age – the one against dead people – by coming to enjoy more of Scott, Hogg and the rest.[4]

---

[1] Alasdair Gray's *A History Maker* makes use of the landscape around James Hogg's haunts at St Mary's Loch. Gray imagines a twenty-third-century matriarchal world in which reivers seek immortality for their skirmishes, not in ballads, but as a televised blood sport.

[2] Tranter (who, undeservedly, now seems to be largely out of print) was not born in the Borders. He was popular (but some might say is now a little out of fashion) and the sheer quantity of his work gives cause to wonder whether it is all of the same quality. Without making any undue comparisons, it must be pointed out now that these same objections could all fairly reasonably be offered up against Scott. So I think Tranter is overdue some recognition.

[3] Tranter is also, incidentally, a clear and acknowledged influence on George R.R. Martin, the author of *Game of Thrones*.

Professor Murray Pittock has remarked that a first-year Scottish literature class at university will often fall upon Scottish texts 'with the hunger of a starved man', so entirely unknown to them is their own country's literature. The situation has been improving, largely thanks to the efforts of many individual teachers. I can only observe, however, that Scott and Hogg went unmentioned to me in secondary school (in those two writers' native Selkirkshire), as did the existence of every other Scottish writer who ever lived.[1] This is not a situation that would be tolerated as anything like normal in very many countries except Scotland.

I am not quite insensitive enough to think that every teacher in Scotland should now find time in their very busy lives to teach their way through Scotland's literature from *Y Gododdin* to Irvine Welsh. However, it would be nice to think that, in the future, more young Scots might at least have the opportunity to discover that a significant body of such Scottish literature *exists*. Walking and reading my way westwards, I have been increasingly made to wonder why we should continue to put up with anything else.

***

I am led to understand that being cool involves showing a studied indifference to the world around you, regardless of how interesting it might be. In Scotland, such a disregard would surely take admirable powers of concentration. This is true not least along the line from Marshall Meadows Bay to Powfoot.

If, however, the reader has some other line they want to walk, then they should just walk it. They will probably unearth at least as much local folklore on their way as I did. However, the things that the reader will see along the Border have a different character to those they might find along some other line, more randomly drawn elsewhere across a map of Scotland. The Border does not just provide events from 'local' history or 'local' literature. Here, the specifically local asserts for itself a claim to a much wider significance. As one Selkirk common riding song puts it:

> Haud up yer heids, ma gallant lads. Ye've come frae naethin sma'.[2]

---

[4] I accept that not everything these writers produce is to be recommended. Scott's *Lady of the Lake*, for example, is never again likely to be considered readable.

[1] I say this without any intended disrespect to the majority of the teachers at Selkirk High School, particularly in the English Department, who sought to teach me about all manner of other things. I also acknowledge that in the last six months of school I did get the option to write a dissertation about a chosen writer who, in my case, was a Scot.

[2] 'Auld Selkirk Toun', by J.B. Selkirk.

I say none of that to avoid a difficult issue. For the avoidance of doubt, my own interest in borders – and my affection for one border in particular – in no way seeks to deflect scrutiny away from the tragic reality of many frontiers. It would be a daunting task – a large book in its own right – to list all the disastrous consequences of inhumane border policy around the globe. The separation of families along the Korean border, the bloodbath following the partition of India and Pakistan, Trump's Mexican wall fantasies, and the sorry consequences of Britain's border-drawing tendencies the world over (and, nearest to hand, in Ireland) can all be brought readily to mind.

Nor do I seek to underplay the reality that communities on each side of the Anglo-Scottish Border have of course always had many social ties that connect them. The Border is not some precipice beyond which there is no communication. As Cameron McNeish has pointed out in his foreword, there are clearly some shared, friendly experiences of the Border from both sides. Another perceptive assessment of the situation is this one:

> Denizens can display almost simultaneous antipathy and affection towards their counterparts on the other side... The degree to which borders theselves were integral to both English and Scottish imaginations [has moved] ...from a purely political boundary to a marker of immutable difference.[1]

Differences, even now-immutable ones like the Scottish Border, are not a bad thing. Recognising and respecting them is good for all friendships. By walking Scotland's Border, my friends and I have been seeking to celebrate a few of the things that continue to make Scotland good-naturedly different – in the face of some formidable prevailing winds which still sometimes howl that she ought not to be different at all.

***

Charles Lamb – not Scotland's most uncritical observer – once commented of the Scot that:

> The twilight of dubiety never falls upon him... Between the affirmative and negative there is no border-land with

---

[1] Bruce, Mark & Terrell, Katerine (eds): *The Anglo Scottish Border: The shaping of identity, 1300-1600.*

him. You cannot hover with him upon the confines of truth or wander in the maze of a probable argument.[1]

There is no hovering among probabilities along Scotland's border line. The matter is not in debate. As I gave warning of at the outset, some of my opinions on that have put me at courteous but unavoidable odds with many others who have written about this most compelling of lines on the map.

As the Solway Firth finally becomes the Irish Sea, it is clearer than ever that the Border very much exists. As for Scotland, she exists more with every tide.

---

[1] From *The Works of Charles and Mary Lamb*, Vol. 2. London, Methuen, 1903. Lamb's views must be treated with caution, given his highly questionable statements about a host of other races. However, he is probably onto something about the Scots.

Timeline

This timeline does not seek to be in any way representative of the major events in Scotland's history over the last two thousand years – just the ones that have directly determined where Scotland's national boundaries have come to lie. Reading this may help Chapter 4 make more sense. It is a complex picture up to the thirteenth century, but (significantly) a much simpler one thereafter.

c130: Hadrian's Wall completed.

c400: Hadrian's Wall abandoned by the Romans.

c500: We think of what is now Scotland as being populated by Scots (meaning here Gaels), Picts, Britons, and the newly-arrived Angles

c700: By this period, the Gaelic kingdom of Dalriada encompasses the west, while Pictland lies in the north and east. The Brythonic kingdom of Alt Clut (later Strathclyde) extends from Dumbarton south-westwards. The Saxon kingdom of Northumbria stretches from the Humber to the Forth on the east coast. It still includes what are now Dumfries and Galloway and Cumbria on the west.

793: Norsemen raid Lindisfarne, an event often taken to represent the beginning of the Viking era in the British Isles.

843: Traditional date for King Kenneth MacAlpin's merger of Pictland and Dalriada, so creating a Scotland lying north of the old Antonine Wall (which runs between the Forth and Clyde).

c900: By around this point, the Kingdom of Strathclyde seems to have wrested control of what we now think of as Dumfries and Galloway and Cumbria from the hands of the Kingdom of Northumbria.

954: Northumbria, weakened by Norse rule to its south, ceases to be an independent kingdom and becomes a (smaller) earldom under increasingly strong English suzerainty.

c1000: The Kingdom of Mann and the Isles stretches by now from Lewis to the Isle of Man. Like Scotland, this is a predominantly Gaelic-speaking people but, in the Isles' case, one under increasingly Norse rule, remaining outside Scotland's control. Orkney and Shetland are, meantime, part of the Kingdom of Norway.

1018: The Battle of Carham ensures that the part of the Earldom of North-umbria lying north of the Tweed comes to form part of Scotland.

c1030: The Kingdom of Strathclyde (still stretching southwards into modern Cumbria) becomes part of Scotland.

1066: Norman conquest of England.

1092: What is today Cumbria is ceded to England, creating a border broadly similar to today's.

1137: Scotland again briefly possesses both Cumbria (as far south as Lancaster) and also Northumbria (as far south as the Tees).

1157: Scotland abandons any claims to northern England, and again settles on boundaries very much like today's (save that Berwick is still in Scotland, and the islands are all still under varying degrees of Norwegian control).

1237: Something close to the 1157 Border (and indeed to the Border of today) is recognised in the Treaty of York, and in border surveys around this time.

1266: The Treaty of Perth brings the Hebrides and the Isle of Man under the Scottish Crown (though Scottish control over the Isle of Man is abandoned in the century thereafter). We now, largely, have the map of modern Scotland.

1297 – 1357: Scottish Wars of Independence.

1332: Large areas of south-eastern Scotland are occupied by England under Edward Balliol's 'Roxburgh Promise', codified as the 1334 Treaty of Newcastle.

1370: Virtually all of the territories occupied in 1332 are by now back in Scottish hands.

1472: Orkney and Shetland are formally annexed from Norway to Scotland, after the non-payment of the Danish royal dowry for which they were security.

1482: Berwick is ceded to England for the final time.

1552: The 'Debatable Lands' at the western end of the Border are officially divided up by a dyke.

16th – 19th centuries: Various very small local disputes and uncertainties are played out along the Border line by landowners and map-makers.

1603: Union of the Crowns means the two kingdoms share a king.

1707: Union of Parliaments brings Scottish independence to an end.

1854 – 63: Ordnance Survey maps out the Border line in final detail.

1976 – 77: The last land-border dispute, on the Solway Firth.

1999: Redefinition in law of Scotland's 'territorial' waters and sea boundaries.

1999: Reconvening of the (devolved) Scottish Parliament.

Scots Glossary

Rather than try to explain every Scots word used as I go, I have provided this glossary. That said, I have generally also offered a footnoted English translation or gloss along the way for some of the older texts quoted.

Scots and English share much vocabulary, and the list below only covers those words found in the book which differ from English. I am resisting any temptation to provide (by way of border-reprisal) a parallel list of the Scots equivalents for all the English words I have used. The spelling here attempts to represent the near-standard that exists for written Scots, rather than to cover all spelling variants.

(adj) adjective; (adv) adverb; (conj) conjugation; (n) noun; (prep) preposition; (pron) pronoun; (v) verb.

A: (pron) I
ablo: (prep) below
ae: (before nouns) one
affrontit: (adj) offended, humiliated[1]
afore: (prep) before
agin: (prep) against
aik: (n) oak
aince: (adv) once
airt: (n) direction, place, (v) direct
alang: (prep) along
an: (conj) and
ane: one
aneuch: (adj, adv) enough
aye: yes
aye: (adj, adv) always. Pronounced differently in most, (but not all), dialects to 'aye' meaning 'yes'.
auld: (adj) old
Auld Nick: (jocular) the Devil
Auld Year's Day: December 31
ava: at all
aw: (adj) all
awa: (adj, adv) away
awbodie: (n) everybody
awfu: (adj) awful, (adv) awfully
ayont: (prep) beyond
bairn: (n) child

[1] 'Black affrontit' is the gravest variety of this situation.

baith: (adj) both

bangister: (n) a violent or lawless person

bauchle: (v) to make a public accusation against a person (not to be confused with its other meaning as a verb, which is to become out of shape)[1]

baw (sometimes baa or ba'): (n) ball

Bells, the: (n) midnight at Hogmanay

Berwicker: (n) a native of Berwick

besom: (n) 1. broom 2. cheeky or disreputable woman

beuk: (n) book

birk: (n) birch

black bun: (n) dense fruit cake covered in denser pastry, eaten at Hogmanay

blaeberry: (n) bilberry

blether: (v) to chatter idly

bleeze: (v) blaze

blyth: (adj) happy, cheerful

bonnie: (adj) good-looking, pretty

bouk: (n) bulk

brak (or brek): (v) break

brae: (n) hill, incline, road up a hill

braw: (adj) good, great, fine

breid: (n) bread

brig: (n) bridge

byre: (n) cowshed

burn: (n) stream, small river

cairn: (n) a loose pile of stones, often used as a boundary marker, etc.

callant: (n) young man

cam: (v) past tense of come

cannie: (adj) cautious, gentle

carlin: (n) witch, or sometimes more generally an old woman

cauld: (n, v) cold

caw: (v) 1. call, 2. drive, propel, push

caw cannie: (v) take care, be cautious

chap: (v) knock (e.g. on a door), (of a bell) chime

clatchie: (adj) (usually of a field, etc.) muddy

claw: (v) scratch

cleuch (or cleugh): (n), ravine

cloot: (n) rag or cloth

clootie well: (n) a holy well or spring at which votive offerings in the form of cloots are left

common riding: (n) a town's annual festival where the boundaries of the common land are ridden on horse

contrair: (adj) contrary

---

[1] Nor is this to be confused with 'bauchle' the noun, which refers either to an old shoe or to a small, clumsy untidy person (at least two of which three qualities are probably necessary to qualify a person as a bauchle).

coonty: (n) county

corbie: (n) crow, raven

conceity: (adj) fancy, fanciful

coory: (v) cuddle

corrie-fistit: (adj) left-handed

cottar: (n) a person with a house, usually tied to his job, but with no land of his own to cultivate

couthie: (adj) agreeable, homely, friendly – but carrying a range of ineffably Scottish associations beyond that

crag, craig: (n) neck

crap: (n) crop

croon: (n,v) crown

crowlin: (n) crawling

daith: (n) death

daud: (n) a lump of something

daunder, dauner: (v, n) wander, stroll

deave: (v) deafen, bore

dee: (v) die

deid: (adj) dead

deil: (n) devil

denner: (n) dinner[1]

ding: (v) beat, conquer

dinna: (v) don't

dool: (n) grief, distress (adj) dismal

doon: (prep) down

dorty: (adj): haughty, sultry, huffy

dreich: (adj) persistently dreary (esp. of a particular type of wet weather)

dreel: (n) a drill or furrow of potatoes

drover: (n) someone who drives cattle (usually from the Highlands to England)

douce: (adj) respectable, prosperous, sedate, tidy

dour: (adj) solemn, grumpy[2]

drookit: (adj) drenched, soaked

drow: (n) a persistent and soaking rain or drizzle

dyke: (n) wall, especially dividing fields. A dry-stane dyke is one made without mortar or cement

echt: eight

ee: (n) eye

elder: (n) in Presbyterian churches, a person ordained to take part in church government, usually in a local kirk session.

eldritch: (adj) spooky, eerie, elfen

een: (n) 1. plural of ee, 2. (n) evening, 3. (adj) even

---

[1] Or (as dinner has increasingly come to be known) lunch.

[2] Rhymes with Eng. 'poor', unless you are American or watch an uncommon amount of US television.

exack: (adj) exact
fack: (n) fact
fain: (adj) (archaic) joyful
fank: (n) sheep pen
far'd: (adj) favoured
Fastern's Een: Shrove Tuesday
faur: (adj) far
fecht: (n,v) fight
fee: (n) often specifically a six-month term of employment as a farm worker
fell: (adj) grievous, cruel
ferlie: (n) wonder, oddity
ferm: (n, v) farm
ferm raw: (n) a row of tied houses for workers on a farm
ferm toun: (n) a large farm with (at one time) a number of workers' houses.
finn: (v) (past tense funn) find
first-fitt (or first foot): (n) the first person to visit a house after the new year. Plural is (strangely) first fitts (or first foots). (v) to visit someone to bring in the new year.
firth: (n) estuary
fitbaw: (n) football
flee: (v) fly
flit: (v) to move house
fodgel: (adj) buxom, plump
follae: (v) follow
forby: in addition to
forfauchen: (adj) exhausted, weary
forrit: (adv) forwards
fowk: (n) people
frae, fae: (prep) from
furth of: (prep) outside, beyond
gae, gang: (v) go
gairden: (n,v) garden
gaed, gaen: (v) sometimes past tenses of gae
gait, gate: (n) way, direction, street
gaun: (v) going (in the Borders, gaun is also used as the infinitive to go)
gie: (v) give
gied: (v) past tense of gie
gin: if
glaur: (n) mud
glen: (n) valley
gless: (n) glass
glesses: (n) glasses (spectacles)
gloamin: (n) twilight
green: (v) (archaic) to long for

grun: (n) ground

guid: (adj) good

guidman: (n) husband

haaf net: (n) type of net traditionally used on Solway for catching salmon and sea trout

haar: (n) sea mist

hae: (v) have

haena (or hinnae): (v) haven't

hail: (adj) whole

hairst: (n) harvest, autumn

haiver: (v) talk nonsense

hame: (n) home

handba': (n) a game of free-for-all handball played in some towns

hantle: (n) handful, small quantity

happ: (v) wrap up, (n) a blanket, warm clothes, etc

haud: (v) hold

hauf: (n, adj) half

haugh (or hauch): (n) river meadow

heid: (n, v, adj) head

herd: (n) shepherd (or sometimes, archaeically, a cow herd)

hert, hairt: (n) heart

hinner: (v) hinder

hinneren: (n) the end, 'in the final event'

hirple: (v) hobble

hizzie: (n) woman (often implying one of questionable character)

Hogmanay (n): the celebration of the New Year (v) to observe Hogmanay

hoose: (n) house

howf: (n) among other meanings, a favoured meeting place, especially a pub

humdudgeon: (n) a sulk

humphy-backit: (adj) hump-backed

hurdums an durdums: (n) uproar, disturbance

hunner: hundred

hurl: (n) a run in a car, etc (v) to move something, esp. something on wheels[1]

ilka: (adj) every

ither: other

Jethart snails: (n) a boiled sweet native to Jedburgh

jing-bang: (n) the whole lot, 'the hail jing-bang'.

kailyaird: (n) cabbage patch, vegetable garden[2]

ken: (v) know

kenspeckle: (adj) conspicuous, well-known

---

[1] This latter meaning lies behind the apocryphal story of the Scottish visitor to an English house, who caused alarm when she offered to 'hurl the piano through to the kitchen'.

[2] Often also used to name a period of nineteenth-century Scottish literature with similarly-limited horizons.

kintra: (n, adj) country
kirk: (n) church
kirkyaird: (n) churchyard
kist: (n) chest, partic. a coffin
knowe: (n) hillock
kythe: (v) appear
laddie: (n) boy, young man
lad o pairts: (n) a boy of humble origins who distinguishes himself in life
lair: (n) burial plot in a cemetery
laird: (n) landowner[1]
lang: (adj) long, or sometimes tall
Langholmite: (n) a native of Langholm
lassie: (n) girl, young woman
law: (n) (usually in place names) hill
leister: (v) to hunt salmon with a spear by night
lenth: (n) length. 'The lenth o' means 'as far as'
licht: (n,v) light
lift: (n) sky
lintwhite, lintie: (n) the linnet (bird)
linn: (n) pool, usually in front of a waterfall
loanin: (n) lane, esp. one into pasture land
loch: (n) 1. lake, 2. fjord
loon: (n) boy
lowp: (v, n) leap
lug: (n) ear
Mains: (usually in place names) home farm
mair: (adj, adv) more
mairch: (n,v) march, border
mak: (v) make
makar: (n) poet
maun: (v) must
maunna: (v) mustn't
meinister: (n) minister
mercat: (n) market
merk: (v, n) mark
micht: (v, n) might
mither: (n) mother
modren: (adj) modern
monie: (adj) many
muckle: (adj) big, (adv) much
mugger: (n) a Romany, especially one working as a hawker
muir: (n) moor
na: no (as in yes and no)

---

[1] Lairds and lords are two different things. Not all lairds (i.e. landowners) are lords (i.e. peers). 'The Lord' (i.e. God) would never be described as 'The Laird' either.

nae: (adv, adj) no, not (but *not* 'no', as in the opposite of 'yes')[1]

naebodie: (n) nobody

naethin: (n) nothing

neep: (n) turnip

nicht: (n) night

nocht: (n) nothing

noo: (adj, adv) now

nor: comparative 'than', as in 'mair nor me' (though in fact people in the Borders are more likely to say 'mair as me')

norie: (n) notion

onie: any

oniebodie: (n) anybody

oo: (n) wool

oobit: (n) caterpillar, generally a 'hairy oobit,' meaning the hairy variety

oor: 1. our, 2. hour

oot: (prep) out

ootby: (adj, adv) outwards, over there, away from home

ower: 1. (prep) over, 2. too (as in too much), e.g. 'There wes ower monie o them'

owerlowp: (n) the right to graze animals occasionally in one's neighbour's fields

pailace: (n) palace

pailmerk: (n) (very) derogatory name used by Selkirk people for people in Galashiels

pech: (v) to pant, e.g. when walking

peel tower: (n) type of heavily-defended farmhouse, often home to Border reivers.

peely wally: (adj) pale, especially of skin,

peewit: (n) lapwing

pey: (v, n) pay

pibroch: (n) classical bagpipe music

piece: (n) sandwich

policies: (n) grounds and outbuildings surrounding an estate house

pooer: (n) power

pow: (n) forehead

puir: (adj) poor

quine: (n) girl

quyk gude, quick good: (n) (archaic) household contents (often as not, those taken by reivers)

raw: (n) row (esp. of houses)

reive: (v) to subject to the attention of Border reivers, to rob.

reiver: (n) a raider of cattle of a type common along both sides of the Border in the 13th to 17th centuries.

---

[1] Unless you are from parts of northern England, Shetland, or are Groundkeeper Willie in *The Simpsons*.

richt: (n, v) right

rickle (or ruckle): (n) a ramshackle pile of objects

rig: (n) a narrow strip of ploughed land

rin: (v, n) run

ruckly: (adj) ramshackle

rydand: (v) (archaeic) lit. 'riding', but often meaning specifically reiving

saltire: (n) heraldic term for a diagonal cross. Used in Scotland to denote the Scottish flag.

saut: (n) salt

scart: (n, v) scratch, cut

scomfish: (v) overcome someone with smoke (or sometimes merely with disgust). The former was often a tactic for smoking people out of their peel towers.

screive: (v) write

sic: (adj) such

siccar: (adj) certain, sure

shank: (n) leg

shortleit: (n) short-list

skite: (v) slide

smaw: (adj) small

smirr: (n) fine, thin rain

smitt: (v) infect, (n) infection

smoor: (v) smother

snaw: (n,v) snow

snell: (adj) (of weather) biting, fierce

sodger: (n) soldier

sonsie: (adj) hearty, cheerful, buxom

Souter: (n) 1. a shoemaker. 2. (in a reference to the town's former trade) a native of Selkirk.

sneck: (n) the catch on a door, etc.

speir: (v) ask (as in to ask a question, but *not* to ask someone to do something, which is likewise 'ask' in Scots)

stane: (n,v, adj) stone

stank: (n) drain

staun: (v) stand

steill: (n) (archaic) pool

strunt: (v) strut

stott: (v) to bounce. 'Tae pit them aff their stott': to put them out of sorts, out of their stride[1]

Suthren (adj): southern, (n) Southerner, Englishman

sweir: 1. (v) swear, 2. (adj) reluctant

syne: then, ago

tacketty: (adj) (of boots) containing tackets (i.e. hobnails)

---

[1] A stotter is someone good-looking, though, paradoxically, stottin can also describe someone who is drunk.

tae: 1. (n) toe, 2. (adj, adv) too, meaning 'as well'. but *not* too meaning 'overly' (which is *ower*, as in 'ower muckle'), 3. (prep) to

tak (past tenses tuik, taen): (v) take

tattie: (n) potato

Terie: (n) a native of Hawick

thir: these

thocht: (n, v) thought

thole: (v) endure, put up with

thon: that (but refering to a further away thing or person than 'that')

threap: (v) persist in debate, (adj) debatable, especially of land

tither: (adj, n) other ('the tane or the tither')

thrawn: (adj) stubborn

thrissel: (n) thistle

toom, tuim: (adj) empty

toon: (n) town

trig: (adj) tidy

tron: (n) place in a town's market place where there was once a weighing machine (and often a place of execution)

twa: two

uise: (v) use

unchancy: (adj) unlucky, ill-omened, supernatural

unco: (adj, adv) unusual, unusually, strange, strangely

verra: (adv, adj) very

wark: (n) work

warld: (n) world

wary: (archaeic) (v) curse

wean: (n) child

wede awa: (archaeic) carried off (by death)

wee: (adj) small

weil: (adv) well

whaur: where

whiles: (adv) sometimes

whins: (n) gorse, broom

whit: what

whit for no?: why not?

widdershins: (adv) anti-clockwise

wyte: (n) blame

youkie: (adj) itchy

yowe: (n) ewe

Bibliography

The reader will, I hope, have realised by now that my footnotes are as often intended as jokes as they are citations.

I have not tried to footnote all of the quotations used, but where a text is quoted, the reference to it in this bibliography or elsewhere is intended as a means of due acknowledgement. Where two editions are mentioned here, it is the older of these which is being cited, and the newer is for information only.

Literary

Aneirin: *Y Gododdin*. Rev. John Williams (ed), William Rees, London, 1853

Auden, W.H.: *Collected Poems*. London, Faber, 1976.

Barbour, John: *The Bruce*, W.M. MacKenzie (ed). London, Adam & Charles Black, 1909.

> See also edition by A.A.M. Duncan (ed), Edinburgh, Canongate Classics, 1997.

Bawcutt, Priscilla and Riddy, Felicity (eds): *Longer Scottish Poems, Volume I, 1375-1650*. Edinburgh, Scottish Academic Press, Edinburgh, 1987.

Bragg, Melvyn: *Credo*. London, Hodder & Stoughten, 1996.

Burns, Robert:

> *The Poems and Songs of Robert Burns*. J.M. Dent & Co, 1905.

> See also *Complete Poems and Songs of Robert Burns*. Glasgow, Harper Collins, 1995.

> *The Letters of Robert Burns*. J. Logie Robertson (ed). London, Walter Scott Company, 1887.

> See also *Robert Burns: The Complete Letters*. James Mackay (ed). Ayr, Alloway Publishing, 1988.

Byers, John: *The Liddesdale Drow*. Hawick, The Express Office, c1945.

Child, Francis James (ed): *The English and Scottish Popular Ballads*. Cambridge, Houghton Mifflin, 1904.

Crockett, S.R.:

> *The Raiders*. London, J.M. Dent & Sons, 1914

> See also as published by Canongate Classics, Edinburgh, 2001.

> *The Smugglers*. London, Hodder & Stoughton, 1911.

Cunninghame Graham, R.B.: *Rodeo: A collection of the tales and sketches of*

R.B. Cunninghame Graham. New York, New York Literary Guild, 1936.

Dunbar, William: *The Poems of William Dunbar.* Edinburgh, William Paterson, 1865.

> See also *The Poems of William Dunbar.* W. MacKay MacKenzie (ed). Edinburgh, James Thin, 1990.

Elliot, Walter (ed): *A New Minstrelsy of the Scottish Border, 1805-2005.* Selkirk, Deer Park Press, 2006.

Gray, Alasdair: *A History Maker.* Edinburgh, Canongate, 1994.

Gray, Alexander: *Selected Poems.* William MacLellan, 1948.

Greig, Andrew: *When they lay bare.* London, Faber & Faber, 2013.

Harry, 'Blind Harry': *The actis and deidis of the illustre and vailyeand campioun Schir William Wallace, Knicht of Ellerslie.* James Moir (ed). London, Blackwood, 1889.

Hay, George Campbell (Deòrsa Mac Iain Dheòrsa): Collected poems and songs of George Campbell Hay (Deòrsa Mac Iain Dheòrsa). Michel Byrne (ed). Edinburgh University Press, 2003.

Hogg, James:

> *The Jacobite Relics of Scotland.* Edinburgh, Blackwood, 1819-21.

> See also *Jacobite Relics.* Murray Pittock (ed) Edinburgh University Press, 2002-2003.

> *The Tales of James Hogg the Ettrick Shepherd.* Glasgow, Eildon Series / Morison, c1870.

> *The Private Memoirs and Confessions of a Justified Sinner.* London, Longman & Hurst, 1824.

> See also as published by Polygon, Edinburgh, 2014.

> *The Three Perils of Man: War, Women and Witchcraft.* London, 1822.

> See also as published by Scottish Academic Press, Edinburgh, 1989.

> *The Poems of James Hogg, the Ettrick Shepherd.* W. Wallace (ed). London, Ibister, 1903.

> See also *James Hogg: Selected Poems and Songs.* David Groves (ed). Edinburgh, Scottish Academic Press, 1986.

Le Clerc, Guillaume: *Roman de Fergus.* Translated and edited by D.D.R. Owen in *Fergus of Galloway: Knight of King Arthur.* Edinburgh, John Donald, 2018.

See also *Fergus: Roman von Guillaume le Clerc*, Ernst Martin (ed). Halle Verlag der Buchhandlung des Waisenhauses, 1872.

Leyden, John:

> *The Poetical Remains of the late Dr John Leyden.* Rev James Morton (ed). London, 1819.

> *Poems and Ballads, with a memoir supplied by Sir Walter Scott.* Kelso, 1875.

Little, Pippa: *Foray: Border reiver women.* Newcastle-upon-Tyne, Biscuit Publishing, 2009.

MacCaig, Norman: *Collected Poems.* London, Chatto & Windus, 1993.

MacDiarmid, Hugh:

> *Selected Poetry.* Alan Riach and Michael Grieve (eds). Manchester, Carcanet, 2000.

> *Complete Poems.* Michael Grieve and William Russell Aitken (eds). Manchester, Carcanet, 1994.

MacIntyre, Donald: *Sporan Dhòmhnaill: Gaelic Poems and Songs by the late Donald Macintyre, the Paisley Bard.* Edinburgh, Scottish Academic Press, for the Scottish Gaelic Texts Society, 1968.

Maitland, Sir Richard: *Ancient Scottish Poems.* Written in sixteenth century and published by Dilly & Creech, Edinburgh, 1786.

Marsden, John (ed): *The Illustrated Border Ballads.* London, Macmillan, 1990.

Massie, Allan: *Arthur the King.* London, Phoenix, 2003.

Miller, Frank: *The Poets of Dumfriesshire.* Glasgow, James Maclehose & Sons, 1910.

Montgomery, Mark: *The Borderer Chronicles.* ruffthedog.com, 2012.

Murray, Les: *Collected Poems.* Manchester, Carcanet, 1991.

Nairne, Carolina Oliphant: *Lays from Strathearn.* Edinburgh, Paterson, 1846.

Ramsay, Allan:

> *The Evergreen.* Edinburgh, Thomas Ruddiman, 1724.

> *The Tea-Table Miscellany: or a Collection of Choice Songs, Scots and English.* Edinburgh, Donaldson and Wilson, 1760.

> *The Poems of Allan Ramsay.* London, Caddell & Davies, 1800.

> See also: *Poems by Allan Ramsay and Robert Ferguson.* Association for Scottish Literary Studies / Chatto & Windus, 1974.

Scott, Sir Walter:

> *Guy Mannering.* Edinburgh, Adam & Charles Black, 1885.
> See also as published by Penguin Books, London, 2003.
> *Letters of Malachi Malagrowther.* Edinburgh, Blackwood, 1981.
> *Marmion: A Tale of Flodden Field,* from *The Poetical Works of Sir Walter Scott.* J.Logie Robertson (ed). Oxford University Press, 1913.
> See also edition of *Marmion* by Palala Press, 2012.
> *Redgauntlet.* Edinburgh, Constable, 1824.
> See also edition by Oxford University Press, 2011.
> *Rob Roy.* Edinburgh, Adam & Charles Black, 1893.
> See also as published by Edinburgh University Press, 2008.
> *Tales of a Grandfather.* Edinburgh, Cadell, 1828.
> *The Chronicles of the Canongate.* Edinburgh, Cadell, 1827
> See also as published by Penguin, London, 2003.
> *The Heart of Midlothian.* London, Adam & Charles Black, 1893.
> See also as published by Oxford University Press, 2008.
> *The Lord of the Isles.* Edinburgh, Constable, 1815.
> *The Lay of the Last Minstrel.* Oxford, Clarendon Press, 1913.
> See also as published by Birlinn, Edinburgh, 2013.
> *The Minstrelsy of the Scottish Border.* Edinburgh, Constable, 1821.
> See also Alfred Noyes (ed). James Thin / Mercat Press, Edinburgh, 1979.
> *The Monastery.* London, Nelson, 1901.
> See also Edinburgh Edition, 2000.

Selkirk, J.B.: *The Complete Poems of J. B. Selkirk (James Brown).* Selkirk, 1932.

Sheldon, Frederick (ed): *The Minstrelsy of the English Border.* London, Longman, 1847.

Smollett, Tobias: *The Expedition of Humphry Clinker.* Dublin, 1771.

> See also version published as *Humphry Clinker.* London, Penguin Classics, 2012.

Stuart, Charles: *Gretna Green: A Comic Opera in two acts, as performed at the Theatre Royal, Smoke Alley.* Dublin, 1783.

Thomson, James: *The Four Seasons and other poems*. London, J. Millan, 1735.

Tranter, Nigel:

> *Sword of State*. London, Coronet, 1999.

> *The Bruce Trilogy*. London, Coronet, 1996.

Welsh, Irvine: *Trainspotting*. London, Secker and Warburg, 1993.

Wilson, John Mackay (ed): *Wilson's Tales of the Borders*. London, Walter Scott Publishing, 1869.

Wilson, Rab (ed): *Chuckies fir the cairn: poems in Scots and Gaelic by contemporary Dumfries and Galloway poets*. Edinburgh, Luath Press, 2009.

History

(Authorship unclear): *The Complaynt of Scotland*. First published 1549. Republished Early English Text Society, London, 1872.

(Authorship unclear): The Declaration of Arbroath. Edinburgh, National Records of Scotland.

> https://www.nrscotland.gov.uk/files//research/declaration-of-arbroath/declaration-of-arbroath-transcription-and-translation.pdf

Banks, F.R.: *The Borders*. London, Batsford, 1977.

Beattie, John: *Prince Charlie and the Border Land*. Carlisle, Thurnam, 1995.

Blake, Brian: *The Solway Firth*. London, Hale, 1982.

Bower, Walter: *Scotichronicon*. Written in 1440s, drawing on earlier material by John of Fordun. See *A History Book for Scots: Walter Bower's Scotichronicon*. D.E.R. Watt (ed). Edinburgh, John Donald, 1998.

Bowie, Karin (ed): *Addresses Against Incorporating Union, 1706-1707*. Aberdeen, Scottish History Society, 2018.

Brockie, William: *The Gypsies of Yetholm: Historical, traditional, philological and humorous*. Kelso, Rutherford, 1884.

Bruce, Mark & Terrell, Katerine (eds): *The Anglo Scottish Border and the shaping of identity 1300 to 1600*. New York, Palgrave Macmillan, 2012.

Byers, John: *Liddesdale*. Galashiels, McQueen, 1952.

Carroll, Emma: *Witches*. Edinburgh University, 2019. witches.is.ed.ac.uk

Craig, Mary: *The Border Burnings: The story of the witchcraft trials in the Scottish Borders 1600-1700*. Stow, Border Voices, 2008.

Duncan: A.A.M.: *Scotland: The making of the kingdom*. Edinburgh, Oliver and Boyd, 1975.

Elliot, Walter: *Selkirkshire and the Borders*. Selkirk, Deerpark Press. 2009.

Fraser, George MacDonald: *The Steel Bonnets*. London, Barrie and Jenkins, 1971.

Fry, Michael: *The Union: England, Scotland and the Treaty of 1707*. Birlinn, Edinburgh, 2006.

Gerber, Pat: *The Search for the Stone of Destiny*. Edinburgh, Canongate, 1992.

Hamilton, Ian: *The Taking of the Stone of Destiny*, Moffat, Lochar Publishing, 1991.

Irvine, Gordon: *The Solway Smugglers*. Dumfries, Robert Dinwiddie, 1971.

Johnstone, Thomas: *The History of Berwick on Tweed* (1817). Reprinted by Berwick History Society, 2004.

Lang, Andrew and John: *Highways and Byways in the Borders*. Macmillan, 1913.

> See also reprinted as *Border life in days gone by*. Newtongrange, Lang Syne Publishers, 1976.

Mackay, James A: *Burns Lore of Dumfries and Galloway*. Ayr, Alloway Publishing, 1988.

McGuigan, Neil and Woolf, Alex (eds): *The Battle of Carham: a thousand years on*. Edinburgh, Birlinn, 2018.

Moffat, Alistair: *The Borders*. Selkirk, Deerpark Press, 2002.

Oram, Richard: *David I: The King who made Scotland*. Stroud, Tempus, 2004.

Prebble, John: *The Lion in the North*. London, Penguin, 1996.

Robb, Graham: *The Debatable Land: The lost world between Scotland and England*. London, Picador, 2018.

Scott, Paul Henderson: *The Union of 1707 – Why and How*. Edinburgh, Saltire Society, 2006.

Statistical Account of Scotland. Published by General Assembly of Church of Scotland between 1791 and 1799. See at: http://stataccscot.edina.ac.uk

New Statistical Account of Scotland. Published by General Assembly of Church of Scotland between 1834 and 1845. See link above.

Third Statistical Account of Scotland. Published by Collins, Oliver and Boyd and others between 1951 and 1992.

Thomas, John: *Gretna: Britain's Worst Railway Disaster (1915)*. Newton Abbot, David & Charles, 1969.

Tokely, A.V: *The Kirk Yetholm Gypsies*. Hawick, Buccleuch Printers, 2004.

Trevor-Roper, Hugh: *The Invention of Scotland*. Yale University Press, 2003.

Unicorn Publishing: *Langholm: the official guide*. Duns, Unicorn Publishing Company, c.1960.

Yetholm Historical Society: *Bygone Yetholm: Portrait of a Border Village*. Yetholm Historical Society, 2009.

Watson, Godfrey: *The Border Reivers*. London, Robert Hale, 1974.

Wyntoun, Andrew of: *The Orygynale Cronykil of Scotland by Androw of Wyntoun*. David Laing (ed). Edinburgh, Scottish Text Society, 1872.

Travel Writing

Boswell, James:

> *Journal of a Tour to the Hebrides with Samuel Johnson.* London, 1785.
>
> *London Journal 1762-1763.* London, Heineman, 1950.
>
> See also edition by Penguin, London, 2010.

Campbell, James: *Invisible Country*. Oxford University Press, 1985.

Crockett, W.S.: *The Scott Country*. London, A. & C. Black, 1902.

Crofton, Ian: *Walking the Border: A Journey between Scotland and England*. Edinburgh, Birlinn, 2014.

Defoe, Daniel: *A Tour thro' the Whole Island of Great Britain (1727)*. London, Parker, 1734.

> See also edition by Penguin, London, 2005.

Greig, Donald & Flint, Darren: *Dumfries and Galloway: Slow Travel Guide*. Chalfont St Peter, Bradt Travel Guides, 2016.

Hall, Alan: *The Border Country: A Walker's Guide*. Milnethorpe, Cicero, 1993.

Lindsay, Maurice: *The Lowlands of Scotland: Edinburgh and the South*. London, Hale, 1956.

Langley, Bob: *Walking the Scottish Border*. London, Hale, 1976.

Mack, James Logan: *The Border Line*. Edinburgh Oliver & Boyd, 1926.

> See also as republished by Grimsay Press, Glasgow, 2011.

McNeish, Cameron: *Scotland's 100 Best Walks*. Edinburgh, Lomond Books, 1999.

Morton, H.V.:

> *In Search of Scotland*. London, Methuen, 1929.
>
> *In Scotland Again*, London, Methuen, 1933.

Pennant, Thomas: *A Tour in Scotland, 1769*. Chester, J. Mark, 1771.

See also as published by Birlinn, Edinburgh, 2000.

Pius II, Pope: *Commentaries.* Published as *Memoirs of a Renaissance Pope*, translated and edited by Florence Gragg and Leona Gabel. New York, Capricorn Books, 1959.

Robson, Eric: *The Border Line: The Story of the Anglo-Scottish Border.* London, Frances Lincoln, 2006.

Russell, Michael: *In Waiting: Travels in the Shadow of Edwin Muir.* Glasgow, Neil Wilson, 1998.

Scott, Alistair: *Native Stranger: a journey in familar and foreign Scotland.* London, Sphere Books. 2013.

Stewart, Rory: *The Marches: A Borderland journey between England and Scotland.* New York, Mariner Books, 2017.

Tranter, Nigel: *The Illustrated Portrait of the Border Country.* London, Robert Hale, 1972.

Warner, Rev Richard: *A Tour through the Northern Counties of England and the Borders of Scotland.* Bath, Cruttwell, 1802.

Other

Beveridge, Craig & Turnbull, Ronald (eds): *The Eclipse of Scottish Culture: Inferiorism and the Intellectuals.* Polygon, Edinburgh, 1989.

Boswell, James: *Boswell's Johnson: The Life of Samuel Johnson.* London, W. Collins, 1924.

Craig, Cairns (ed): *The History of Scottish Literature.* Aberdeen University Press, 1987.

Crawford, Thomas: *Walter Scott.* Edinburgh, Scottish Academic Press, 1982.

Darton, Mike: *The Dictionary of Place Names in Scotland.* Moffat, Lochar Publishing, 1992.

Hutchinson, Peter Orlando: *The Chronicles of Gretna Green.* London, Richard Bentley, 1844.

Kay, Billy: *The Mither Tongue.* Edinburgh, Mainstream Publishing, 1986.

Keay, John & Julia (eds): *Collins Encyclopaedia of Scotland.* London, Harper Collins, 1994.

Loxley, James: *Ben Jonson's Walk to Scotland.* Cambridge University Press, 2015.

MacCormick, John: *The Flag in the Wind: The Story of the National Movement in Scotland.* London, 1955.

See also as published by Birlinn, Edinburgh, 2008.

Osborne, Brian D. & Armstrong, Ronald: *Scotch Obsessions*. Edinburgh, Birlinn, 1996.

Reed, James: *Sir Walter Scott: Landscape and Locality*. London, Bloomsbury Academic, 2013.

Ross, David: *Scottish Place Names*. Edinburgh, Birlinn, 2001.

Scottish Government: *Scotland's Future*. Edinburgh, Scottish Government, 2013.

Scottish National Dictionary Association: *The Concise Scots Dictionary*. Mairi Robinson (ed) Aberdeen University Press, 1991.

Scottish Parliament: *Official Report*. parliament.scot

UK Government: *Scottish Adjacent Waters Boundary Order (Statutory Instrument 1999, No. 1126)*

Warbrick, Colin: 'The Boundary between England and Scotland in the Solway Firth', in *British Yearbook of International Law* (Volume 51, Issue 1) 1980.

Wolter, Allan B: *John Duns Scotus' Political and Economic Philosophy*. New York, Franciscan Institute, 2001.

Ziccardi, M James: *Medieval Philosophy: A Practical Guide to Duns Scotus*. Amazon, 2011.

Search for other works by these authors on:

Oxford Academic: https://academic.oup.com/

Google Scholar: https://scholar.google.com/

Index

Bowes, Sir Walter, border surveyor 96, 102, 103, 106, 117, 133, 194
Bowmont Water 5, 105, 108, 113, 127, 210
Bowness-on-Solway 216, 232, 234,
Bowness Wath 234
Bragg, Melvyn, writer 239
Brexit 48, 144, 193, 221
Britons, ancient people 30, 31, 158, 243
Broons, The, comic characters 216
Bruce, Marjory, daughter of Robert the Bruce 84
Bruce, Robert the, See Robert I
Bruce, The, long poem by John Barbour 66, 136, 233
Brus, Robert de, father of Robert I 63, 66
Brythonic people, See Britons
Buccleuch, Dukes of 93, 131
Buchan, Countess of 21
Buchan, John, writer 70
Burgh, Elizabeth de, *See* Elizabeth, Queen of Robert the Bruce
Burgh by Sands 230
Burnmouth 48
Burns, Robert, poet 25, 72, 84, 86, 87, 92, 115, 145, 148, 191-193, 221, 227, 228
Byers, John, writer 153, 166, 178, 193

Calvinism 147
Canny Island 71
Canonbie 14, 40, 193-195, 199, 200, 203, 204, 209
Carey, John, Governor of Berwick 104
Carham 43, 95-97, 105, 120
        Battle of (1018) 32-35, 39, 95, 96, 243
Carlin's Tooth 148, 150
Carter Bar 5, 6, 11, 113, 135-142, 144-146, 151, 232
Carter Fell 156
Carwinlay 205
Castleton 153, 161, 162
Castra Exploratum, *See* Netherby
Catraeth, Battle of (c.600 AD) 158
Catrail, earthworks 158, 159
Ceolwulf, Saint 67
Chain Bridge, *See* Union Bridge, Paxton
Chapelcross nuclear power station 231
Chariots of Fire, film 59
Charles II, King of Scotland and England 77
Charles II Faa Blythe, King of the Yetholm Gypsies 110
Charles Edward Stuart, Prince ('Bonnie Prince Charlie') 58, 111, 151, 193, 198, 216, 222, 230, 235
'Charlie's Monument', Coldstream 82, 83
Cheviots 5, 26, 54, 77, 113, 114, 116, 118, 120, 124, 127, 135, 141
'Chevy Chase', poem 135
Chew Green, Roman camp 132
Chirnside 61

Redgauntlet, novel by Sir Walter Scott 208, 230, 235